FRANCHISE ORGANIZATIONS

FRANCHISE ORGANIZATIONS

Jeffrey L. Bradach

Harvard Business School Press   Boston, Massachusetts

Library of Congress Cataloging-in-Publication Data

Bradach, Jeffrey L.
    Franchise organizations / Jeffrey L. Bradach.
      p. cm.
    Includes bibliographical references and index.
    ISBN 0-87584-832-X (alk. paper)
    1. Chain restaurants—Management.   2. Franchises (Retail trade)—
Management.   I. Title.
    TX911.3.M27B72   1998
    647.95′068′8—dc21   97-28868
                                                             CIP

Contents

Preface and Acknowledgments   vii

1 Introduction   1

2 The Management Challenges Facing Restaurant Chains   15

3 Building Blocks of Chain Organizations: Company
and Franchise Arrangements   31

4 Unit Growth   61

5 Uniformity   83

6 Local Responsiveness   111

7 Systemwide Adaptation   133

8 Conclusion   167

APPENDIXES

A The Literature on Owning or Franchising   187

B The Research Design   191

C The Role of the Field Visit   195

Notes   201

References   219

Index   229

About the Author   238

Preface and Acknowledgments

This book represents the culmination of an in-depth study of the management of chain organizations. Although we patronize local units of national chains every day—McDonald's, Pizza Hut, Starbucks, Holiday Inn, and Texaco gas stations, to name just a few—we tend to forget that these local units are part of systems that often span the United States, and sometimes even reach across the globe. Despite the fact that chain organizations pervade the business landscape, little has been written about this way of conducting business. The primary aim of this book is to present a model of management for chain organizations.

I originally became interested in chain organizations because they are a good example of a compelling practical and theoretical problem: Why do firms make or buy certain activities? Chain-restaurant organizations are fertile ground for studying this question because, as we shall see, most large restaurant chains consist of company-owned or franchised units—a variation of the make-or-buy choice. What I quickly learned, though, was that executives of chains did not see this as an "either-or" decision; indeed, most large chains both owned *and* franchised their restaurants. Even more interesting was the observation of executives and franchisees that the two sides of a chain affected each other in a variety of ways. It was at this point that I decided to shift the focus of the research from the simple question of own-or-franchise to the broader and more basic question of how chain-restaurant organizations are managed to achieve their objectives.

The primary idea I develop in this book is that the simultaneous use of these two different arrangements—an organizational configuration I label the plural form—enables a set of processes that strengthens each arrangement and makes the whole more than the sum of the parts. Drawing on my in-depth study of five large restaurant chains, this book lays out a model of management that is built on the processes enabled by the plural form. While one must be careful when generalizing from such a small sample, this approach offers fresh insights into why chains use company and franchise arrangements. More broadly, the book illuminates an important form of organization that has gone largely unnoticed, offering a new perspective for understanding the behavior and performance of other complex organizational designs that involve the use of internal and external relationships.

A host of people have contributed to the ideas presented in this book. Most important, the companies I studied and the managers and franchisees I interviewed were consistently helpful and tolerated with extraordinary patience my repeated visits and phone calls. I particularly want to thank the following people for their assistance throughout the project (I note the titles they held during the project): from KFC, John Cranor, president, and Gregg Reynolds, vice-president for government and environmental affairs; from Pizza Hut, Steve Reinemund, president, and Scott Mackey, vice-president for franchising; from Hardee's, Robert Autry, president, Lynn Summers, vice-president for executive development, and George Kelsey, area vice-president; from Jack in the Box, Mohammad Iqbal, executive vice-president of marketing, and Bruce Frazer, vice-president of product marketing.

The research reported here was conducted largely when I was a doctoral student in the Organizational Behavior program at Harvard University. As I gathered and analyzed data, Patrick Kaufmann, Paul Lawrence, and Peter Marsden, members of the faculty at Harvard, asked challenging questions and pushed me to sharpen my arguments. Robert Eccles provided guidance throughout the project and offered insightful comments on nearly every draft of every chapter. This research would not have been possible without the generous financial support provided by Harvard Business School.

Since joining the faculty at Harvard Business School, I have benefited greatly from many discussions about this work with my colleague Nitin Nohria. Nitin convinced me that this project should culminate in a book—advice that over the last few months I sometimes wished he had kept to himself! Several people have assisted in editing and preparing the final manuscript—Barbara Feinberg, Stephanie Woerner, Corey Sheehy, and Dan Erikson.

Finally, I want to thank my family and friends for their support while I worked on this project. I am especially grateful for the support given to me by my wife, Kristin. Whether I was stuck and could not begin to write or was on a roll and could not stop writing, she understood.

Jeffrey L. Bradach
August 1997

FRANCHISE ORGANIZATIONS

*The company-franchise relationship is like a marriage. You
    agree to enter the relationship, there are some basic rules,
    but there are a whole lot of things you have to work out as
    you go.*

*The company arrangement is organized as a military
    model. . . . If there are eleven people in the room who
    think one way and I think the other, then we may still
    do it my way.*

Chapter 1

Introduction

IN 1996, 40 percent of retail sales passed through chains that engage
in franchising, a proportion that some analysts expect to reach 50 percent
by the turn of the century. Industry after industry has been transformed,
as the local units of a chain replace the mom-and-pop proprietors that used
to sit on every street corner.[1] Chains are one of the dominant forms of
organization of our times, with a single chain often having hundreds, even
thousands, of units operating under a common trademark in diverse locations. Yet despite their importance we know very little about how chains
work. What are the challenges to operating such an organization? And
what kinds of practices have developed to meet those challenges? This book
addresses those two questions by studying five chain organizations in the
fast-food segment of the restaurant industry.

Managing a chain is more complicated than it looks. To an outside
observer, the local units in a chain appear the same. A McDonald's restaurant in Chicago looks largely the same as a McDonald's in Paris. Yet beneath
this veneer of similarity reside two entirely different types of units—company and franchise—exemplified by the quotes, at the head of this chapter,
from two executives. A manager of a company unit conforms to our
conventional notions of management: his or her superior exercises authority and the manager follows those directions. Franchisees, in contrast, view
themselves as independent businesspeople and see their relationship with
the chain as one between business partners. The job descriptions for corporate field personnel at the restaurant chain KFC suggest the managerial

implications of this difference: while the chain "manages" company employees, it "works with" franchisees. A frequently repeated industry adage captures the contrast: "You can tell company people, but you have to sell franchisees." Company and franchise arrangements embody different structures, systems, and processes, and each one has particular strengths and weaknesses. This book describes the characteristics of each arrangement and how they meet the challenges facing managers of chains.

While the differences between company and franchise units often tempt managers and academics into trying to determine which one is better, this book takes a different tack. I argue that company and franchise arrangements offer complementary attributes, with each one providing some strengths that are not available from the other. Chains composed of both company and franchise units—an organizational arrangement I label the *plural form*—can and do take advantage of these complementary attributes through a variety of processes that lead each side to influence the other; the overall performance of the chain is thereby strengthened. One CEO I interviewed explained the benefit of the plural form: "The chain [company units] gives you a system perspective, while the franchisees give you a local perspective. We are constantly working to balance both of these perspectives. By having both company and franchise units, we are able to do that." The challenge facing managers, then, is *not* to pick either company or franchise units but instead to use both and ensure that processes exist that leverage the strengths and ameliorate the weaknesses of each one.

The objective of this book is twofold. First, I offer a model for how a restaurant chain is organized and managed. It highlights how company and franchise units are managed, and identifies the key organizational variables that influence performance. Significantly, no such understanding exists in the academic literature; scholars have tended to focus on why chains should own or franchise units, not on how they are managed once they are in place (see Brickley and Dark 1987; Caves and Murphy 1976; Oxenfeldt and Kelly 1969; Rubin 1978). (Appendix A briefly reviews this literature.) The model presented here shows how chain organizations meet their four primary management challenges: (1) adding new units, (2) maintaining uniformity across units, (3) responding locally when appropriate, and (4) adapting the system as a whole when threats or opportunities arise. Company and franchise units meet each challenge differently, but the model offered here shows how the simultaneous use of both arrangements enhances a chain's ability to meet each challenge. This model should help practitioners and theorists better understand the underlying dynamics affecting the behavior and performance of chain organizations.

The second objective overlaps with the first. This book describes a new organizational category: the plural form (Bradach and Eccles 1989; Bradach 1997). The plural form is not unique to the restaurant industry; indeed, several business sectors exhibit structures and processes similar to those reported here (these are discussed in Chapter 8). By ignoring the distinctive properties of the plural form, academics and practitioners have overlooked important dynamics that may help to explain the long-term performance of organizations. The plural form, with its dissonant internal structures, enables an organization to produce variations in performance and behavior, which are essential to a manager's efforts to exercise control and promote innovation in a balanced way. The plural form also offers multiple flows of information, from within and outside the organization, which can enhance performance. The beauty of this arrangement is that these dynamics are embedded in the organizational structure; that is, the plural form provides a context that supports self-correction and self-renewal.

THE CHAIN INDUSTRY

Chains represent one of the dominant organizational forms of our time. Think about driving to work today. You were probably bombarded by signs advertising a unit of a chain organization—restaurants, hotels, pet shops, gas stations, tax-preparation services, and convenience stores. The sales of chain organizations have increased 94 percent over the past decade (Hoffman and Preble 1993). Since their explosive rise early in this century, the growth of chain organizations has outpaced the growth of the economy, reflecting the marketing power of these organizations and the value consumers place in them (Luxemberg 1985). For example, during the first three months of 1997, restaurant chains were consistently represented among the most advertised brands on prime-time network television, often accounting for five out of the top ten ("CMR Top 50" 1997). In the United States, a chain organization opens a new outlet every eight minutes (Sabir 1996)!

Franchising constitutes a vital facet of these chain operations. Franchisees purchase the right to operate a unit under the chain's brand name. Typically, the franchisee agrees to follow certain operating guidelines (to preserve the value of the brand), pays the chain operator a royalty fee based on revenue, and receives the income produced by the unit. In 1996 franchising contributed $800 billion to the U.S. economy, employing more than eight million people and generating, as noted, more than 40 percent of retail sales ("Franchising Guide" 1996). Franchised systems represent the most dynamic component of chain organizations. A poll by the International Franchise Association (IFA) documents that they are expanding at approximately twice the rate of company-owned enterprises ("Strong Franchising Growth Projected" 1996).

The role chains play in the economy is perhaps best illustrated by taking a look at the most famous chain of all: McDonald's. Ray Kroc founded the modern McDonald's Corporation in 1955, and the restaurant behemoth eventually earned him a spot on *Life*'s list of the "100 Most Important Americans of the 20th Century" ("Welcome to McDonald's" 1996). By 1963 the company was selling one million hamburgers daily, and by the mid-1990s the chain could easily boast "Way Over 100 Billion Served!" McDonald's staggering rate of expansion has left an indelible imprint on American society. Fully 96 percent of the U.S. population has visited McDonald's at least once, and 8 percent of our nation has eaten there today. Over half of the American population lives within three miles of a McDonald's restaurant, and eighteen million people are served daily in the United States, with a total of thirty million served daily worldwide. Furthermore, the company is a veritable employment powerhouse, with former and present employees constituting one-eighth of the current U.S. workforce. During the last forty years McDonald's has employed more than sixteen million people, and the company has recently superseded the U.S. Army as the institution that trains the greatest number of American youth—nearly 700,000 teenagers annually.

Every three hours, a new McDonald's restaurant opens somewhere in the world. Operating in nearly one hundred countries worldwide, McDonald's has also become a key player in the national and global economy, generating $30 billion in annual sales that produce a net income of more than $1.4 billion. McDonald's is one of the thirty key stocks that compose the Dow Jones Industrial Average; it is listed on the stock exchanges in New York, Chicago, Paris, Frankfurt, Munich, Tokyo, Zurich, Geneva, and Basel. The company itself manages roughly 15 percent of its twenty thousand restaurants worldwide, leaving the remaining 85 percent in the hands of 4,500 franchisees and affiliates. Many franchisees belong to advisory boards that advise senior management with input on the company's strategy and programs, and such collaboration often leads to innovative and successful new product lines. The Big Mac, Filet-O-Fish, and Egg McMuffin were all originally conceived by McDonald's franchisees.

Few chains can match the sweeping scope of McDonald's, of course. But these organizations nevertheless constitute a vital economic force that will pose managerial challenges for the foreseeable future. The chain-management model presented in this book is rooted in detailed research of five major restaurant chains. As a microcosm of the industry as a whole, these organizations serve as a window through which the problems and opportunities of chain management may be more fully understood. Of particular significance is the fact that restaurant chains represent the largest segment of chains based around a "business format" (for example, restaurants and hotels), in contrast to chains organized as vehicles for distributing products (for example, automobile dealerships and gas stations). While distribution chains account for the bulk of the revenue that passes through chain organizations, business-format chains are growing faster; more than 75 percent of all units are of the business-format variety, totaling over $250 billion in annual sales (Sabir 1996).

Restaurant chains constitute an especially powerful force even within the dynamic context of the franchise industry. Fifteen of the twenty largest franchised chains are restaurants ("Top 50 Franchisers" 1995), and in 1995, nineteen restaurant chains exceeded sales of $1 billion (Lombardi 1996). In addition, restaurant sales represent 50.6 percent of the money spent at business-format franchises (U.S. Department of Commerce 1987). In the restaurant industry, between 1975 and 1985, the share of sales captured by chains larger than 150 units grew from 20 percent to over 30 percent (Emerson 1990), reflecting the growing dominance of large chains. The largest chains have continued to experience rapid growth through the 1990s, with the fifty largest chains experiencing 8.6 percent sales growth in 1995, more than double the industry average ("Top 50 Franchisers" 1995).

In addition to their impressive market power, restaurant chains are especially useful to study because they represent a relatively mature segment of the fast-growing business-format chain industry. These organizations exemplify the policies, practices, and challenges associated with managing company and franchise arrangements. The maturity of the industry has also caused its leaders to focus more attention on management than is the case in some other industries where the attention of executives is almost exclusively focused on unit growth.

OVERVIEW OF THE MODEL

The argument made in this book is that the simultaneous use of company and franchise arrangements enables a set of processes that help a chain meet its four basic management challenges. The first indication of the plural form's significance is found in a survey of the structure of chain organizations. Among the 100 restaurant chains with the most units in the

United States in 1995, thirteen were composed entirely of company restaurants, eight were composed entirely of franchise restaurants, and seventy-nine used both types.[2] Table 1-1 shows that the plural form is especially prevalent among the largest chains that dominate the chain-restaurant industry. Furthermore, the plural form is stable over time. Among the top twenty-five chains in 1995, twenty-one out of the twenty-two plural forms were also plural forms in 1988; Subway became the sole exception by shedding its thirty company units to become a pure franchise chain. The plural form is a pervasive and enduring structure used by major restaurant chains.

A close examination of how chains are organized and managed suggests why the plural form may dominate. Figure 1-1 maps the key relationships among the management challenges and company and franchise arrangements. The process of unit growth (the top box), which produces the architecture of relationships, is distinct from the management processes associated with operating a chain on a daily basis (the bottom box). The columns labeled "Company" and "Franchise" offer a stylized representation of how each arrangement meets the challenge. The columns in italic type highlight the plural processes that link the two sides and lead the whole to be greater than the sum of its parts.

Table 1-1   The Mix of Company-Owned and Franchise Units in Restaurant Chains, 1995

Quartile	Pure Form	Plural Form
Quartile 1	5	20
166–249 units	20%	80%
Quartile 2	9	16
250–416 units	36%	64%
Quartile 3	4	21
435–711 units	16%	84%
Quartile 4	3	22
735–11,368 units	12%	88%

My research shows that the plural form facilitated the *unit growth process* by enabling a chain to escape some of the constraints of each form. Chains used three sources of growth to add units to the chain: company units, new franchisees that added a unit, and existing franchisees that added units. Each source of growth offered the chain operator different economic benefits and was associated with different costs; at the same time, each source of growth was constrained by different factors. The simultaneous use of company and franchise units enabled faster growth than either one by itself; I call this the *additive process*. Underpinning this additive dynamic were more subtle processes. For example, new markets were sometimes seeded with company units preceding the solicitation of franchisees to enter that market. The other major plural dynamic was the *socialization process*, which involved using company people as franchisees. This helped solve the problem of identifying new franchisees who understood the demands of the system, were proven performers, and were easy to "work with" (since persuasion was the main source of influence a chain operator used with franchisees).

Once in place, a chain's company and franchise arrangements were

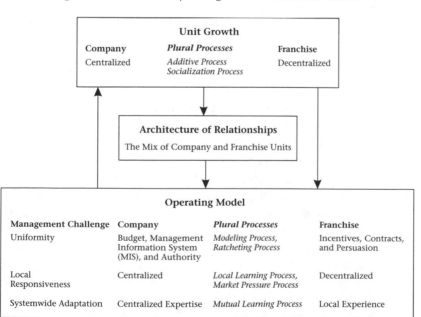

Figure 1-1   The Model of Management in Restaurant Chains

Unit Growth

Company	***Plural Processes***	**Franchise**
Centralized	*Additive Process*	Decentralized
	Socialization Process	

Architecture of Relationships

The Mix of Company and Franchise Units

Operating Model

Management Challenge	**Company**	***Plural Processes***	**Franchise**
Uniformity	Budget, Management Information System (MIS), and Authority	*Modeling Process, Ratcheting Process*	Incentives, Contracts, and Persuasion
Local Responsiveness	Centralized	*Local Learning Process, Market Pressure Process*	Decentralized
Systemwide Adaptation	Centralized Expertise	*Mutual Learning Process*	Local Experience

equally effective at maintaining *uniformity,* although different organizational mechanisms were used to meet this challenge. In general, the chain operator used more intensive monitoring to maintain uniformity in company units. Ironically, this incessant emphasis on uniformity was one of the reasons that its maintenance was such a problem: unintended consequences of tight control plagued the company arrangement. However, one of the key plural dynamics that affected uniformity—*the modeling process*—may have been contingent on the company arrangement's strict adherence to standards. In this process, franchisees who owned multiple units (which accounted for most franchise units) replicated the practices of company management. The *ratcheting process* also increased the system's overall level of uniformity by having each arrangement serve as a benchmark for the other on a variety of performance measures. These comparisons set in motion a process that increased—ratcheted up—performance.

Local responsiveness was higher in the franchise arrangement than in the company arrangement. The franchise contract motivated franchisees to look for opportunities to innovate, since they were recipients of the unit's profits; the contract also tended to give them some latitude in exercising local control. The franchise contract and industry norms allowed franchisees to make decisions on a variety of issues, while the company arrangement, with its high degree of centralization, inhibited local responsiveness. One of the benefits of the plural form could be seen in mixed markets (that is, where both arrangements existed): company units sometimes copied the local responses of nearby franchisees, what I label the *local learning* process. More subtly, the chain operator's staff, which directly and indirectly affected local responsiveness in both company-owned and franchise units, was more effective when operating in a plural form than in a pure company or franchise arrangement. I label this the *external control* process. Nevertheless, despite this dynamic and the existence of multi-unit franchising, which tended to weaken local responses in the franchise arrangement, local responsiveness remained higher in franchise arrangements.

The plural form played a crucial role in meeting the challenge of *systemwide adaptation.* A shift in the industry's competitive dynamics at the end of the 1980s toward greater emphasis on managing existing units (rather than growing simply by adding units) had made systemwide adaptation particularly important. Company and franchise arrangements complemented each other through all four stages of the systemwide-adaptation process: generating ideas, testing them, selecting them, and implementing them. Put simply, the plural form allowed a chain to produce a greater variety of ideas and apply a more thorough selection criteria to them than could be accomplished by either company or franchise units by themselves.

The complementary nature of the two arrangements extended to the implementation phase, too. Company-owned units were used to demonstrate the chain's commitment to a new idea, and franchisees continued to evaluate the feasibility and desirability of the proposed change. I call this the *mutual learning process.*

The arrows linking the growth and operating challenges boxes in Figure 1-1 highlight how chain operators actively used the growth process to influence the management of the chain, and in turn, how the management of the chain shaped the growth process. For example, every chain operator used its ability to control a franchisee's growth (which is a standard part of the franchisee's contract) as a source of influence to help it induce the franchisee to meet the other management challenges. At the same time, efforts to meet the management challenges sometimes affected the growth process. One chain, for example, pursued a strategy of placing company units in every major market so it could "show franchisees how to run their restaurants right," increasing the level of uniformity in the chain. An important contribution of this work is identifying how company and franchise units interact in the context of the four management challenges to make the entire chain operate more effectively.

THE PLURAL FORM

The basic definition of the plural form is straightforward: the simultaneous operation of two different structures—in this case, company and franchise arrangements—to perform similar tasks (Bradach and Eccles 1989). Each structure has strengths and weaknesses, and if an organization can use each to leverage the strengths and weaknesses of the other, then the overall structure will be stronger than either one operating by itself. The plural processes described in this book illuminate how a chain takes advantage of those complementary characteristics.

One of the most powerful features of the plural form in the restaurant setting is its capacity to provide both uniformity and systemwide adaptation, control and innovation. The difficulty of achieving both in any single organizational structure has often been noted in the literature (Burns and Stalker 1961; Duncan 1976; Kanter 1983; Leonard-Barton 1992; Tushman and O'Reilly 1997). The plural form's capacity to overcome this dilemma hinges on two features of the form: (1) balancing the amount of similarity and difference between the two arrangements, and (2) building processes that link both arrangements. Similarity permits managers in the chain operator's organization and franchisees to make valid comparisons across units and structures; differences—in this case produced by the different ownership and management structures—encourage the kinds of variations that are the source of control *and* innovation. The challenge facing the chain operator is to strike a balance between similarity and difference: too much similarity will diminish variety, while too much difference will overwhelm the organization's ability to maintain uniformity.

The tensions inherent in an organization that encompasses sharply differing structures can be difficult to manage, but those tensions also provide a mechanism for self-correction and self-renewal. Managing the two arrangements simultaneously helps the hierarchical company structure overcome its tendency toward ossification; it helps the franchise arrangement, with its looser "federal" structure, overcome its tendency toward entropy. In the final chapter of this book, I will explore these deep patterns of the plural form.

THE PLURAL FORM IN OTHER SETTINGS

The plural processes described here are specific to restaurant chains, but there is reason to believe that the underlying patterns of the plural form exist in other settings. Theories of tapered integration, which is the simultaneous use of in-house production and outside suppliers, underscore the benefits of such plural processes. The key advantages for the company include a more powerful bargaining position relative to suppliers, a good "feel" for costs, protection from strikes and opportunistic behavior of suppliers, and access to outside research and development activities (Scherer 1970; Porter 1980; Harrigan 1983). Walker and Weber (1984), using similar reasoning about the make-or-buy choice, argued that a firm's production knowledge and information reduces the risk of suppliers engaging in opportunistic behavior. The emphasis in all of these arguments is on the control benefits provided by the simultaneous operation of two structures—preventing supplier opportunism through the possession of good information and the credible threat of being able to terminate the relationship. The research reported in this book indicates that these defensive measures represent only a small part of the benefits of using a plural form.

Architectures of relationships similar to the plural form have been observed in other settings, too. For example, Monteverde and Teece (1982) reported that many manufacturers make and buy the same automobile component. Anderson and Schmittlein (1984) found that many companies simultaneously employ a direct sales force and utilize third-party distributors. Donahue's study of privatization of government services (1989) highlighted cases where local governments relied on public and private services for the same activities. In all of these cases, however, the research question was posed as one of institutional choice: which arrangement works best under what conditions? But this question overlooks the possibility that using different arrangements simultaneously might yield benefits unavailable to either one by itself.

More broadly, the plural processes cast light on a phenomenon that has gained attention recently: network organizations. Prognosticators say that the future belongs to firms that can effectively manage arrangements such as joint ventures, dynamic networks (Miles and Snow 1986), strategic partnerships (Kanter 1989), global coalitions (Porter and Fuller 1986), and federations of firms (Handy 1990). A pressing issue facing organizations utilizing these complex structures is how to manage them, since there is ample evidence that network arrangements often fail. The argument presented here suggests that the architecture of arrangements—specifically, the blending of a network relationship with a hierarchical one that constitutes the plural form—may offer a possible solution to this problem. Just as a franchise relationship by itself suffers from certain limitations, so too do many of these network arrangements; and just as the plural form remedies some of those problems in the case of chains, it may do the same in these other cases.

THE RESEARCH PROJECT

This book reports the results of an in-depth study of five chain restaurant organizations. The project was originally intended as an investigation into why chains owned or franchised their units. I was initially attracted to chains that both owned and franchised their units because they allowed me to examine the causes and consequences of using different governance structures, holding constant the industry, firm, and technology. In the first phase of the project, I visited three major restaurant chains (which asked not to be identified) to learn how they managed each arrangement. While respondents noted a variety of management structures and processes unique to each form, they also highlighted numerous examples of how company and franchise arrangements influenced each other. It became clear to me that viewing company and franchise arrangements as autonomous entities ignored some of the most important ways these arrangements contributed to overall organizational performance.

I studied five major restaurant chains: KFC (formerly known as Kentucky Fried Chicken), Pizza Hut, Hardee's, Jack in the Box, and Fishermen's

Landing* (see Table 1-2). The three largest chains in the sample were among the four largest chains in the United States in terms of revenue in the early 1990s; the other two, Jack in the Box and Fishermen's Landing, were ranked in the top 50. Each chain was a plural form, with the mix of units ranging from 26 percent company-owned to 65 percent company-owned. Except for Jack in the Box, the other four chains had been plural forms for over a decade and had maintained roughly the mix shown in Table 1-2 during that period. Jack in the Box had been entirely company-owned until 1980, when it began to franchise units. Through the early 1990s, these chains represented a few of the success stories in the chain-restaurant industry.[3]

In each chain, I conducted interviews with a vertical slice of the organization, starting with the CEO and moving down the ranks to company managers and franchisees. In all, I interviewed ninety people who worked for the companies and twenty-one franchisees; many of these people were interviewed several times. I also went on field visits with managers to company and franchise units, attended marketing cooperative meetings with company and franchise people, and interviewed leaders of the franchise councils that represented the franchise perspective to the company. My objective was to hear and see how chains actually functioned in practice, what the challenges facing managers were, and how they met them. A full description of the research process can be found in Appendix B.

THE ORGANIZATION OF THE BOOK

This book is organized around the four major challenges facing restaurant chains: unit growth (Chapter 4), uniformity (Chapter 5), local responsiveness (Chapter 6), and systemwide adaptation (Chapter 7). Each chapter details how the particular challenge is met by the company arrangement and by the franchise arrangement, then shows how the processes of the plural form influence the challenge.

The next two chapters set the stage for those analyses. Chapter 2 describes the characteristics of the chain-restaurant industry. The shared identity of restaurants; the local production of the product, service, and physical plant; and the use of small, geographically dispersed units lead to the four management challenges. Using industry data, I describe the shift in the emphasis of management from adding units to managing existing units, which makes the accomplishment of uniformity, local responsiveness, and systemwide adaptation increasingly important. Chapter 3 discusses the

---

* Fishermen's Landing is a disguised company name. Data related to the characteristics of the chain have been altered slightly to protect the anonymity of the chain, but these changes do not affect the arguments presented here.

building blocks of a chain organization: company and franchise arrangements. I identify and describe the key characteristics of each arrangement. The rest of the book builds on the characterizations offered in this chapter.

Chapter 8 summarizes the arguments and speculates about this study's implications for chains with different mixes of company and franchise arrangements. I then propose that plurality may be a strategy for resolving the dilemma of obtaining control and innovation within a single organizational design, and more broadly, may be a strategy for achieving self-correction and self-renewal in chain organizations. The chapter also compares the plural form to other organizational designs—"ambidextrous" and "hybrid" forms—that are attempts to generate patterns of organizational behavior that are similar to the plural form.

Chapter 8 devotes considerable space to exploring the theoretical implications of the research. Throughout the book, in an effort to make the text easily read, I have relegated to endnotes many of the theoretical issues that are raised by particular findings. Academics and consultants studying franchising and chain organizations may find the endnotes to each chapter and Chapter 8 especially interesting.

Table 1-2   *Descriptive Statistics on Chains in the Sample, 1989*

Company	Product Description	Total Units	Company Units	Franchise Units	Sales ($ millions)
KFC	Chicken, sandwiches	4,899	1,262 (26%)	3,637 (74%)	2,900
Pizza Hut	Pizza, pasta, sandwiches	5,707	2,770 (48%)	2,937 (52%)	2,800
Hardee's	Burgers, specialty meals, breakfast	3,076	1,018 (33%)	2,058 (67%)	2,725
Jack in the Box	Burgers, specialty meals, breakfast	957	637 (65%)	320 (35%)	775
Fishermen's Landing	Fish and chips	800	440 (55%)	360 (45%)	310

Chapter 2

The Management Challenges Facing Restaurant Chains

W E ARE IN essence managing six thousand identical factories spread around the world," said Steven Reinemund, CEO and president of Pizza Hut.* This succinct description highlights how chains differ from conventional organizations. While the implications of mass production and large-scale administration fill the literature on organizations, the mass production of organization itself—the cloning of a common set of practices in geographically dispersed units, which is what a chain does—has gone largely unnoticed. One explanation for this oversight is that people confuse the management of a unit, which is what they see down the street, with the management of a chain of identical units, which is what distinguishes chains from other forms of organization. The unique characteristics of chains lead to four challenges: adding units, uniformity, local responsiveness, and systemwide adaptation.[1] They reflect the local and system nature of managing chains—ensuring the efficient and effective operation of each local outlet (responding to local conditions and adding a new unit), while at the same time dealing with a set of problems at the level of the system (uniformity and systemwide adaptation).

The centrality of the four management challenges emerged as I conducted my research. Notably, the two streams of research discussed in Appendix A—agency cost theory and ownership redirection theory— encompass all four of the challenges in their arguments for the use of company and franchise units. Agency cost theory hinges on issues related to uniformity and local responsiveness, and ownership redirection theory focuses on the challenges of systemwide adaptation and the desire to add new units. When framed in this way, it is clear that the two theories do not compete with each other; they simply focus on different variables. One

---

* All of the people cited in the text will be identified by the titles they held when I conducted the research.

of the aims of my research is to bring all these variables into a single theoretical framework and clarify how each organizational arrangement, company or franchise, is organized to achieve *all* of these objectives. The importance of each challenge for a chain is influenced by several factors, such as a chain's corporate strategy, its size, and the competitive dynamics of its market segment. But all successful chains must to some extent accomplish all four challenges.

In the competitive environment that had developed in the early 1990s in the restaurant industry, the relative importance of the challenges changed. Historically, chain restaurants relied almost entirely on the addition of new units for growth (Emerson 1990). However, the saturation of restaurants in many markets, the rise in the cost of real estate and construction, and the emergence of strong competitors in every market segment forced chains to change their strategy and focus more on managing their existing units effectively. It was no longer the case, as one executive put it, that "We just have to build 'em and the people will come."

CHARACTERISTICS OF THE BUSINESS

The four management requirements emerge from three basic characteristics of chain restaurant organizations: (1) the shared identity of restaurants, (2) the local production of the product, service, and physical plant, and (3) the use of small and geographically dispersed units. All chain restaurants exhibit these characteristics, and they produce the management challenges discussed later in this chapter. Each characteristic is discussed below.

Shared Identity

By definition, the restaurants in a chain share a common identity. In their study of franchising, Caves and Murphy (1976, 572) stated that the operator of a unit "cloaks himself in the identity" of the chain's trademark. The shared identity manifests itself most obviously in the visual markings of a chain: McDonald's golden arches; KFC's red-and-white bucket; and Pizza Hut's red roofs. The same identifying marks are found in every unit of a chain. The value of sharing an identity across units comes from the message it sends to customers and the expectation it creates in them, just like the branding of a consumer product (Caves and Murphy 1976). Customers know what to expect when they enter a KFC restaurant to purchase a bucket of Original Recipe KFC chicken with eleven herbs and spices. Gregg Reynolds, vice-president of public affairs at KFC, emphasized the point: "KFC chicken should taste the same and be served with the same friendly service regardless of whether it is purchased in Tiananmen Square in Beijing, China, or in Louisville, Kentucky."

In their article about franchising, Caves and Murphy explained the role played by the trademark in chain organizations:

> Some franchised goods and services are purchased by mobile customers in local markets where they do not regularly shop. The cost of search for them is very high relative to the expected benefit; the assurance provided by the franchise trademark of a minimum level of quality in an alien market becomes particularly valuable to the buyer and thus can yield a rent to the producer (p. 574).

Some of the earliest chains were formed in the hotel and motel businesses and the fast-food restaurant business, where transient consumers are common and the power of trademarks is particularly useful (Luxenberg 1985). McDonald's, the largest chain-restaurant organization in the world, exemplifies the role of shared identity and consistency in a chain organization: "You may not think their food is the best, but you always know that a Big Mac will be a Big Mac," said one executive in another chain. Evidence of the trademark's importance was offered by Tom Dolan, formerly a Burger Chef franchisee, who converted to Hardee's when his old chain was acquired. He recalled that several Burger Chef franchisees decided not to convert but to operate independently: "They are no longer in business. They underestimated the value of the sign."

The shared visual identity of a chain's units mirrors the shared operational identity. In their textbook on the design and functioning of marketing channels, Stern and El-Ansary (1988) categorize fast-food chains as "business format" operations and contrast them to product-distribution channels.[2] The shared identity encompasses the "methods of doing business" because that is how a chain operator ensures the provision of the uniform product and services represented by the common visual identity. In my research, participants in chain organizations were emphatic that the "product" in restaurant chains almost always was more than the food a unit provided. A common performance measurement tool (discussed in Chapter 5) was the QSC audit, which measured the quality of the food, service, and cleanliness of the restaurant. All these elements were deemed essential aspects of the product. Even the label "fast food" captures an essential characteristic of the product for most chains. The shared identity of units in a chain encompasses not only visual markings but also the physical design of the unit, the menu, the production processes, and the service.

An important way restaurant chains build and reinforce their shared identity is through advertising. For example, during the first three months of 1997, restaurant chains were consistently represented among the most advertised brands on prime-time network television, often accounting for five out of the top ten ("CMR Top 50" 1997). The advertising spending of four of the five chains in my sample placed them among the top 200 brands in the United States in 1988. KFC, for example, spent over $100 million in 1988 on advertising. The economies of scale associated with television advertising provide large chains with an important source of competitive advantage, and in part explains the growing concentration of the restaurant business in large chains (Caves and Murphy 1976; Emerson 1990). The unit-growth process in chains was in part shaped by the need to obtain a critical mass of units in a market to make advertising economical. Advertising was not a necessary condition for success—Fishermen's Landing did no advertising, for example—but for many chains it built and reinforced the chain's shared identity and influenced other management processes.

The Local Production of the Product, Service, and Plant

In the chain-restaurant industry, the product, service, and plant are produced and maintained for the most part at the local level. Behind the outward features of a shared identity, a variety of local activities are required to operate a unit and a chain. While the shared identity creates the appearance of mass production, Steven Reinemund's assertion that his chain is composed of thousands of identical factories implies a local dimension to chains that is often missed. The physical production of the food, for example, displays the local nature of organizational activity:

- Every Pizza Hut restaurant prepares fresh dough twice a day.

- Every Hardee's restaurant begins work at 5 a.m. by making biscuits from scratch.

- Every KFC restaurant cleans, breads, and fries chicken throughout the day and night.

- Every Fishermen's Landing restaurant cooks the customer's order when it is placed.

- Every Jack in the Box restaurant cooks, dresses, and packages the hamburgers as customers place their orders.

The physical product in a restaurant chain is largely created in each local unit, unlike a distribution chain, which sells centrally produced items like cars, sweaters, or ice cream. The management challenges presented by these different situations varies widely, with the former type requiring a variety of management mechanisms to maintain the presentation of a shared identity. The chains I studied used detailed procedure manuals, automated equipment, centrally preprepared supplies, and training to ensure the creation of identical products, but a large part of the production process nonetheless was local.

The service component of a chain restaurant's business format is also an inherently local production. Service involves activities that are created and delivered in individual restaurants, for example, speed of delivery, friendliness of employees, and cleanliness of restrooms. In the chain-restaurant industry, service is integral to the business format. For example, the successful fast delivery of fresh food to customers, a central aspect of the fast-food segment of the restaurant industry, depends on a range of factors in each restaurant. Given the perishable nature of the physical product, small buffer inventories separate the market (in the form of customers' orders) and the production process. If the local manager does not respond to shifts in demand promptly and appropriately, product shortages or excesses occur quickly and lead either to slow service (because the product must be made) or to high levels of waste (because products must be thrown out). "Service time," like other elements of a chain restaurant's services, is a result of activities that happen in each particular outlet.

Finally, the physical plant—the siting and building of a unit—is "produced" locally. Selecting restaurant locations and negotiating for them occurs locally, even if the central office sometimes has control over the final decisions. In any case, knowledge of local conditions is a critical success factor in these activities. Patterns of automobile and foot traffic, for example, and the opening or closing of nearby businesses that provide potential customers, are among the local factors that determine the success of a site. As the director of development at Jack in the Box, Bill Motts, remarked: "If you don't factor in the effect of the installation of a traffic island, for example, you might overstate the potential of a site. A seemingly small oversight like that can determine whether a unit can reach break even." Along with selecting a site for a restaurant, the actual building of a unit is a local production. Chain operators often must approach community zoning commissions for variances (for example, for drive-through windows), and local building contractors must be selected and managed during construction. Indeed, as Gerald McGuiness, executive vice-president of development for Hardee's, observed, "If you make a mistake at the beginning, it doesn't matter how well you run the unit because it won't make money."

Small, Geographically Dispersed Units

Convenience is a key attribute of the fast-food business. Consumers will not go far out of their way for a fast-food meal. Convenient location is the top reason for choosing a quick-service restaurant, followed by fast service, according to ADVO's consumer survey on fast-food restaurants.[3] Consistent with that finding, Emerson (1982) reports that brand loyalty is weak among fast-food patrons, with the typical consumer eating in 3.4 different chains in a six-month period. The explosive growth of drive-through windows in chain restaurants and the widespread experimentation with delivery, carts, kiosks, vans, and other means of bringing the product closer to customers reflect how chains have tried to make themselves more accessible and convenient to consumers. In fact, the key factor chains in my research used in evaluating the viability of a potential restaurant location was the number of cars that had direct access to the site.

The need to be convenient for consumers has two important organizational implications: first, firms must disperse their units across different locations, and second, the minimum efficient scale of a unit must be small. Chains locate their units where the customers are (for example, malls and schools) or are likely to pass by (for example, exits off major roads). McDonald's has located its outlets such that 50 percent of the U.S. population lives within three miles of a McDonald's restaurant (Love 1986). Customers will not go too far out of their way to visit a fast-food chain—even a McDonald's!

As a consequence, chains reach customers by building and operating numerous geographically dispersed small units rather than a few large units. The relatively constricted market reach of a unit is reflected in the typical franchise contract. It usually specifies that no unit may be located within a one- or two-mile radius of an existing unit. The logic is that if units were located closer, they would cannibalize each other's sales; put another way, if consumers are farther than a mile or two from a unit, they are not likely to visit it.

Conclusion: Characteristics of Restaurant Chains

The shared identity of units; the local production of products, services, and plant; and the use of small and geographically dispersed units combine to create a complex set of management challenges for managers. Yet these dynamics are not often discussed in the existing literature on organizations. In most organizational theory, the key to understanding the design of an organization revolves around the concept of specialization.[4] While the internal operation of a restaurant displays a high degree of specialization— in fact, it might be viewed as the modern-day version of Adam Smith's pin factory—the relationship among units in a chain displays a different organizing principle. Chain organizations are built on the principle of cloning: replicating a business format with fidelity. This basic organizing principle, the product of the three characteristics of the industry, leads to the four management challenges faced by chain operators.

THE FOUR MANAGEMENT CHALLENGES

Meeting these challenges is a necessary but not sufficient condition for success: while a poor business proposition cannot be salvaged by simply fulfilling the management requirements, a sound business concept surely will be subverted by *not* meeting them. Later, we will see that the last three challenges have grown in importance with the maturation of the chain-restaurant industry. Growth by adding units remains important, but success now depends more heavily on meeting the challenges associated with managing existing units—uniformity, local responsiveness, and system-wide adaptation.

Growth by Adding Units

The revenue of an individual restaurant is difficult to increase beyond a certain level since convenience is an immutable characteristic of a site. Once a site is established, it is difficult to change its convenience to stimulate further growth.[5] The inherent economic constraints posed by a given location help explain the finding that new stores in major chains achieve their "maximum attainable volume" in just a few months (Emerson 1982); it also accounts for the classic answer to the question, "What is the key to success?"—location, location, location. It is extremely hard work to boost the sales of existing units. Accordingly, chains rely heavily on the addition of new units to grow their business. Table 2-1 shows data for four of the chains I studied, which highlights their reliance on new units for growth.

In each chain, the growth in the number of units far exceeded the growth in the revenue generated by existing units. In an informative analysis, Emerson (1982) found that the real sales growth of existing units at McDonald's had been flat for over twenty years and that its revenue and profit increases—which had been monumental through the 1960s, 1970s, and 1980s—had come almost exclusively from unit additions. The tight relationship between adding units and chain growth suggests that the business format itself is the product, one that is essentially "sold" with the opening of each new outlet. In fact, it is precisely this product—the business format—that a franchisee buys when joining a chain.

Several other factors reinforce the penchant of chains to grow by adding units. First, the addition of a unit increases a chain's market presence, a form of advertising itself that reinforces a chain's identity; at the same time, a new unit benefits from the already established identity of the chain. The rapid achievement of the "maximum achievable sales" mentioned above is in part a function of the preexisting identity, conveyed through the trademark, that provides a new unit with an automatic reputation before it even begins operating. Adding units in a market is also motivated by a chain's desire to capitalize on the synergy created by clustering units together and presenting customers with a pervasive visual presence.[6]

Furthermore, each new unit benefits from the accumulated expertise of the chain. Most of the costs incurred by the chain to create and refine a business format occur early in the life of a chain. Later in a chain's life cycle, the chain operator clones units, which in essence spreads the cost of research and development for the format over a larger base with the addition of each unit. On top of that, the accumulated expertise developed during the cloning process itself, such as improved criteria for selecting sites, faster plans for building restaurants, and more efficient operating strategies, enables chain operators to upgrade their chain's overall performance as new franchises open. Emerson (1990, 109) notes that McDonald's

Table 2-1   Average Annual Growth in Sales and Units, 1983–1988

Chain	Unit Sales in Real $ (increase)	Number of Units (increase)
KFC	−1.4%	1.8%
Pizza Hut	0.7%	7.3%
Hardee's	0.1%	9.9%
Jack in the Box	1.1%	4.1%

Source: *1989 Technomic 100*, Technomic, Inc., Chicago, Ill., and estimates of Technomic analysts.

opens new units at performance levels slightly higher than those of its existing restaurants, a pattern that is in part explained by the continuous improvement and application of knowledge to new units. (Chapter 4 describes in detail the strengths and weaknesses of adding company and franchise units to the system, and the advantages that accrued to chains that did both at once.)

Uniformity

Maintaining the uniformity of units in a chain is what preserves its shared identity. In a business-format chain, uniformity permeates almost every aspect of a unit's operation. What makes this challenge particularly daunting is that key elements of the business format require a variety of local activities to execute. Lovelock (1984, 480) highlighted the difficulties inherent in managing even a single-site service business: "Producing a service typically involves assembling and delivering the output of a mix of physical facilities and mental or physical labor. . . . These factors make it hard for service organizations to control for quality and to deliver consumers a consistent product." Lovelock emphasized the difficulty of managing a single service-based unit, but the challenge facing a restaurant chain is even more complex. James Randall, CEO of Fishermen's Landing, explained the importance of achieving consistency:

> By maintaining consistent, high quality operations *across all our units* while at the same time maintaining that same level of consistency *in the same units over time,* we are able to insure that our customers get what they come for: a high quality meal in a pleasant environment. Next time they see the Fishermen's Landing sign, they'll think of us and stop by. This is a tough thing to do, but it is our objective.

The local production of the product, service, and plant, coupled with the geographic dispersion of units, made the maintenance of uniformity a constant challenge for chain operators.

Regardless of whether an outlet is owned by the company or a franchisee, several common measures are taken to imprint uniformity into the business format. Voluminous operating manuals, for example, specify virtually every aspect of a unit's operation. As we shall see in Chapter 5, these uniform operational standards are intensively detailed, breaking down the activities involved in managing a unit into minute parts and prescribing procedures for performing each part. In my study, local operators (both in the company and franchise arrangement) followed the procedures because they were simple, easy, and (usually) proven, and also because they created an interlocking set of activities that discouraged improvisation. One franchisee put it this way: "Why venture into the unknown? Once you start screwing around with the format, things get really complicated."

These chains promoted uniformity in several other indirect ways. For instance, all restaurant sites in a chain were selected on the basis of similar criteria, the same architectural plans were used to build units (with some allowance for customization), and the equipment and its layout were almost identical in all units. The uniform physical layout of the restaurant and the automated pace of the equipment channeled the behavior of local operators into uniform patterns, whether they were company managers or franchisees. As Kaufmann (1989) pointed out, uniformity also reduces the cost of monitoring, since comparisons of units that subscribe to a standard format make it relatively easy to detect deviations. Comparisons were integral to the management of chains.

Local Responsiveness

Because individual restaurants operate in diverse local markets, local responsiveness is a critical factor in managing any specific outlet. Each unit may face different competitive circumstances, such as small regional competitors or competitive units located next door; each unit may face different customer tastes, such as the demand for Mexican cuisine in south Texas or for pork products in Iowa; and each unit may face different dynamics related to the factors of production, such as the difficulty of finding crew personnel in urban markets or finding a reliable supplier for a perishable item in remote markets. Therefore, each unit must be responsive to local conditions—sometimes as part of the effort to maintain uniformity (for example, finding appropriate factors of production) and sometimes to alter the uniform format to better match a local market.

Local responses can be grouped into two categories. First, *tactical local responses* involve adapting various business policies and practices to a market. These business policies and practices operate beneath the cloak of systemwide uniformity. For example, selecting local produce and dairy vendors, pricing, and hiring employees are responsive to the particularities of local markets but do not change the uniform format. Second, *strategic local responses* alter the uniform business format in an effort to better meet the needs of the local context. For example, Hardee's served pork sandwiches in Iowa in response to, and in support of, local pork producers. Every KFC restaurant served the standard "Original Recipe," along with either "Extra Tasty Crispy" or "Hot and Spicy" chicken depending on the characteristics of local markets. The boundaries dividing these two types of local responses were sometimes vague in practice. Pricing, for example, was a tactical local response at KFC and Pizza Hut, but with the national advertising of prices in these chains, prices were increasingly becoming part of the uniform format. Similarly, capital investments may be a tactical local response—replacing an old oven, for example—or may be part of a system-wide movement toward a new image—installing new ovens to produce a new product for a market.

Every unit in a chain must generate tactical local responses, which are an inevitable outgrowth of the local production of products and services and the geographic dispersion of units. In contrast, chains and/or individual franchisees choose to engage in strategic local responses. Fishermen's Landing and Jack in the Box, with very few exceptions, subscribed to a strategy that permitted no strategic local responses: almost all units throughout the chain, for example, served exactly the same menu. The strategies at KFC, Pizza Hut, and Hardee's allowed for greater latitude in varying elements of the uniform format in response to local circumstances, particularly in the menu. By definition, of course, strategic local responses reduced the uniformity of a chain. Whether this tradeoff was seen as worth making often depended on the extent to which it increased a unit's ability to meet the demands of a local market.

Systemwide Adaptation

Systemwide adaptation is how threats to and opportunities for the chain as a whole are translated into management action. A systemwide adaptation changes the shared identity of a chain, establishing a new standard of uniformity. The introduction of a new product in a chain is the most visible and common systemwide adaptation. These adaptations take many other forms, as well: implementing new operating procedures for making pizzas, installing new menu boards in Jack in the Box restaurants, replacing conventional ovens at Hardee's with "top-side cookers" that simultaneously cook both sides of a hamburger, and advertising a promotion for KFC's "Hot Wings" product. Systemwide adaptation is a complex management challenge because an adaptation must be applicable, at least to some extent, to units competing in diverse local markets and at the same time be easy to implement uniformly in thousands of units.

My research concentrated mostly on product innovations, although the underlying process is similar for other types of adaptations. Product innovations I observed ranged from major additions to the menu, like the Hardee's Broiled Chicken Sandwich, to minor variations such as Pizza Hut's Cheese Lover and Pepperoni Lover pizzas, which simply added more cheese or pepperoni to an existing product. Even these minor variations, however, can affect the production process in major ways. Pizza Hut had to devise production methods that allowed for the addition of cheese to a pizza but that would not increase the pizza's cooking time; otherwise, the conveyor system that moved pizzas through the oven would have to be slowed, which would diminish the restaurant's production capacity. When a chain operates thousands of restaurants and serves two million meals per day, as is the case with KFC, very small effects in a single local unit multiply into enormous effects for the system. In the testing process, the operational impact of an adaptation has to be considered along with determining whether the adaptation meets the needs of enough consumers in enough different markets to be profitable.

While the entire business format is integral to a chain's identity, the core element of the identity of most chains is the menu. The names of many chains reflected this emphasis (*Burger* King, *Pizza* Hut). Moreover, from a financial perspective, adding or deleting items from a menu has an immediate and direct impact on a chain's revenue and profits. In hard economic times, chains search for new products to attract more customers. Along with inducing chains to add items that fit into the existing menu, competitive pressure can lead to more radical menu shifts: for example, the testing of pizza and chicken at McDonald's. Similarly, Hardee's, traditionally a hamburger chain, introduced fried chicken in some of its units in 1989; in fact, the company's primary motivation in acquiring the Roy Rogers chain was to obtain the expertise required for the production of chicken. Another important factor causing chains to change their menus has been the American public's growing concern with health and nutrition (Emerson 1990). Over the past decade, chicken sandwiches were added to the menu at Hardee's, salad bars were added at Pizza Hut, prepackaged salads were introduced at Jack in the Box, and KFC experimented with a skinless "Lite 'n Crispy" product.

A chain's strategy influences its need for systemwide adaptation. Fishermen's Landing competes in a market segment that is largely insulated from strong competitors, and therefore has changed its format little since its founding. Even so, the firm has prepared for future systemwide adaptations, as illustrated in its 1989 franchise contract, which was renegotiated to give the chain operator the right to collect advertising fees from franchisees. At the other extreme of systemwide adaptation is Jack in the Box, where innovation was constant during the period of my study; new products were added to the menu approximately every three months. "Constant innovation is the core of our business strategy," said Mo Iqbal, executive vice-president for marketing at Jack in the Box. KFC, Pizza Hut, and Hardee's fell between the extremes of Fishermen's Landing and Jack in the Box. All three chains aggressively added products, improved production processes, upgraded facilities, and advertised their businesses to meet the growing competition in their markets.

Managers I spoke with in all the chains believed that systemwide adaptation was gaining in importance. George Kelsey, an area vice-president at Hardee's, summarized the common sentiment: "The capacity to act will determine the winners and losers in the industry." Managers also stated that systemwide adaptation was the most complex and difficult of all the challenges. The rest of Reinemund's comments from the first sentence in this chapter emphasize this point: "We are in essence managing six thousand identical factories around the world. When an idea is proposed we have to evaluate whether it will work in all the different contexts. With franchisees this process is even more complicated because they are interested in a unit while we are managing a system." As the ability of chains to grow by adding units has diminished, systemwide adaptation has become increasingly important. And it is in this context that the crucial role played by the plural form becomes most evident.

Conclusion: The Four Management Challenges

While all chains must address the four management challenges, the previous discussion highlights a few factors that influence the salience of each challenge for any given chain. The most obvious mediating factor is a chain's *business strategy*. For example, the chains in my study varied in the emphasis they placed on strategic local responsiveness and systemwide adaptation. Fishermen's Landing allowed few strategic local responses and it adapted the system very infrequently, though it was preparing itself for future adaptations. In contrast, Jack in the Box's strategy called for continuous innovation, which made systemwide adaptation a central challenge. The other three chains fell in between these two extremes. A chain's business strategy also influenced its decision of whether to add units quickly or slowly. Still, a chain had to add units if it wanted to grow. Uniformity and tactical local responses were less susceptible to variation across chains. Although the importance of each challenge varied by chain, all four of them played a vital managerial role.

The *size of a chain* also influenced the importance of the challenges. All the chains in my sample were large, so this factor is difficult to discern from my data, but it is clear that the management challenges are affected by a chain's size. Maintaining uniformity and local responsiveness grow more difficult as a chain expands into new and more varied markets. For the same reasons, identifying and implementing systemwide adaptations that fit the varied markets become more complicated as a chain grows larger. Not only do the challenges shift with unit growth, but the nature of organization itself changes with size, as discussed in Chapter 7.

Finally, the *competitive dynamics* of a market segment and of the industry influenced the importance of each challenge. Fishermen's Landing's relatively competition-free segment allowed it to worry less about systemwide adaptation and focus more intensively on uniformity. In contrast, the fierce competition that existed in the chicken, pizza, and hamburger businesses made it important for the other chains to adapt quickly to opportunities and threats.[7] The aggressive discounting that was then occurring in these segments, for example, made it important for a chain to be able to react quickly to new advertising by a competitor. While the strategy of a chain, its size, and the competitive dynamics of its market segment moderated the emphasis placed on each challenge, all of the challenges played a role in the successful management of a chain.

THE NEW BASIS OF COMPETITION: MANAGING EXISTING UNITS

The dynamics of the chain-restaurant industry in the 1980s shifted the emphasis from adding new units to managing existing units. Robert Autry, CEO at Hardee's, offered an observation shared by many industry participants:

> In the past, the almost sole objective of a chain was to build as many units as fast as possible. It was a race to get key locations. Today, real estate is expensive, we have saturated many of our markets with units, and competitors are everywhere—including right next door to our units. We now have to step back and give more thought to how to run units—or else we won't be around too long.

John Roberts, founder and chairman of Fishermen's Landing, agreed: "In the old days you just put up the unit and went to the bank. Today, it's a lot more complicated. You have to do things right." The competitive nature of the industry is perhaps captured best by a common sight on America's roadways today: several fast-food outlets standing side by side, all vying for the same customer.

Over the second half of the 1980s, chains maintained their historical growth rates largely through unit additions. As the decade progressed, though, this source of growth slowed. In 1985, among the one hundred largest chains, unit growth was 8.3 percent and real sales growth was

6 percent. By 1990, unit growth had fallen to 4 percent and real sales growth dropped to 1.5 percent. Ironically, as this data shows, the addition of units compounds the problem of weakening existing unit performance: "There is a continuation of growth in supply [of units] coupled with very little growth in demand," noted an industry expert, which implied increased competitive pressure on existing units ("The NRN Top 100" 1989). Malcolm Knapp, a leading industry analyst, highlighted the significance of the shift: "In the '70s you just needed to be clean and consistent to be profitable. Today, the easy pickings are gone" (Deutsch 1988). As the decade ended, the increased use of discounting and promotions signaled the growing intensity of competition.[8] Also, during this time the unit-growth process itself became more expensive as real estate and construction prices escalated faster than the growth in revenues of the average unit (Emerson 1990).[9]

While unit growth remained important at the end of the decade, through the 1980s a chain's success came to depend more heavily on implementing uniformity, local responsiveness, and systemwide adaptation. Consumers had more choices in selecting a place to eat, and chains had to better meet the expectations of consumers by maintaining uniformity or risk losing them. There was heated competition in most local markets, which required more effective local responses. And shifting consumer tastes, new competitors, and increased market pressures made systemwide adaptation an organizational necessity. Chain operators had to reshuffle the priority of the management challenges: managing existing units effectively became just as important, if not more important, to a chain's success as adding new units.

These management challenges are not a simple checklist. From the perspective of a chain operator, managing a restaurant chain entails balancing the tensions and tradeoffs involved with these complicated relationships. Organizational theory must therefore address how the design and functioning of a chain circumscribes these dynamics. The next chapter describes the characteristics of the franchise and company organizational arrangements, while chapters 4 through 7 go into more detail about the dynamics involved in meeting each management challenge.

Chapter 3

Building Blocks of Chain Organizations: Company and Franchise Arrangements

COMPANY AND franchise restaurants in a chain look alike from the outside, but this appearance masks major differences in how each arrangement is organized and managed. As my research showed, these differences in structure and management provided a chain with distinctive strengths and weaknesses in relation to meeting the management challenges. This chapter describes the arrangements in detail by comparing their key characteristics.

A chain's organization chart reflected the distinctiveness of company and franchise arrangements. In four of the chains I studied, the organization assigned responsibility for managing company and franchise units to separate departments. The only exception to this structure was Fishermen's Landing, which instead assigned senior managers in the company arrangement to franchisees. Whether using specialized or senior personnel, the organizational design of chains reflected a simple fact: company and franchise arrangements were not interchangeable and required different skills to manage. Indeed, the titles and job descriptions for the chain operator's field personnel assigned to the franchise and operations (company) departments—"franchise consultants" and "area managers," respectively—indicated the contrasting management strategies used in each arrangement: area managers "managed" company employees, and franchise consultants "worked with" franchisees.

Each arrangement's distinctive characteristics lead to different organizational designs. Figure 3-1 summarizes the complex constellation of economic, organizational, and normative characteristics that differentiate company and franchise arrangements. Reading down each column highlights the internal coherence of each arrangement; reading across each row outlines the contrast between the two arrangements. The box at the bottom of the chart identifies two crucial aspects of chains that are not easily categorized as either company or franchise elements; they are products of both. Many franchisees own multiple units; I refer to them as multi-unit franchisees. They typically have internal structures that replicate many of the characteristics of the company arrangement. Cross-cutting career paths often move people from one arrangement to the other.

CHARACTERISTICS OF THE COMPANY AND FRANCHISE ARRANGEMENTS

The characteristics of each arrangement highlighted in Figure 3-1 transcended the specific management challenges of unit growth, uniformity, local responsiveness, and systemwide adaptation, but they nevertheless were integral to each arrangement's capacity to achieve them. These characteristics serve as the foundation for the analysis in the following chapters.

Figure 3-1   Characteristics of Company and Franchise Arrangements

Characteristic	Company	Franchise
Contractual Relationship	Employee Zone of acceptance	Partner Formal contract
Chain Operator's Economics	Profits	Fees Royalties
Local Operator Rewards and Orientation	Salary Internal system	Net income External market
Source of Chain Operator Influence	Authority	Persuasion
Architecture of Information	Transparent operation "Less-rich"	Opaque operation "Rich"
Structural Type	Hierarchy Stable structure People move	Federation Fluid structure People stable

Multi-Unit Franchise:
Hierarchy within federation

Cross-cutting Career Paths:
"Making" franchisees

The Contractual Relationship

The labels "employee" and "franchisee" imply a relationship between the chain operator and local operator. The two relationships can be usefully characterized as different types of contracts: an employment contract with company personnel, and a business contract with franchisees. These different kinds of contracts support different types of relationships—company employees are subordinates of the chain operator, and franchisees are partners with the chain operator. A quick glance at the classified section of a newspaper illustrates this dichotomy: chain operators advertise for employees in the "Employment" section, while solicitations for franchisees are found in the "Business Opportunities" section.

In the company arrangement of the chains I studied, the contract between employees and the firm was implicit; rarely did a written employment contract exist. The nature of the employment contract is aptly captured by Simon's concept (1976) of a "zone of acceptance," an area where the subordinate is willing to accept the decisions made by a superior. A managerial translation of this academic jargon was provided by a division vice-president who noted: "If there are eleven people in the room who think one way and I think the other, then we may still do it my way."

The zone of acceptance is at the center of Williamson's assessment of the advantages of hierarchy (1985, 78): "[In hierarchy,] adaptations can be made in a sequential way without the need to consult, complete, or revise interfirm agreements." A superior may choose to explain his or her decision to subordinates, but that is not necessary since they must comply with the dictates of the superior. A vice-president of marketing in one chain posed the issue clearly: "Sometimes company people complain about new products or marketing programs, but you accepted the paycheck so you better get on board." The right of the chain operator to exercise authority to achieve objectives that fall within the zone of acceptance facilitated the rapid implementation of systemwide adaptations.

In contrast, the chain operator–franchisee relationship was a partnership between owners. As a franchisee who owned forty-seven units stated, "I never have worked for anybody in my life." He elaborated on his relationship with the chain: "They do most of the marketing; they're the experts. Also, in the site selection process they remind us of things we might overlook. They ask lots of questions. A lot of us [franchisees] probably think we know more than they do, but they certainly can help. I am independent but a partner with the company." Judy Ross, a Fishermen's Landing franchisee, described her relationship to the chain operator in similar terms: "I am an independent owner, but the company is a phone call away." This description echoed the comments of yet another franchisee: "In the company you can go belly up and still have a job. Not here. The difference is that I'm an independent businessperson. I'm on my own." All franchisees I talked to asserted their independence and identified themselves as an owner.

These characterizations were not self-delusions on the part of franchisees; chain operators agreed with them. George Kelsey, an area vice-president at Hardee's, observed, "For company people, this is a job; for franchisees, this is their business—they may have their life savings at stake." John Cranor, CEO of KFC, described the relationship this way: "We share a joint enterprise where we have different responsibilities and have different roles."

Scholars and practitioners agree that this characterization of the franchise relationship is at odds with the terms of the written contract, which slants in favor of the chain operator.[1] The franchise contract for the chains in this study was usually between thirty and fifty pages long, and was for fifteen to twenty years in duration. It included a variety of specific provisions concerning the operation of the franchisee's unit(s), such as the hours of operation, the training required of franchisees and provided by franchisors, the products on the menu, the financial obligations of the parties, and the conditions for termination of the contract. In an analysis of franchise contracts, Hadfield (1991, 943) finds "the great weighting of the clauses towards the obligations of the franchisee." A franchisee told me that "I showed the contract to my lawyer and he said, 'Forget it.' He said it was incredibly one-sided, but the company won't alter a single word, so I just signed it."

The contract sets the expectations of the parties and creates a framework for the relationship, but it does not reflect fully the actual conduct of the relationship (Macauley 1963; Macneil 1978). Indeed, while the franchise contract appeared to create the functional equivalent of the employment relationship, the conduct of the relationship in practice revealed that the two were entirely different.[2] Participants agreed that the franchise contract was important, but they argued that its role was often exaggerated. A division vice-president stated that "Despite the fact that the contract is very one-sided in the franchisor's favor, it is not clear who would win if these provisions went to court." An assistant director of legal affairs for Hardee's, Dave Gordon, explained further why disputes rarely ended up in litigation:

Usually a useful response is elicited before anything gets that far. Not only is it not in the interest of the franchisee to get kicked out, but we [the corporation] can end up without a royalty from that unit if we kick them out. On top of that, it is by no means clear who would win in litigation. The big company picking on the small entrepreneur does not usually play well in front of juries.

John Cranor, of KFC, agreed with this line of reasoning, although he argued, "Sometimes you have to pursue an issue even if it is incredibly expensive. It sends a signal that we are monitoring the system. But things really have to get bad before we go that far."

Despite the contention among some scholars that termination is the central tool that chain operators use to manage franchisees (see Rubin 1978; Klein 1980; Brickley and Dark 1987), my data suggest that it played a minor role in the day-to-day management of franchisees.[3] The most common litigated issue was the nonpayment of royalties, not "operational defaults" such as compromising uniformity. Dave Gordon explained why: "It is easy to prove in court whether a franchisee has paid or not. It is really hard, though, to make an operational default stick. They might still be making $700,000 per year, so a judge will often not buy the argument that the operation is failing." Ken Williams, the chief operating officer at Jack in the Box, concurred, saying only somewhat facetiously that, "You need a dead rat in the kitchen, and preferably three or four, if you want a chance of winning."

In sum, the formal contract was a limited, and sometimes misleading, map to understanding how the chain operator–franchise relationship was conducted in practice.[4] One of the central puzzles this research addresses is how franchisees are managed by the chain operator in the absence of strong, easily enforceable contracts.

The metaphor used most frequently by managers to describe the franchise relationship was borrowed from the closest and most complex of human partnerships: marriage. A director of franchising for one chain described it this way: "It is a big decision to join a chain. You're hooking up for life—or at least for a long time. You really need to make sure you're compatible so you can work together. I equate the relationship to a successful marriage. Communication is key. And that is why we listen." This conceptualization of the relationship helps explain the importance of selecting the "right" franchisee. Franchisees and chain executives did not characterize the relationship by referring to the contract, for reasons that will become clearer when the methods of influence are discussed later in this chapter. When discussing the business partnership, chain-operator personnel and franchisees talked about the complex, personal, and emergent dynamics that embodied the relationship.[5]

The contrasting relationships that existed in company and franchise arrangements were reflected in the position titles used by the chain operator. The title "manager" was attached to almost all positions in the company arrangement: area manager, district manager, regional manager, and so on. In contrast, the chain-operator personnel that worked with franchisees were usually called "consultants" or "representatives." The titles were not just rhetorical devices but reflected the basic differences in the contractual relationships that existed between the chain and local operator in each arrangement.

Chain Operator's Economic Benefit

In the company arrangement, the chain operator invested capital and received the net income from its units; in the franchise arrangement, franchisees invested capital, paid the chain operator an initial franchise fee and ongoing royalties, and received the income from the unit. Each of these economic structures presented the chain operator with different incentives, which manifested themselves in the management of each arrangement. The economics of the franchise arrangement created an interesting management problem that was solved by the plural form.

The economic structure of the franchise arrangement creates a potential conflict of interest between a chain operator and franchisee. Franchisees benefit from the profits of a unit; chain operators benefit from a royalty based on a franchisee's revenue. This arrangement, say scholars and practitioners alike, can lead the chain operator to engage in activities that boost revenue but adversely affect profit. This would obviously occur if the chain operator sold two franchises for nearby areas, a move that might maximize the revenue potential of the total area but likely would make both units unprofitable because each would cannibalize the sales of the other. Not surprisingly, most franchise contracts give franchisees an exclusive territory of one or two miles around their restaurant. Similarly, a conflict of interest could manifest itself in the introduction of a product that generated high volume but yielded low margins.

A hidden but crucial aspect of the plural form that emerged in this study is that it largely resolves this potential conflict of interest between the chain operator and franchisee. When the chain operator owned enough units, the economic incentives of the chain operator and the franchise arrangement became aligned. A new product, for example, that generated high sales and low margins was something that both the chain operator and franchisees sought to avoid. While conflicts of interest sometimes still occurred, as we will see, they were not built into the plural form. This obvious but ignored aspect of the plural form forces us to reevaluate whether the chain operator–franchise relationship is shaped by a fundamental conflict of interest (see Chapter 7).

Local Operator Rewards and Orientation

The chain operator's economics is only half the equation: we must also consider the economics from the local operator's perspective. In the company arrangement, managers were rewarded mainly on the basis of a fixed salary and promotions to higher positions. A company manager's performance was typically evaluated based on several well-specified operating and financial standards. In contrast, a franchisee's rewards were derived from the income generated by his or her unit(s). The chain operator's right to grant franchisees new units was in some ways comparable to a company manager receiving a promotion, but the central economic consideration for a franchisee remained the income of existing units. The different reward systems influenced the local operator's performance goals and objectives. In general, company employees were oriented to the internal system, while franchisees were oriented to the external market.

A company manager's compensation was composed mainly of a fixed salary and a small bonus component. At Hardee's and Jack in the Box, for example, the average bonus for company managers was 14 percent of salary, and was based on behaviors and results. In one chain, for example, the bonus for a position was based 40 percent on "financial targets" and 60 percent on "personal job objectives." The financial targets encompassed both inputs and outputs, including revenue and income targets as well as specific ratios of revenue to costs (food, labor, waste, and so forth). The personal job objectives included four categories: (1) customer service, (2) food variance, (3) labor hours, and (4) staff development. The use of several specific performance measures to evaluate the performance of company managers was common to all the chains I studied and reflected their abiding concern with maintaining uniformity.

When company managers described how they were evaluated, they explicitly emphasized the maintenance of standards. One restaurant manager described his job as follows: "I make sure everything is ready and standards are followed, like opening on time." Said another, "The manager is responsible to see that food isn't being taken out the back door, the cash is being handled properly, and customers aren't waiting in line for ten minutes." Meeting the standards dominated the attention of managers in all chains, and this was clearly a consequence of the reward system. Chain operators supported this approach because they feared uniformity might be compromised if emphasis were placed on financial measures. As one executive put it, "We would have chaos if people were given too much of an incentive to maximize financial results. They would screw up the business concept in their attempt to get the bonus." Consequently, bonuses were usually relatively small and were based largely on meeting the standards. In practice, the main reward in the company arrangement was promotion, not pay-for-performance compensation in a given position.[6]

This reward system produced an internal orientation in company managers that focused them on the standards and procedures specified by the chain operator. Three other factors contributed to this internal orientation. First, the financial aspects of the bonus programs were often so complex that managers barely grasped them. In one chain, for example, managers received $250 for each quarter they achieved the targeted "profit as a percentage of sales," and they earned 4 percent of all profit dollars "over profit as a percentage of sales up to $3000." And this was just one of several elements of the bonus program! Second, the bonus programs were constantly changing, which compounded the problem of understanding their complexity. In four of the five chains, the compensation system for managers changed during the research project, which lasted less than two years. As one manager put it, "Compensation is easy to play with but hard to get right. So we're constantly changing it." Finally, the specialization of functions left the restaurant manager with control over few of the decisions affecting the financial status of a unit. An area manager complained that bonus programs often ignored this feature of the company arrangement: "While the gross profit number is important, my managers can't be held responsible for marketing programs like couponing that screw up that number."

In contrast, a franchisee's rewards were determined by how well his or her restaurants performed on a financial basis. "The cash register has to ring for me to succeed," said Spike Erhardt, a Hardee's franchisee. Mike Walters, a Fishermen's Landing franchisee who had formerly worked in the company arrangement, described the difference between being an employee and franchisee: "My name is on the bank loan. I can't walk away, because it is my business. If things go bad for the company manager they don't lose the house and car, but as a franchisee I would. I have to make this work." Making "this work" meant generating profit so that the franchisee could pay the bank loan and royalty and build the business. Franchisees received the profit stream of the business directly, and they also benefited from the capital value of the business (itself a function of the profit stream) by being able to sell the franchise contingent on the approval of the chain operator. Bill McDonald, senior vice-president of marketing at KFC, nicely summarized the franchisee orientation: "The franchisee says to himself every day: What do I need to pay attention to? And the answer is always the same—restaurant operating profit." That mindset was reinforced

by the franchise contract, which fixed the simple economics of the arrangement (profits minus the royalty) for ten or twenty years. The confusion
caused by constant change in the company arrangement did not occur
here.

Because of the economics of the franchise arrangement, franchisees displayed an external orientation and were sensitive to the conditions they
faced in their local markets. Maintaining operating standards mattered, but
the central challenge facing franchisees was to generate profit by competing
effectively in their local market. The meetings I observed in each arrangement during my research reflected these contrasting orientations: meetings
between company managers and area managers typically revolved around
the budget and the cleanliness of the restaurant, while meetings between
franchisees and franchise consultants focused on competitors and new
products, both of which affected the financial performance of the unit. This
contrast existed even if the standards were used directly to grant a franchisee the right to add new units. (Interestingly, as we shall see in Chapter 5,
uniformity was approximately the same in each arrangement despite the
apparent difference in attention given to the standards.)

Source of Chain Operator Influence

The chain operator exercised its influence over local operators through
authority in the company arrangement and persuasion in the franchise
arrangement. The local operator's response to such actions was consistent
with the source of influence: company managers complied, and franchisees
exercised choice. Recall the quote in the introduction: "You can *tell* company people, but you have to *sell* franchisees." Jay Willoughby, a division
vice-president at Pizza Hut, also stressed the contrast between managing
each arrangement: "The difference between working with franchisees and
the company is the difference between the wiggly-line way of getting things
done versus the straight-line way."

An executive vice-president captured how influence was exercised in the
company arrangement: "We essentially have a military organization in
company units—we tell them and they do it." Authority complements the
zone of acceptance discussed earlier: authority determines what actions will
fill the zone. In company units, authority is grounded in a person's position, what Weber (1971) called the "legally established impersonal order."
The holder of a position is obeyed by virtue of residing in a higher office.

Several people reported that the primary job of the local operator was to
"comply with what the boss tells me to do." The reward system, which
revolved around following rules laid down by top management, reinforced

the use of authority in the company arrangement. (Chapter 8 discusses the efforts of a few chains to "empower" managers and involve them in the decision-making process, but in general these initiatives had modest objectives and met with limited success.) Company unit managers rarely exercised choice over important business issues, and never was their range of choice analogous to a franchisee's. One manager confirmed the limited nature of choice in the company arrangement when he said, "Selling to company managers is a stylistic thing; selling to franchisees is a necessity." Simon's work (1976, 129) helps explain the contrast: "It is this 'right to the last word' which is usually meant in speaking of 'lines of authority' in administrative organization." In company units, the right to the last word belonged to superiors, and they usually exercised it.

In the franchise arrangement, the chain operator used persuasion rather than authority to influence the behavior of franchisees. As noted, the franchise contract provided the chain operator with only limited authority and few practical sanctions. Read what two long-time franchise consultants from different chains said about working with franchisees:

> We have no authority, so we must be able to convince the entrepreneur—many who are extremely successful businesspeople—to do things. Communication, negotiation, and listening skills are the key to the relationship.

> On the company side, we can put restrictions on people. In contrast, with franchisees we suggest, nurture, and prod to achieve our goals. Relationships are crucial, and when they deteriorate it becomes extremely frustrating to try to get the company's goals across.

Influencing a franchisee's behavior was critical, given that franchisees exercised choice over a wide range of policy areas. Sometimes those choices adversely affected the uniformity of the chain or impeded the implementation of a systemwide adaptation. The right of franchisees to make choices (by virtue of the contract and industry norms), coupled with their reward system, made Simon's description of authority inapplicable: franchisees never simply gave the franchisor the "last word." In most instances, the chain operator had to persuade franchisees to change their behavior.

The persuasion process took a variety of forms. Ron Rehahn, a Hardee's regional general manager who worked closely with franchisees, described a few of the persuasion strategies available to the chain operator: "The company identifies things that could be improved and passes along that information to the franchisee. Controlling growth is an important power button to get them to move, but the key power button is greed. If we propose things that make economic sense, they will do them." Sharing information, presenting economic rationales, and controlling growth were used by chain operators to convince franchisees to adopt a course of action. Scott Mackey, director of franchise operations at Pizza Hut, warned of the danger of trying to circumvent the persuasion process: "The worst thing you can do is treat a franchisee like an employee. Then they'll never stop being a problem for you. We treat them like business partners." In the day-to-day conduct of the relationship, franchise consultants relied heavily on "selling" franchisees, showing them the "business case" that supported a course of action.

Controlling the growth of a franchisee was the most coercive strategy used by the chain operator (excepting legal remedies, which were infrequently used). Paul Headley, a KFC franchise consultant responsible for working with franchisees, summarized this management technique in one sentence: "The key way we manage franchisees that don't follow the standards is that we don't let them grow." At Jack in the Box, a franchisee's existing units had to meet certain quantitative performance levels before the chain operator granted the franchisee the right to add new units. The unit growth of franchisees not only provided the chain operator with financial benefits in the form of additional royalties, but it also was an important management tool (see Chapter 4).

In summary, the source of influence was unilateral in company arrangements, with company superiors initiating action and directing subordinates, and was bilateral in franchise arrangements, with the chain operator often proposing a course of action and selling franchisees on it. The company arrangement was built on local compliance, while the franchise arrangement hinged on local choice and, ultimately, local consent.[7] From this perspective, Williamson's arguments (1985) about the relatively high transaction costs associated with contractual relationships hold true here. The "straight line" versus "wiggle line" comparison offered by Willoughby helps explain the disparity between transaction costs. A complete view of the situation, however, must also include the "transaction benefits" produced by the franchise arrangements; what Assael (1969) calls constructive conflict. We will see that this plays a big role in the systemwide-adaptation process (see Chapter 7).

Architecture of Information

The information architecture represents where, how, and what kind of information is captured by an organization. In chain organizations, the architecture of information made the company arrangement transparent from top to bottom, while it left the franchisee's operation largely opaque from the perspective of the chain operator. The chain operator routinely received a massive amount of information about company operations and performance and very little about franchise performance. The company-generated information gave the chain operator considerable leverage in the persuasion process with franchisees. A crude estimate of the amount of information that flowed to the chain operator, however, tells only part of the story. The information produced by each arrangement also varied in terms of its source (for example, MIS, face-to-face meetings, and so forth), its type (for example, its "media richness"), and its flow (for example, number of points of reproduction before reaching decision makers). These differences and others had major consequences for the management and decision-making processes in chain organizations—and for the accomplishment of uniformity, local responsiveness, and systemwide adaptation.

In the company arrangement, the MIS served as the foundation of the information architecture. Four of the chains had computerized cash registers ("point-of-sale systems") that automatically captured data on the performance of company units; Fishermen's Landing gathered similar data manually. The cash registers tracked sales by individual products and time of day. The MIS also compiled information on the two major costs of a restaurant, food and labor, through nightly inventories and employee time-cards. These data were "polled" by a central computer each night, so that on a daily basis people at the different levels in the company hierarchy had access to the previous day's data.

Company managers always brought their profit-and-loss statement to the interview when I told them I was interested in how company units were managed. Each person in the hierarchy had performance data for the units reporting to him or her. Performance evaluations were based in large part on these numbers. Along with these detailed profit-and-loss data, a wealth of operating data was collected that related to issues like product mix, volumes by time of day, and the results of product promotions. The amount of data gathered by the company arrangement can be voluminous: every month, for example, Hardee's published a book over two hundred pages long, filled with charts and graphs based on this information. The automated MIS was the key element of the information architecture in company arrangements, but other means of acquiring information also existed. Frequent field audits captured information on the quality, service, and cleanliness of units, which was aggregated and rolled-up like the financial measures. A less formal source was the "field visit," which entailed executives making regular appearances at local units. All told, the information architecture in the company arrangement made a unit's operation virtually transparent to senior levels in the hierarchy.[8]

In the franchise arrangement, the chain operator captured less information. In three of the chains, the chain operator received only a royalty payment based on the revenue number each month. Franchisees in the other two chains sent profit-and-loss statements to the chain operator on either a quarterly or annual basis. No chain integrated franchisees into its automated MIS, and hence, little detailed operating data flowed between them. Franchisees often had their own MIS, depending on the size of their organization, but those data were not routinely shared with the chain operator. I observed meetings in three chains that centered on the chain operator asking franchisees to share their operating data. In one instance, in the franchisee's office, the division director of franchising asked the franchisee how a recent promotion had performed. The franchisee turned to the credenza, pulled out a ledger, ran his finger down the page and said, "It pushed volume up about 5 percent." He then placed the book back in his credenza.

When I asked people to explain why more data did not routinely flow between the chain operator and franchisees, they were usually puzzled; it was a taken-for-granted part of the relationship. The response of one franchisee, however, may shed some light on the question: "How I run my business is not the company's affair. My business is *my* business." Information played a role in defining what it meant to be an independent businessperson. This situation is visible in other contexts, such as when management refuses to "open the books" to the scrutiny of labor unions or when subcontractors refuse to share information with partners. The economics of the franchise relationship also may account for the chain operator's reduced need for detailed operating data. The chain operator's economic benefit was derived from revenue (through the royalty), which was less affected by local management issues than profit and therefore was less necessary to monitor. Still, a variety of business policy issues depended on data that were unavailable through the franchise arrangement. Regardless of the reason, the result was the same: a franchisee's operation was opaque to the chain operator.

Although detailed operating information was not acquired by the chain operator, the franchisees delivered information to the chain operator when issues of concern arose. Numerous meetings, forums, and private discussions, described in the next section, ensured that the chain operator's top executives and franchisees exchanged information and debated policy proposals. Steven Reinemund, the CEO of Pizza Hut, offered an explanation for the value of this source of information, which was reiterated by all the top executives I interviewed: "In most businesses, there is a risk to complaining. People tell their bosses what they think the boss wants to hear. The franchisee, though, does not work for you and has no hesitation to call you directly and let you know what he thinks. The franchisees make us better." This perspective calls into question an important assumption of transaction-cost economics, which contends that marketlike relationships generate distorted information as compared to hierarchical structures (Williamson 1985). To the contrary, executives in these organizations reported that it was the company arrangement that often produced distorted information, although it also must be recognized that the franchise arrangement produced no information at all regarding many issues. Although the local interests of franchisees clearly shaped the views they expressed on given management issues, executives still viewed this source of information as crucial and compared it favorably to that offered by company managers.

The Reinemund quote above suggests that the distortion of information in the company arrangement occurred because its flow was embedded in hierarchy: subordinates adjusted information—either purposefully or unwittingly—to suit their bosses. A less jaundiced explanation may also help explain the phenomenon. The serial reproduction of information, which occurs when information flows through multiple levels in the hierarchy, can lead to unintended distortions (Williamson 1970). The frequent face-to-face meetings between chain executives and franchisees prevented distortions of that sort from occurring. One CEO made this point when he observed, "You don't have to spend time wondering what franchisees think, since if they don't like something, they will immediately call you up." Essentially, franchisees provided the senior executives in the chain operator organization with an undistorted flow of information directly from the local level. The familiarity of franchisees with their local markets coupled with their typically extensive business experience enhanced the value of this information. "We really need the input of franchisees," said Don Mucci, director of franchising at Hardee's. "They're the ones that know the business."[9]

The medium of communication was almost always verbal and usually face to face in the franchise arrangement, which in itself helped shape the type of information that was exchanged. Daft and Lengel (1984) argued that the medium of communication affects the "information richness" of the data; they defined information richness as the "information-carrying capacity of the data" (p. 196). The franchise arrangement provided a chain with narrowly focused, rich information through personal interactions, while the company arrangement provided the chain with a more complete picture composed of less rich information through its MIS. A similar contrast is suggested by Jensen and Meckling's typology of information types (1991). The company arrangement's MIS generated vast amounts of "general information," which was easy to summarize and communicate in statistical form, while the franchise arrangement produced "specific information," which conveyed the particularities of their local markets and was costly to communicate. Chain organizations often had to balance the needs of the system with the demands of varied local markets, and these different types of information aided in that process.

The different amounts, sources, flows, and types of information produced by each arrangement had major implications for the systemwide-adaptation process. As we shall see, the two architectures of information complemented each other, and this complementarity was one of the central benefits of the plural form. Quite simply, each arrangement provided different and useful information. The common analytic approach of trying to identify the best architecture for a firm or problem overlooks the possible advantage of utilizing multiple architectures. It is important to realize that the information architectures were intertwined with the other features of each arrangement. For example, the fact that franchisees were essentially granted tenure when they joined a chain enabled them to exercise voice without fear of repercussions. Conversely, the internal orientation of company managers gave them little incentive to share information with superiors about what was happening in local markets. Moreover, superiors did not expect such information from them. In the chain-restaurant industry, the relationship between the information architecture and the organizational arrangement may run even deeper: the use of MIS may be incompatible with rich, specific, and accurate face-to-face information exchanges.[10] I discuss this conundrum in Chapter 8 in the context of chain operators' attempts to create a hybrid arrangement.

Structural Type

Company and franchise arrangements used different structural mechanisms to achieve their objectives. Broadly speaking, for company units the structure was hierarchical; for franchisees, it was federal. These labels encapsulate the characteristics described above for each arrangement and reveal how firms comprising hundreds or even thousands of units organized themselves to meet the management challenges.

Table 3-1 displays the spans of control used by the chain operator in the management of company and franchise units. The franchise consultant's span of control, measured in terms of either individual franchisees or franchise units, was wider than the span in the company arrangement. A variety of factors account for this difference. The employment relationship in the company arrangement, built on fixed salaries for rewards and authority for influence, required superiors to exercise authority in guiding action. In contrast, franchisees exercised more local autonomy, by virtue of the franchise contract and industry convention, which reduced the need for the chain operator's involvement. The franchise arrangement's complexity was revealed by the fact that chain operators described themselves as organized around both franchise units and franchisees. The persuasion process focused on franchisees. As Paul Headley, a KFC franchise consultant, put it, "You sell franchisees, not their units." The wide spans of control in the franchise arrangement compared to the company arrangement was also the result of multi-unit franchisees employing the same management structures as the company arrangement. Between the franchisees' incentives and their own management structures, franchisees in large part monitored and managed themselves, which reduced the need for chain-operator control.

At the corporate level, divisional structures were common. This structure

---

Table 3-1   Span of Control of Chain Operator's Field Staff

	Franchise Consultant		Company Area Manager
	---	---	---
Company	Number of Franchisees	Number of Franchise Units	Number of Company Units
KFC	15	90	6
Pizza Hut	9	175	7
Hardee's	6	35	6
Jack in the Box	8	45	8

Note: Fishermen's Landing did not use a specialized field structure to manage finances.

looked much like the semiautonomous business units described by Chandler (1962) in his classic book *Strategy and Structure*. Like the managers of divisions in Chandler's book, the division vice-presidents in my study were evaluated largely on the financial performance of their areas, and they had all the functions reporting to them. In contrast to companies Chandler studied, however, the corporate office of a chain was responsible for more than resource allocation and divisional performance evaluation; in practice, a chain's divisions had only limited autonomy. Indeed, the division heads of finance, marketing, human resources, and real estate had dotted-line reporting relationships to the directors of each function in the corporate office. These dotted-line relationships were very strong, essentially creating a centralized shadow hierarchy.

The proposition that centralization casts a shadow over the divisions of the company arrangement was also supported by the widely varying and frequently changing sizes of divisions. The average number of company units in a division ranged from 750 at Pizza Hut to 186 at Hardee's. During the time of my research, KFC switched from twelve divisions to eight and Hardee's eliminated one division office entirely and melded its units into an existing division. With the center dominant, the divisional structure of the company units was somewhat superfluous. The functional heads in each division were constrained by corporate marketing decisions, pay and promotion policies, and real-estate development standards; the functional departments in each division, for the most part, ensured compliance with corporate policies. The chain operator's concern with the management challenge of uniformity was largely accountable for this structure.

The franchise arrangement displayed a very different structure, which can be usefully described as federal. Individuals owned and operated one or several units and they controlled many of the activities that occurred in them. As one franchise consultant put it, "With franchisees there is no chain of command." While one of the corporation's franchise consultants was assigned to every franchisee, in no way could the relationship be described as a reporting relationship. Instead, franchise consultants generally focused on trying to persuade franchisees to adopt programs and improve performance. The process of making decisions about advertising was the most vivid example of the federal structure at work in most chains. Four of the five chains I studied advertised on television, and in three of them advertising decisions were made on the basis of majority-rule voting arrangements. Quarterly meetings about advertising were held, wherein the chain operator presented its advertising strategy to franchisees for their input and approval. While the chain operator's specialists played a role in this process, unlike the company arrangement, they did not make the decisions. One chain executive described the franchise arrangement, only half jokingly, as "democratic anarchy."

Many activities encompassed by the federal structure were not contained on the organizational chart. In the franchise arrangement, decisions were often made through face-to-face interactions between the chain operator's executives and franchisees in a variety of forums. All the chains had annual or semiannual franchise conventions where the top executives of the chain met with all the franchisees and discussed key business issues. In the three largest chains, similar meetings occurred more frequently at the regional level. The agenda for these meetings was typically set jointly, or the chain operator and franchisees took turns hosting and running the meetings. Four chains had a "franchise association" or "franchise advisory committee," represented by elected franchisees, that met regularly with top chain operator executives. Fishermen's Landing had no formal association, but its small size (nineteen franchisees) made it easy for the top executives to keep in close contact with franchisees.

At the same time, ongoing and ad hoc task forces of franchisees worked on different issues. In one chain, eight committees of franchisees worked in concert with the chain operator on issues ranging from quality assurance to advertising. In another firm, the chain operator convened a joint advisory committee (JAC) made up of franchisees and chain personnel whenever important issues arose. The corporate staffer with responsibility for working with franchisees in that chain noted that, "We need the input of franchisees up front. At the franchise convention when the proposal is being discussed we want franchisees on the stage selling their fellow franchisees." These formal means of contact were complemented by a variety of informal one-on-one meetings between franchisees and chain executives. To facilitate these interactions, executives in one chain took franchisees fly-fishing, while another chain took franchisees on ski trips.

The federal structure was the outcome of pressures generated by both the chain operator and franchisees. The chain operator's need to sell franchisees led to a lot of personal contact between the two entities. The effective use of persuasion as a means of influence depended in large part on sharing sound analysis with franchisees and maintaining a strong relationship—the marriage metaphor discussed earlier reflected this characteristic.[11] One executive explained the underlying dynamic of the federal structure this way: "Franchisees fear that their fate will be somehow compromised by a screw-up in the corporate office. They want to know what we are doing and thinking. Remember, many of them have all their money tied up in their restaurants. We have to always be communicating with them." The incentives facing franchisees—the need to "make the cash register ring"— led them to deal directly with key decision makers whenever they felt that important business issues were at stake. The federal structure was an important aspect of the architecture of information that linked franchisees with top executives.

Finally, the hierarchical and federal structures were built with different kinds of people who spent different lengths of time with the chain. Company restaurant managers were usually high school and sometimes college graduates in their midtwenties. Often the job with the chain was their first professional experience. In contrast, franchisees were older when they joined the chain—often in their late thirties or early forties. This is not surprising, since the capital required to purchase a franchise was considerable and took time to save. A franchisee formerly may have been a mid- to senior-level manager in a company, an airline pilot, an independent businessperson, or a franchisee in another chain. The more peerlike relationship between the chain operator and local operator in the franchise arrangement was in part attributable to the social similarity of executives and franchisees and the potential value a franchisee could add to the decision-making process based on his or her experience.

The two structures revealed another subtle dynamic related to their people: the company structure was stable but people flowed through it, while the franchise structure was fluid but the people were stable. On the company side, there was a constant flow of people up the structure: promotion was the main way company people boosted their compensation. At Hardee's, for example, restaurant managers stayed in their restaurant on average for eighteen months before being promoted. Along with promotion, turnover among restaurant managers ranged from 20 percent to 40 percent in the chains I studied. Even at the top of the organization, turnover was common: during the two years of my research, three of the chains changed their CEOs. People moved in, out, and through the hierarchical structure.

In contrast, the franchise structure was anchored by a stable base of franchisees. More than one franchisee commented, "I have been here longer than almost anyone in the company organization." Recall that the franchise contract ranged from fifteen to twenty years, usually with renewal provisions. Franchisees joined the chain with a long-term investment in mind; a franchise was not simply an investment to be held and sold. They were essentially granted tenure upon entry. In all of the chains except Jack in the Box, which had started franchising relatively recently, there were franchisees who had been affiliated with the chain since its inception. This long association gave franchisees a familiarity with their local markets that was unmatched in the company arrangement, and it provided them with experiences that made a major contribution to the systemwide-adaptation process. In contrast to the conventional view that a firm's long-term perspective must be lodged in its uppermost hierarchical positions (see Jacques 1990), the long time horizon in this arrangement resided with individuals (franchisees) who had a long-standing relationship with the chain.

The divergence between the hierarchical and federal structures was vividly illustrated when I arranged the interviews for this research. Company units were often identified by a number, while franchise units were identified by the franchisee's name. My discussions with top executives made clear how substantially the relationships differed. After telling me in detail about the business and personal history of a franchisee I had met who owned five units, one CEO confessed that he knew little about company managers two levels below him, each of whom was responsible for hundreds of units. Bob Haberkamp, an area vice-president at Hardee's, characterized the difference between the management of the arrangements this way: "The management of company units is more systems-oriented and the management of franchisees more people-oriented." The relative experience and tenure of the people occupying each structure accounts in part for this difference.

Summary of the Characteristics

It is risky to try to sum up a complex phenomenon, but let me offer a broad visual image of each arrangement that reveals a fundamental asymmetry between them. In the company arrangement, the details of the local operation were transparent to the chain operator, while the chain operator's decision process was opaque to the local manager. The reverse was true for the franchise arrangement: the details of the local operation were opaque to the chain operator, but the chain operator's decision process was transparent to franchisees. This contrast emanates from the characteristics described in this chapter. I will show in later chapters that the different nature of transparency helps explain how and to what extent each arrangement met the management challenges. At the same time, the neat asymmetry suggests the advantage of operating both arrangements simultaneously as a plural form, a point that will become clearer as each management challenge is discussed.

Even though company and franchise arrangements embodied sharply differing economic and organizational characteristics, each arrangement can also be seen as an integrated social system. For example, in the franchise arrangement the economics of the contract led to the external market orientation, and franchisee autonomy forced the chain operator to engage in persuasion processes. The same connections were visible among the characteristics of the company arrangement. Changing any single component may affect several other variables, or alternatively, may have no affect at all because of the reinforcing and redundant nature of the characteristics. I discuss the implications of trying to alter these characteristics or combine them in other ways in Chapter 8.

BLENDING THE CHARACTERISTICS

Although the company and franchise arrangements each displayed distinct characteristics, there were two principal ways that the arrangements affected each other: by multi-unit franchisees replicating the management structures observed in the company arrangement and through career paths that cut across each arrangement. These two plural dynamics created an organizational context that directly influenced a chain's ability to meet each of the management challenges.

Multi-Unit Franchisees: Hierarchy within the Federal Structure

Multi-unit franchisees represented the vast majority of franchise units. Most significantly, multi-unit franchisees replicated in their organizations many of the structures, systems, and processes used in the company arrangement: hierarchy was used by franchisees to manage the units in their minichains. While the structure of the franchise arrangement was a federation of franchisees, a hierarchical structure usually governed franchise units. In essence, hierarchy was nested within the federal structure.

The prevalence of multi-unit franchising suggests the importance of understanding this phenomenon. The vast majority of franchise units in the chains I studied were part of a franchisee's multi-unit minichain. Table 3-2 describes the composition of the franchise base in each chain. The average number of units owned by a franchisee ranged from 2.7 to 22.5. To fully appreciate the role played by multi-unit franchising in these chains, however, it is important to note the concentration of units among franchisees. The largest franchisees at KFC, Pizza Hut, and Hardee's had 270, 339, and 432 units, respectively. Each of these franchisees generated revenue of over $100 million. The largest franchisee at Jack in the Box owned only 30 units, but recall that the chain had begun franchising

Table 3.2 *Descriptive Data on Franchise Arrangements*

Company	Number of Franchise Units	Number of Franchisees	Average Size of a Franchise (units)	Size of Largest Franchisee	Percentage of Franchisees That Own 50% of Franchise Units	Number of Franchisees That Own 50% of Franchise Units	Number of Franchisees That Own One Unit
KFC	3,592	778	4.6	270	11	17	350
Pizza Hut	2,984	149	20.0	339	4	29	18
Hardee's	2,058	250	8.2	432	3	8	88
Jack in the Box	320	120	2.7	30	16	19	51
Fishermen's Landing	360	16	22.5	100	19	3	0

relatively recently. The preponderance of franchise units resided in minichains owned and operated by franchisees.

The concentration of units among a few franchisees is further illustrated by the percentage of franchisees owning half of the franchise units in a chain. At Hardee's, only 3 percent of the franchisees owned 50 percent of the franchise units. In the chain with the lowest concentration, Fishermen's Landing, only 19 percent of its franchisees owned half of the franchise units. The managerial implication of such concentration becomes clear when we translate the percentages into the number of franchisees; that is, the number of people the chain operator had to work with and influence. At Fishermen's Landing, three individuals owned half the franchise units. Pizza Hut was the other extreme, but even there only twenty-nine franchisees represented half of its units.

These chains still had a large number of franchisees who owned single units, but these franchisees accounted for a relatively small fraction of the franchise units. The last column in Table 3-2 shows that the number of single-unit franchisees ranged from 350 at KFC to only 18 at Pizza Hut. Single-unit franchisees as a percentage of total franchise units varied from less than 1 percent (Pizza Hut) to 16 percent (Jack in the Box). Single-unit franchisees were the exception, not the norm, and as we will see in the next chapter this form was transitory; single-unit franchisees were likely to become multi-unit operators.[12] Despite the pervasiveness and managerial significance of this phenomenon, multi-unit franchising is routinely dismissed by existing research as either inconsequential or inefficient—an assumption that this research clearly disproves (for an exception to this oversight, see Kaufmann 1991; Kaufmann and Dant 1996).[13]

The implications of multi-unit franchising are traced throughout the book. Here, I want to highlight some of the key aspects of this phenomenon. Almost every franchisee I interviewed said that they used the same management practices as the company arrangement—for example, the same spans of control, performance-evaluation systems, and operations reporting schemes. One franchisee said, "It would be hard for me to point to many things where my people do things differently than their people. We all belong to the same company." Another franchisee noted, "The company has a lot of experience managing multiple units, so we can learn from that." Virtually every chain executive and franchisee that I interviewed agreed with Fishermen's Landing executive vice-president Robert Brown when he said, "Big franchisees look just like us."[14] The replication of the company arrangement in the franchise arrangement helps explain the similar levels of uniformity across arrangements I observed in the chains I studied. We might predict that the external market orientation of franchisees and the absence of chain-operator authority would lead to less uniformity, but multi-unit franchising was a counterweight to those forces. This "modeling effect" is explored in Chapter 5.

Multi-unit franchising not only transformed the internal operating dynamics of the franchise arrangement, but it also reconfigured the relationship between the chain operator and the franchise community. The means of influence—persuasion—made it a virtual necessity to deal individually with franchisees. Multi-unit franchising transformed the monumental task of managing hundreds and even thousands of relationships (if individual units were the unit of management) into a more reasonable management responsibility.[15] Many of the executives and franchisees said that a chain comprising a small number of medium- to large-sized franchisees was preferable to a chain comprising a large number of small franchisees. As one executive vice-president put it, "We would never get anything done if we had to deal with a zillion small franchisees." The benefits of having fewer people to "work with" were seen in all of the management challenges but especially in systemwide adaptation, where exercising persuasive influence over franchisees was of paramount importance. A countervailing dynamic was that large franchisees sometimes were more difficult to persuade because they were less dependent on the chain operator, in part because they had their own infrastructure. The advantages and disadvantages of multi-unit franchisees will be vividly apparent in the discussion of the systemwide-adaptation process.

Scholars have traditionally emphasized the advantages of franchisees in terms of their ability to operate efficiently in local markets without close supervision (Rubin 1978; Brickley and Dark 1987). As the multi-unit franchisees grow large, however, this presumed efficiency advantage dissipates, which often leads researchers to devalue its influence. As we shall see, however, a variety of compensating advantages accrue to the chain operator that used multi-unit franchisees: faster and less costly growth, greater levels of uniformity, and fewer relationships to manage.

Cross-Cutting Career Paths

Another plural process that affected the behavior and performance of chains occurred when career paths cut across the two arrangements. The conventional view of careers in chains is that company people ascend the hierarchy, and franchisees remain independent small businesspeople. In fact, most company personnel did flow through the company hierarchy, with the relatively narrow spans of control and the scalar structure providing a natural career ladder. The typical career path of a franchisee, however, differed, as suggested by Table 3-2: a franchisee who excelled at operating his or her existing units added new ones and built a minihierarchy. Franchisees devoted a large portion of almost every interview to explaining their plans for adding units.

Along with these two distinct and separate career paths were three other paths that cut across the two arrangements and deeply affected the chain's functioning (see Figure 3-2 for illustrative paths): (1) company people becoming franchisees, (2) company managers becoming franchise consultants, and (3) company managers becoming managers in a franchisee's organization. In each case, the franchise arrangement was gaining people who had been socialized into the policies and practices of company units. Thus, all three career paths directly influenced the chain operator's ability to exercise control over the franchise arrangement. For that reason, it will be useful to look at the particular factors involved in each career path.

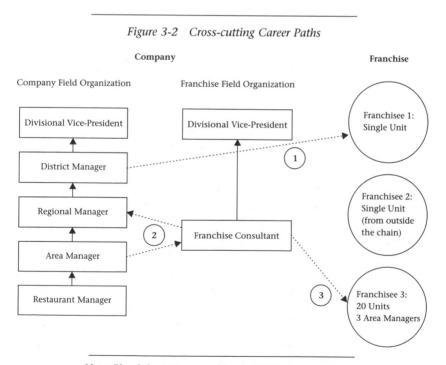

Figure 3-2   Cross-cutting Career Paths

Note: Plural dynamics noted by dashed line: (1) company people becoming franchisees, (2) company managers becoming franchise consultants, and (3) company managers becoming managers in a franchise's organization.

Company person to franchisee. A key constraint facing chain operators as they sought to grow was finding interested and qualified franchisees. The plural form offered a means of escaping this constraint by utilizing company people as franchisees. The chief operating officer of one chain explained the benefits of this approach: "The company people know the system. They are proven operators and they appreciate the importance of maintaining standards and running the business right. There is much less risk in terms of getting a bad apple with company people because we know them well." Company managers understood what was required to operate a restaurant in the chain; moreover, their experience as company managers inculcated in them an appreciation of the importance of following the chain's standards, thereby reducing the likelihood they would become a management "problem" as a franchisee. This process resembles Ouchi's "clan" form of organization (1980), whereby socialization into an organization reduces the need for hierarchical or market mechanisms of control. Here, however, the clan form extends across market boundaries. In addition, this path provided both the company and the prospective franchisee with information about each other. Executives from all five chains remarked on the advantage of selecting company people whom they were confident they would be able to work with. The long preexisting relationship built a foundation of trust between the employee and the organization, which supported the efficient conduct of the relationship when that person became a franchisee (Arrow 1974).[16]

All five chains used this career path. At Fishermen's Landing, eight of the nine most recent new franchisees were former company employees. Jack in the Box executives estimated that 40 percent of the 90 franchisees joining the chain between 1987 and 1989 had been with the company before. Hardee's developed its "American Dream Program" in 1990 to enable selected company employees to become franchisees, and eighteen of the most recent new franchisees were from company ranks. KFC relied less on this pattern, although its minority franchising program recruited some company employees to become franchisees. KFC's history may help explain the absence of this path, since it had hundreds of franchisees before it started company units. Pizza Hut had sold almost no franchises since 1977, but before then, executives reported, many of the old franchisees were former company people and two of the five franchisees I interviewed fit that category.

The company arrangement obviously incurred a cost when good people were "lost" to the franchise arrangement, but the different mechanisms of control still made this a sensible strategy. Recall how one executive put it:

"The management of company units is more systems-oriented and the management of franchisees more people-oriented." Since chain operators relied heavily on personal relationships to manage franchisees, it was particularly useful if the person had a tie with the organization. This factor was less crucial on the company side.

Company manager to franchise consultant. The chains drew almost exclusively on the ranks of area managers to become franchise consultants. Fishermen's Landing did not use this path, but its reliance on senior company managers to work with franchisees led to the same result as the other chains: experienced operators worked with franchisees. One division vice-president explained the importance of this career path: "The entire franchise consultant–franchisee relationship is based on credibility. The credibility of that person depends on their operations experience and their ability to solve problems." The CEO of another chain elaborated: "The franchise consultant must have the maturity to deal with franchisees without having to resort to authority. The person needs to know the business and earn the respect of the franchisee." One franchise consultant at KFC recalled, "When you first meet franchisees they always want to know if they have more time [in the chain] than you. Once I say I've been doing chicken for eighteen years, they are willing to work together."

Both chain operators and franchisees deemed company-specific experience important, and chains rarely hired franchise consultants from outside. Noted one franchisee: "I'll talk to them [franchise consultants] if I think that they can help me." Managers of plural-form chains firmly believed that to be credible in persuading franchisees to change their behavior, franchise consultants had to have operating experience with the chain: "Franchise consultants need to really understand our business, and that comes from running one of our restaurants," said one chain executive.

At the same time that the move from the company to the franchise side provided credibility to the franchise consultant, the move back to the company may have enhanced their effectiveness as company managers. A division manager remarked that the franchise consultant position "teaches people a distinct set of skills, in a particular setting, that helps them be better managers when they return to the company side of the organization." Another company executive took a more ambivalent view: "Sometimes the transition back is difficult. As a franchise consultant, a person has access to corporate information and plans and a degree of freedom that does not exist on the company side. At the same time, they've gained a broader set of skills which allows them to be more effective when they return to the company side." Despite the difficult transition, this executive also noted that the experience as a franchise consultant served as an important developmental experience for some company executives.

Company manager to franchisee manager. The final career path that affected the performance of the franchise arrangement was the movement of people from the company hierarchy to a franchisee's minihierarchy. Franchise consultants were seen as the best candidates for this move, since they often developed close relationships with franchisees. During my study, nearly half the franchise consultants in one division of one company joined franchise organizations. This path was not as common in other chains, but each had examples of it occurring. Tony Deluca, a division director of franchising at KFC, pointed to the advantage of this path: "We hate to lose good people, but at least now we'll have some real operating expertise in those franchise organizations." The director of franchising in another chain remarked that he often tried to dissuade people from making this switch (in fact, it was contractually prohibited for franchisees to "pirate" company people), but conceded, "It's better that we keep the expertise within the chain than lose it altogether."

These three career paths played a major role in helping a chain operator accomplish its objectives, such as maintaining standards (by diffusing people who had been socialized to company policies and practices into the franchise arrangement) and controlling the behavior of franchisees (by strengthening the credibility of the franchise consultants). These findings agree with Larson's argument (1992) that the social dimensions of inter-organizational relationships play a crucial role in controlling and coordinating behavior in these transactions. In her study of entrepreneurial businesses, Larson identified personal reputations and prior relations as critical preconditions for establishing an effective relationship. The use of company people as franchisees satisfies these two conditions, with the additional advantage that their reputations are based on having first-hand experience in the chain. The other two career paths also supported the exercise of social control by providing actors the credibility and prior relationships on which effective relationships could be built.

CONCLUSION

This chapter described how company and franchise arrangements were organized and managed in the chains I studied. The company arrangement was an almost textbook hierarchy; in contrast, the franchise arrangement, held together by formal contracts and informal relationships, formed a federal structure. Although the two arrangements were sharply differentiated, multi-unit franchisees and career paths that cut across arrangements created dynamics that affected the functioning of the other.

The remainder of this book explains how company and franchise arrangements met the four management challenges discussed earlier. Each arrangement took different approaches and met with different degrees of success. The treatment of each challenge in a separate chapter should not obscure the reader's recognition of some of the tensions and tradeoffs that existed between these approaches: the capacity of an arrangement to handle one challenge sometimes affected its capacity to accomplish another one. For example, the hierarchical structure used by the company arrangement can be effective at achieving uniformity but less effective at generating local responsiveness. Similarly, the organizational design used to maintain uniformity may enable the rapid diffusion of systemwide adaptations, but at the same time it may stifle the production of novel ideas for systemwide adaptations—which themselves are often initially local responses! Although there are tradeoffs, all four management challenges must be met to some degree in order to achieve success.

Chapter 4

Unit Growth

ADDING UNITS to a restaurant chain plays a crucial role in its success and management. The direct financial implications of new units are obvious: more revenue and profits from additional company units, and more fees and royalties from new franchise units. Unit growth also produces important indirect effects in the form of leveraging the trademark to the benefit of existing and new units, increasing market presence and identity, and generating more funds for advertising.[1] Even in the increasingly competitive environment of the early 1990s and the saturation of many local markets with a chain's units, the addition of units remained a key way chains grew.

Despite the importance of unit growth to the success of chains, it has not attracted the direct attention of scholars of organizations.[2] Yet the addition of units is a management objective in itself and has its own dynamics; moreover, it is the process through which the mix of company and franchise units is created. A major finding of this research is that multi-unit franchisees are a relatively inexpensive source of growth for chain organizations. Rather than view a chain as composed of two potential sources of growth, company units and franchise units, my data clearly indicated the importance of distinguishing between growth provided by new franchisees and existing franchisees. The tendency of researchers to dismiss multi-unit franchising as an inefficient organizational form overlooks the advantages of using existing franchisees as a source of growth.[3] The first half of this chapter discusses the ways a chain can grow, showing that each strategy has different strengths and weaknesses and faces different constraints.

The second half of the chapter discusses how the plural form enabled a chain to overcome some of the constraints limiting growth. Most simply, the additive process highlights how the simultaneous use of different strategies can help a chain grow. The second important process is socialization, which was touched on in the previous chapter, whereby the chain recruits company personnel to become franchisees. Both processes suggest that plural-form chains will grow faster than pure forms.

The final section of the chapter explores the connection between adding units and managing franchisees. The growth process provided the chain operator with a base of power to use with franchisees: the chain operator had the right to award new units to franchisees—what French and Raven (1959) call "reward power." The explicit provisions of the franchise contract were difficult to enforce, so the leverage deriving from the right of the chain operator to regulate a franchisee's growth was viewed by participants as the most important means they had for influencing the franchisees' behavior. Like the process of growth itself, this element of multi-unit franchising has received little attention from scholars (for an exception see Kaufmann 1991).

THE GROWTH PROCESS

Chains obtained new units from three sources: (1) adding a company unit, (2) adding a franchisee and a franchise unit, and (3) adding a franchise unit to an existing franchisee's organization. Figure 4-1 shows the relative size of each source of unit growth for Hardee's from 1984 to 1988. The most notable aspect of Figure 4-1 is that existing franchisees accounted for most of the unit growth at Hardee's. This pattern is representative of the five chains. Although exact data were not available, KFC and Fishermen's Landing roughly matched these proportions. Pizza Hut had not added a new

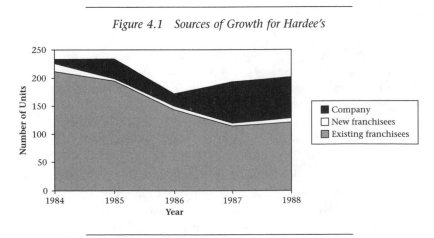

Figure 4.1   Sources of Growth for Hardee's

Source: Company documents.

franchisee since 1977, so its restaurant growth consisted solely of units built by the company and existing franchisees. Jack in the Box had begun franchising in the mid-1980s, and it still relied more heavily than the others on new franchisees, but its existing franchisees were quick to add new units, thereby moving the balance more in line with the Hardee's mix.

The addition of units from each source of growth involved different management processes. Each process reflected economic and management considerations unique to each source, and each was constrained by different factors. Regardless of the source of growth, however, it is critical to understand that in all three cases the chain operator controlled the growth process. The chain operator had the right to approve the addition of every unit, regardless of its source, and it was the chain operator who weighed the costs and benefits of using each source.

Table 4-1 highlights the key characteristics of the unit-growth process for each source. It compares each source on the basis of the three dimensions listed in the left-hand column: (1) the chain operator's economics, (2) the chain operator's organizational resources required for growth, and (3) the key constraints affecting the use of the source of growth. The focus on the chain operator is warranted because it was the decision maker in the growth process.

The Addition of a Company Unit

The addition of a company unit involves a capital investment by the chain operator of between $350,000 to over $1 million. This investment includes expenditures for the real estate, building, equipment, and signs. The addition of company units consumes most of a chain's capital. As Mo Iqbal, executive vice-president of marketing at Jack in the Box, stated, "Each site is a big investment. Locating a restaurant is the most important decision made by a chain." The financial return on investment produced by a company unit is the net income of a unit. For example, Hardee's reported that the average pretax profit margin on a company unit, not counting corporate overhead, was approximately 16 percent in 1988 ("Franchise Offering Circular" 1989, 42). (Considerable overhead expense was devoted to the management of company units, as is discussed in the next chapter.)

Every chain dedicated specialized organizational resources to adding company units. The CEOs in all five chains had people reporting directly to them who were responsible for the addition of company units. At Jack in the Box, for example, Bill Motts, the vice-president for restaurant development, reported to Robert Nugent, the CEO. Motts's direct reports included a director of real-estate development, director of construction and

Table 4-1   Characteristics of Sources of Unit Growth

Dimension	Company Units	New Franchisee	Existing Franchisee
Chain Operator Economics	–Capital investment +Net income	+Initial franchisee fee +Royalty income	+Initial franchisee fee +Royalty income
Chain Operator Organizational Resources Required	High Staff for developing real estate and restaurants	Medium Staff for finding franchisees Review of site development	Low Pro forma review of site
Key Constraints on Growth	Capital Management	Appropriate franchisees	Exclusive territories (in some chains)

energy, director of architecture and engineering, manager of equipment purchasing, and an administrative coordinator. More than sixty people worked in Jack in the Box's restaurant-development group, most of whom were dedicated to adding company units to the chain. Although other responsibilities such as remodeling existing units consumed some of the staff's time, in the three years prior to 1989 the company averaged forty new company units per year, which meant that more than one full-time specialist was devoted to growth for each additional company unit.

This commitment of organizational resources reflected the significance of the unit-growth process, and more specifically, the importance of selecting and developing the right site. All chains used aerial photographs to identify and map "traffic generators" (such as nearby factories or department stores) and competitors. Chains also employed firms to estimate traffic flows and volumes around the proposed site, and conducted research on the area's demographics and the community's growth plans. The personnel in development departments, often in consultation with people in the operations department, analyzed the viability of a site based on their estimates of land and building prices and the site's revenue potential. Although these activities occurred locally, the reports were compiled and sent to corporate headquarters for review and approval. At KFC, Jack in the Box, and Fishermen's Landing, the CEO personally approved all new sites. In fact, the CEOs in the latter two chains personally visited every proposed site. At Hardee's and Pizza Hut, a committee of top executives signed off on new company sites. The large capital investments involved with adding a new unit justified the significant amount of organizational resources devoted to unit growth.

This brief description suggests two key constraints facing growth in the company arrangement: capital and management. The extent to which these constraints limited chains varied depending on their financial situation and their corporate strategy. Hardee's, for example, was limited by its corporate parent (Imasco) to a growth rate consistent with the level of capital generated by the chain. The leveraged buyout at Jack in the Box in 1987 constrained capital and company growth, since capital had to be directed toward paying down the LBO debt. On the other hand, top executives at Pizza Hut, KFC, and Fishermen's Landing emphasized that limited managerial capacity rather than capital constrained their growth. The deep pockets of Pepsico, Inc., which owned both Pizza Hut and KFC, and the private ownership of Fishermen's Landing and its self-imposed slow growth rate, accounted in part for their focus on management constraints.

In all the chains, however, executives remarked on how limited managerial resources constrained the unit-growth process in the company arrangement. Jack Laughery, the chairman of Hardee's, said, "We'll only open as many units as our internal management team can handle" (Van Warner 1987). A Pizza Hut division vice-president offered a similar perspective: "The real issue is how many units can we build before it significantly impacts our base. We added three units to one market last year and it simply was too fast—we're still trying to get things settled down there." Opening a new restaurant required a disproportionate amount of management time compared to managing existing units, which limited the number of new units a chain could open. Among the activities required to open a restaurant were transferring, promoting, or hiring new restaurant managers; hiring and training new employees; establishing vendor relationships; troubleshooting the new building and equipment; and implementing the initial marketing programs to acquaint local customers with the unit. While the specialized resources mentioned earlier assisted with some of these activities, a major burden was placed on the existing management team.

The expertise required to accomplish these activities resided mainly with existing managers in the company hierarchy. The involvement of the CEOs in site selection, given their limited time, was a dramatic example of a constraint imposed by existing management. In one chain, local managers complained about how long it took to get the CEO's approval. The involvement of less-senior local managers in expansion planning was intensive and similarly constrained. For example, Debbie Stewart, a district manager at Hardee's, estimated that over half of her time for several weeks was devoted to opening a single unit. At the same time, she was responsible for the management of several existing units. She personified the Pizza Hut vice-president's worry that excessive growth could cause a firm to lose control of its base. Nugent, CEO of Jack in the Box, put it in even stronger terms: "You can kill a company by growing it too fast."[4]

Two factors in the company arrangement of a chain, both involving uniformity, made the managerial constraint especially pronounced. First, each new company unit required the installation of a panoply of mechanisms used to monitor and manage uniform standards. All new units also required an elaboration of the management hierarchy (because spans of control were narrow), new field auditors, and a complex MIS. The growth rate had to be consistent with a chain's capacity to implement all those mechanisms simultaneously, otherwise uniformity, and more generally the performance of the new units, would be compromised. (See Chapter 5 for a more detailed discussion of how the companies managed uniformity.)

The second element of the managerial constraint also hinged on accomplishing the management challenge of uniformity. This constraint existed because company-unit uniformity was highly dependent on tight supervision. (Indeed, when one chain halted field audits of its company units, performance fell precipitously.) This left the existing management staff with little time for developing and opening new units. Accordingly, to the extent they directed their attention away from managing existing units to adding new ones, the chain risked a decline in performance in the existing units. Chain operators walked a fine line between obtaining the benefits of adding new units and doing so at a rate that would keep systemwide performance levels intact.

Another managerial constraint to company growth existed in the development department. To accelerate the growth process, a chain had to hire more of the types of people found in Motts's department at Jack in the Box described earlier. Executives in all the chains I visited remarked that these departments were extremely difficult to manage effectively. One division vice-president explained that it was a constant struggle to "keep G&A [general and administrative expenses] down and grow efficiently." The kinds of people needed to find and develop real-estate sites fit uneasily in the rule-bound world of a chain organization. Managers stated that turnover was high among personnel in these departments, which was particularly damaging to growth since long lead times—between eighteen and thirty-six months—were needed to develop a site. The ever-shifting growth strategies of a chain also complicated the management of these departments because it was tough to staff at efficient levels. One chain staffed the real-estate department to the baseline level of unit growth to avoid the inevitable peaks and valleys. This staffing strategy obviously imposed a limit on unit growth in the company arrangement.

Finally, the specialization of functions in the company arrangement—especially the separation of real-estate development and operations—sometimes led to suboptimal siting decisions. The real-estate department's goal was usually the rapid addition of units; the operation department's objective was to operate profitable units. "You constantly have to pay attention to both aspects of this equation," said Gary McCain, a division vice-president of KFC, "otherwise you could get lots of unprofitable units or very slow growth."

Chain operators used three mechanisms to deal with this potential problem. First, growth decisions were often made by top executives responsible for both development and operations. Second, operations managers were sometimes responsible for providing the sales estimates for new sites, effectively giving them veto power over potentially unprofitable sites that might be proposed by the development department. Third, development departments sometimes had profit-and-loss responsibility for a new unit for the first year of operation, after which time it transferred to the operations department. This assured that the site-decision process included operating issues in its calculus. While the three organizational design remedies helped balance the tension between growth and management, the turnover of personnel in company arrangements exacerbated the tension, since few people lived with the consequences of their decisions. On the other hand, the decision-making process in the company arrangement benefited from the expertise of specialists in real estate, construction, and operations, and the accumulated experience of having built hundreds of units, which were resources less accessible to franchisees.

Adding a New Franchisee and New Franchise Unit

For the chain operator, the economic impact of adding a new franchise and thereby a franchise unit came in two parts. It received an initial franchise fee for each outlet. At Hardee's the fee was $15,000; Jack in the Box, $25,000; KFC, $20,000; Pizza Hut, $25,000; and Fishermen's Landing, approximately $20,000. The franchisee also paid an annual royalty fee to the chain operator, usually 4 percent of yearly revenue. If a unit generated sales of $500,000 per year, then the annual royalty payment from the franchisee to the chain operator was $20,000. The profits of the unit accrued to the franchisee, not to the chain operator.

People summarized the economic difference between company and franchise units in a similar way. The comments of Robert Brown, executive vice-president at Fishermen's Landing, and CEO Robert Nugent of Jack in the Box, were representative:

> With company units, you have a big margin and cash flow but also a significant investment; with franchise units, you receive a smaller margin but the return on investment approaches infinity because there is no investment.

> The economic advantage to franchising is that there is less risk to our income statement because we're not affected by cost pressure; we have no capital at stake; and the cost to support franchisees is much lower than company units.

The conventional wisdom offered by these executives is somewhat misleading. As we shall see, the resources required to manage franchisees were substantial, although less than in the company arrangement. One executive observed that "people way underestimate how much time and energy it takes to manage franchisees." Still, the basic contrast between the economics of each arrangement holds true.[5]

The chain operator's organizational resources for this source of growth were devoted mainly to the search for new franchisees. KFC, Hardee's, and Jack in the Box were actively soliciting new franchisees during my research; Pizza Hut and Fishermen's Landing were no longer adding new franchisees to their chains. The franchise sales departments in the first three chains searched for new franchisees. The Hardee's department consisted of five people in the headquarters and one or two people in each region; Jack in the Box had three staffers who recruited franchisees. The expenses involved in finding qualified franchisees can be substantial: in an aggressive campaign to grow its franchise operation, Hardee's spent $350,000 in marketing to obtain fifty "qualified" franchisees, yet significantly fewer than that ultimately joined the chain. In all three chains, division vice-presidents interviewed and approved all new franchisees, with final approval resting with the executive vice-president of franchising at the corporate level. Still, this commitment of resources was less than that devoted to adding company units.

It became clear from these conversations that the key constraint to using new franchisees as a source of growth was finding appropriate ones. George Kelsey, an area vice-president at Hardee's, put it this way: "The franchise agreement is very flexible and you have to be able to work with these people. The bottom line is that you better pick the right people." Bill Thelen, director of franchising at Jack in the Box, concurred: "You have to be extremely careful about who you let in because it's hard to get them out of the system if you make a mistake." As noted in the previous chapter, persuasion—not authority, as in the company arrangement—was the prevailing source of influence used by the chain operator in the franchise arrangement. In that context, it was essential for the chain operator to be comfortable with the prospective franchisee.

Roger Attanas, director of franchise sales at Hardee's, noted: "We have to be sure that we are able to work with the person. A bad choice can lead to years of headaches for the company." When I asked people involved in selling franchisees what kinds of people exhibited the characteristic of "being easy to work with" they inevitably said, "We have all types." They did, however, mention some types of people that they were inclined to avoid. One director of franchising said to me: "We stay away from lawyers. They are too independent. Professor types like you are the same way. Before long they think they know the system better than we do. We look for hardworking people who are willing to work within the rules." In a context where little authority existed, individual attributes were a crucial factor in assessing the qualifications of potential franchisees. As Jerry Prinds, director of franchise sales at Jack in the Box, observed, "We're really honest with people. We want them to know what they're getting into and we want to know about them. Essentially, we are giving them tenure. Better they get out now than later."[6]

To ensure that prospective franchisees understood the demands of the system, they were typically required to work in an existing unit anywhere from a week to several weeks before the chain operator would approve them. The primary reason was so that candidates knew exactly what they were getting into. Attanas of Hardee's recalled, "We've had a few people lose interest after a few days of making biscuits at 5 a.m." People also found out how detailed the rules were in the management of the restaurant; they learned that there was a difference between being an independent business-person and a franchisee. (McDonald's and Domino's have pushed this initiation process to the extreme, instituting trial periods for prospective franchisees that can last up to two years.) The trial period not only educated prospective franchisees about the chain but also socialized them into norms and practices that were acceptable to the chain operator. By the time these people became franchisees, they had internalized the norms and practices of the chain.

Another constraint limiting franchise expansion was the increased com-petition for good prospects among chains. As Bill Evans, director of fran-chising at KFC, observed, "There is no longer a long line of super people waiting to be franchisees." Bill Thelen of Jack in the Box offered an expla-nation for this frequently made point: "There has been a lot of bad press about franchising and about fast food.[7] We don't get nearly the inquiries we used to. On top of that, the industry is really competitive—everybody is selling franchises. You don't come in with nothing and become a mil-lionaire anymore." The explosion in the number of opportunities was reflected in the popular press. *Entrepreneur* magazine publishes an annual list of the top 500 franchise opportunities. *The Franchise Opportunities Hand-book,* a government publication, lists 2,000 franchise opportunities. Pro-spective franchisees shopped among these alternatives, which made it increasingly costly and difficult to attract the best candidates.[8]

The high cost of entering the fast-food business also narrowed the range of qualified candidates. Don Mucci, director of franchising at Hardee's, estimated that 1 percent to 2 percent of the people who made initial inquiries were approved by the company, and only a fraction of that number actually ended up owning a unit. The low percentage was in part a consequence of the management concerns mentioned above, but it also reflects the difficulty of finding people "with a million dollars who want to be up to their elbows in flour in a restaurant," said Tony Deluca, a division manager at KFC. For precisely that reason, the evaluation process typically required that the prospective franchisee work in an existing unit for a few days. KFC, Jack in the Box, and Hardee's were all seeking franchisees who would be owner-operators, but they would occasionally help a particularly good employee with the up-front investment. In general, though, while partnerships with passive investors were occasionally permitted, a significant part of the ownership had to reside with the day-to-day manager of the franchise.

Along with needing considerable organizational resources to find new franchisees, the chain operator also committed some resources to help them develop sites and open their restaurants. The ability of franchisees to find and develop sites was viewed by some managers as the major contribution of franchisees to a chain: "They know local conditions and we rely on this. Furthermore, it is *their* investment so they're pretty careful and thoughtful about making it work," said Mo Iqbal of Jack in the Box. John Cranor, chairman of KFC, was less sanguine about the abilities of franchisees: "The outcomes vary widely with franchisees. Sometimes they find the best sites and the best deals, but they sometimes get into the worst deals too." Both these assessments were likely true and reflected the disparate backgrounds franchisees brought to the chain.

Most chain operators provided resources to assist inexperienced franchisees in identifying and developing sites. Jack in the Box dedicated two people to the task of helping its new and existing franchisees develop real estate. Motts's group mentioned above provided franchisees with architectural drawings for their units (a service specified in the franchise contract) and helped them deal with construction-related issues. Howard Crossan, division director of development, described a similar arrangement at KFC: "We consult with new franchisees, help them out when needed, but they do most of the work." The franchise contract often specified that the chain operator provide operational assistance for a new store opening, a resource that was particularly valuable to new franchisees. Several of the chain operators' managers reported that they worked with new franchisees intensively for a few days before and after opening a unit. One area where the chain operator consciously avoided much involvement was estimating the business potential of a site. Gerald McGuiness of Hardee's explained why: "We might warn a franchisee that they are too optimistic about the sales potential of a site, but we stay away from offering any number; otherwise we might be sued for misleading the franchisee. The final decision about a site is theirs."

In summary, the organizational resources required to add franchise units by adding a new franchisee were somewhat less than those required to add company units. The cost advantage of the franchise source of growth came from the fact that some franchisees required little assistance and therefore consumed few resources. Moreover, most franchisees made decisions (for example, selecting vendors) and undertook activities (for example, hiring staff) that in the company arrangement would have required the involvement of existing managers.

Existing Franchisees Add a Unit

In all five chains, existing franchisees added a large number of units to their organizations. In fact, this source of growth far outpaced the units added by new franchisees. The result of this growth is evident in the average number of units operated by a franchisee, ranging from 2.7 (Jack in the Box) to 22.5 (Fishermen's Landing). Most franchisees were motivated to grow because the opportunity to expand the business in existing units was inherently limited; to grow, a franchisee usually had to add new units. Another more subtle but powerful motivation for growth was franchisees' desire to "build a business." KFC's John Cranor noted that as franchisees grew they went from "owning a job to owning a business." Kelsey of Hardee's elaborated on this point: "Often a franchisee's goal is to get away from running a restaurant and being able to hire a district manager. It is the other things like finance, construction, and real estate that a lot of franchisees really like." For many franchisees, "doing deals" was more exciting than managing restaurants. For others, the goal was building an organization of their own. Spike Erhardt, a Hardee's franchisee who owned over forty units, talked about "his" marketing person and his plan to add a training person. Adding units involved more than a simple economic calculation; it also involved the creation of one's "own business" and moving away from working in the restaurant to managing a business.[9]

From the perspective of the chain operator, the economics are the same as for adding new franchisees: with each new unit, the chain operator received the franchisee fee and royalty income. In contrast to the two previous sources of growth, however, the demand on the chain operator's organizational resources was considerably less. Steven Reinemund, the CEO of Pizza Hut, which relied almost solely on existing franchisees for adding units, argued that "franchisees are good at striking deals, finding sites, supervising construction, and such things." It stands to reason that these people were better at these activities than new franchisees because they had already done them at least once. A large franchisee in another chain put it this way: "I've built more units than anyone in the company. I don't need their help." The chain operator reviewed and approved the sites of multi-unit franchisees, but its commitment of resources to that activity was relatively small and typically involved no more than a drive-by visit to the site.

Growing through existing franchisees overcame the main constraint associated with adding new franchisees—the risk that a person would be difficult to work with. As Gerald McGuiness of Hardee's explained, "We get the same royalty and fees, and we get an experienced guy rather than a new guy." Frank Puthoff, the director of franchise development at Pizza Hut, made a similar point: "Adding units to existing franchisees is a less risky way to grow than adding new franchisees where you never know what you are getting." This perspective was shared by all the people I interviewed and was reflected in the growth strategies of Jack in the Box and Hardee's, both of which not only grew through existing franchisees but also by searching for new franchisees who were capable of running multiple units. Jack in the Box's Thelen remarked, "We want people who can add a couple of units every year. In the development agreement we give them a positive incentive to grow. If they build faster than the agreed-to rate, then they get breaks on their franchise fee." The Hardee's strategy reflected a similar emphasis. McGuiness stated, "Ideally, we want people who can open one to five units per year." These types of franchise contracts, referred to in the industry as "development agreements," showed that a primary motivation for using existing franchisees was to accomplish the management challenge of unit growth. Growth from this source required less chain-operator resources compared to the other two sources of growth.

Chain executives emphasized another advantage of relying on existing franchisees for growth. Jay Willoughby, a division vice-president at Pizza Hut, summarized the argument: "It is much easier to have 140 franchisees add 1 unit per year than to have the company add 140 units per year." This contention was repeated to me in many interviews. Managers perceived that the decentralization of the unit-growth process accelerated the overall growth of a chain. Their argument implied that a diseconomy of scale adversely affected the growth process in the company arrangement. The diseconomy might be due to the local nature of the growth process—finding and making deals for sites, negotiating with local zoning commissions, managing construction contractors, hiring and training managers, and weathering the rocky start-up phase—and the difficulty the company arrangement had in managing more than a few of these local decisions and activities. This issue warrants much more research.[10]

The experienced franchisee usually developed his or her own units, which made growth from this source an almost costless proposition for the chain operator. In fact, the most serious constraint on growth with existing franchisees occurred when a franchisee owned an exclusive territory and did *not* develop it. All of Pizza Hut's franchisees owned territories; KFC, Hardee's, and Fishermen's Landing had some old franchisees that owned territories, although most franchisees (and all new ones) owned franchise rights only for specific restaurants; and Jack in the Box sought franchisees capable of meeting a development agreement that provided an area to the franchisee but only so long as he or she met a schedule of adding new units. In these chains, the exclusive territories were the result of commitments made early in the chain's life. John Roberts, the founder of Fishermen's Landing, recalled that the selling of franchise territories was not part of a grand strategy: "We did what we had to do to get the chain going. At that time, we didn't imagine it would be a big chain." Pizza Hut territories had been granted in a similar fashion; between 1961 and 1965 the chain divided up the entire country between the company and franchisees. Colonel Sanders at KFC granted territories on the basis of a handshake in the early 1960s, before the chain became well-established. It was thought at the time that such arrangements would enable the rapid development of a territory at a low cost to the chain operator.

In recent years, however, chain operators have recognized that this approach can actually place a constraint on growth, because the franchisee controls the rate of growth for an exclusive territory, where no other type of unit can be located. To circumvent this potential obstacle, Pizza Hut and Fishermen's Landing renegotiated the franchise contracts in the 1980s to specify growth rates for territorial franchisees. "These agreements were worked out individually," said Ken Staab, a Pizza Hut franchisee. "For most of us, it wasn't a big deal because we want to grow." In some cases, though, a franchisee did not wish to grow, due to financial problems or alternative investment opportunities. A common reason chain operators acquired franchisees was because they failed (from the perspective of the chain operator) to develop a market to its full potential in terms of adding units. No chain I studied continued to grant exclusive territories.

It is clear that from the perspective of managing unit growth, granting new units to existing franchisees had significant advantages over the other two approaches. These experienced franchisees typically knew what they were doing, having added units in the past, which put less demand on the chain operator's resources. Just as important, the chain operator had good information on existing franchisees, which made them much less of a risk than new franchisees. This rationale suggests that franchise arrangements composed of multi-unit franchisees will grow faster than franchise arrangements that add units by adding new franchisees.

Later, we will see that growth through existing franchisees may come at a cost in terms of operating performance. Agency cost theorists argue that the incentives of local franchisees in large part explain the use of franchising. With each additional unit in a franchisee's organization, however, these incentive effects are diluted, which is why these theorists argue against multi-unit franchising—if they admit it exists at all (see Brickley and Dark 1987). Later I will suggest that large franchisees may actually contribute to the objectives of the organization, but for now let me focus on the role of multi-unit franchising in the growth process. By leaving out the advantages related to growth, agency cost theorists miss one of the key reasons for multi-unit franchising.

PROCESSES OF THE PLURAL FORM

This section shows that the plural form helped the first two sources of growth—company units and new franchisees—overcome the constraints that limited them. While scholars construe the central growth problem facing the chain operator as choosing between company and franchise units, that formulation ignores a simple matter of addition: growth from two sources is faster than growth from either source alone, especially when each is bound by different constraints. The plural form also helped chains overcome a key constraint on the franchise arrangement—finding qualified franchisees—by creating a career path that led some company managers to become franchisees.

The Additive Process

When managers talked about their growth strategies and their use of company and franchise units, they spoke in terms of adding the two sources together. The comments of executives from three chains were representatives of others I interviewed:

> When we are at the maximum pace of adding new company units, then everything the franchisee does is gravy.

> Our strategic goal is to become the number-two competitor in every market by 1994. To do that, we must have franchisees filling in markets with us.

> We use franchisees to fill in the gap between our targeted objective for new units in a market and our ability to add company units.

The sources of growth operated autonomously from each other: franchisees searched for good sites that they then proposed to the chain operator; concurrently, the chain operator searched for new locations. Each source was constrained by different factors, so using more than one source enabled a chain to grow faster than by growing solely with either one. Gerald McGuiness of Hardee's put it this way: "Essentially we have two engines of growth—company and franchise units. We grow faster by using both, rather than just one."

The value of the plural form in the additive process hinges on two assumptions: first, that constraints existed on each source, and second, that unit growth needed to occur rapidly, thereby making the constraints binding. The first assumption was discussed in the previous section. Capital and managerial constraints limited the growth of the company arrangement, and the difficulty of finding qualified new franchisees limited the growth of the franchise arrangement. Growth through existing franchisees was less constrained, although the obvious point that all existing franchise growth *began* as new franchise growth did impose a constraint.

The need to grow fast was what made the constraints binding; otherwise, a chain could simply accept the constraints of an arrangement and grow at a slower rate.[11] The general pressure to increase revenue and profits motivated chain operators to grow as rapidly as possible. But it was strategic considerations that made accelerated growth in new markets important and that pushed chain operators against the constraints imposed by each arrangement. The relevance of the speed of growth for Jack in the Box was highlighted by Mo Iqbal: "We try to codevelop markets [use both company and franchise units] to get the needed market penetration quickly. The key to success is getting on television and you need a lot of units to make that economical." Don Mucci made the same argument for Hardee's: "Until you are able to get on television, you are probably losing money. So the length of time it takes to build enough units to make TV economical is the length of time you lose money. Speed is critical." These dynamics were less relevant to KFC and Pizza Hut because they already had a presence in most major markets. Still, they too noted the need to develop markets fully to build and leverage funds for advertising and preempt competitive intrusion. (Fishermen's Landing did no television advertising, which placed it under less pressure to grow fast. In addition, Fishermen's Landing was the only privately held company in the study, which also reduced the pressure to grow.) Advertising spending was based on a contribution per unit for both company and franchise units; hence, a critical mass of units in a market was required before advertising was economically feasible. This means of funding advertising necessitated that markets be developed quickly. Most chain executives and franchisees agreed that advertising was vital to a unit's success.[12]

The codevelopment strategies of local markets reflected in some cases an even more subtle dynamic of the plural form in the growth process, as Mucci explained: "Hardee's used to want pure company markets, but no more. As long as we still control the market [advertising decisions were made based on a majority vote] it doesn't make any difference what the mix is. We want franchisees to fill in markets. This strategy enables us to free our capital to seed other markets." The concept of "seeding" markets with company units was mentioned by Jack in the Box, too. Thelen noted, "Franchisees always ask what our plans are for a market they are considering. They want to make sure we are committed to it." Chain operators signaled their commitment to a market by building units, a signal that influenced a franchisee's decision to invest in the chain and enter the market. Also, lenders often asked for data on a company's historic performance in a market before making loans to franchisees, which again encouraged the kind of seeding strategy mentioned by Mucci. Although agency theory does not discuss the growth process, it does implicitly argue that plural chains can grow faster than pure company chains. The central finding of the theory is that chains use franchisees to operate in remote locations or in small markets because franchisees require a less elaborate management infrastructure to manage. Put another way, the use of franchisees enabled a chain to add units in places that otherwise would have been inaccessible to company units. This additive plural dynamic did not necessarily foster faster growth, but it did enable entry into otherwise inaccessible markets.[13]

Finally, in some chains company personnel and franchisees competed for sites, another dynamic of the plural form. This accelerated growth by inducing each side to search aggressively for growth opportunities. McCain's growth strategy at KFC built explicitly on this dynamic: "We have an underpenetrated market and we need to grow it. It's first come, first served. But when a franchisee comes to us with a proposed site, I want to know why my real-estate people [company people] didn't know about it." The process worked in reverse too; if an existing franchisee did not actively add units (assuming he or she did have an exclusive territory), then the chain operator sometimes stimulated growth by threatening to add a new franchise or company unit nearby.

Company People as Franchisees

The key constraint inhibiting the growth process with new franchisees was finding qualified and interested people. As noted in Chapter 3, the plural form provided chain operators with a partial solution to this problem: using company personnel to become franchisees. The chain operator had better information about the company person than with an outsider, especially concerning the vital question of whether they would be easy to work with. Also, by using company people, the franchise relationship was created in the context of a longstanding personal relationship. "I know everyone in the company arrangement from John [the founder] on down," said Mike Walters, a Fishermen's Landing franchisee who had formerly worked for the company fifteen years. "We all know where the other is coming from." With an outside franchisee, trust had to be created; with the company manager-turned-franchisee, trust already existed.

Along with the information advantages that accrued to the chain operator about company people, these people had better information, too, enabling a more informed "self-selection" process. James Randall, the CEO of Fishermen's Landing, emphasized the importance of selecting franchisees who understood the demands of the system: "This is a hard job. You're essentially on call 24 hours a day, 365 days a year. It is not uncommon to work 80 hours a week. We want to make sure that people understand the commitment they're making, and with company people they know what is involved." As noted, the franchisee selection process tried to educate prospective franchisees about the rigors of restaurant management, but that was no substitute for actually having worked for the chain for several years. With company people, the chain operator was less likely to be selecting franchisees who later decided they did not want to make biscuits at 5:00 A.M.; similarly, it was less likely that a prospective franchisee joined the system under a misconception of what was involved.

The use of company people as franchisees was also driven in large part by a practical consideration: the shortage of qualified prospective franchisees that had both the capital and the expertise to operate a restaurant. The escalating cost of real estate and construction led to the conundrum noted by Robert Nugent, the CEO of Jack in the Box: "People with enough money to become a franchisee usually don't want to run a restaurant." While company people rarely had the required capital, they were proven operators. In these cases, the chain operator or a passive investor often assisted the company people in buying the franchise.[14] For instance, Hardee's made loans to employees that were repaid over the first few years of the contract. Similarly, Fishermen's Landing offset the cost of acquiring a franchise by buying the land and building; the only capital cost facing the employee-turned-franchisee was the equipment, signs, and franchise fee. The chain operator preferred owner-operators to passive investors, but chain operators appeared more comfortable permitting these hybrid ownership arrangements for their own employees. The chain operator's confidence in the quality of the company people was key to this hybrid arrangement.

Selecting company personnel to serve as franchisees helped solve the difficult problem of finding qualified franchisees. Using company people as franchisees was the functional equivalent of using existing franchisees for growth: the chain operator selected proven operators to add units in both cases. This strategy might appear to exacerbate the managerial constraint facing company units by cutting into its base of seasoned managers, but the emphasis on systems and routines in company units made it less sensitive to the turnover of qualified personnel than the franchise arrangement. Paradoxically, this career path might even strengthen the performance of the company arrangement. Robert Brown, Fishermen's Landing's executive vice-president for development, argued that this career path "is a great motivator on the company side. You have to be a top performer to become a franchisee."

In summary, the employee-turned-franchisee career path yielded several benefits: better informed decisions on the part of both the chain operator and the manager to engage in the franchise contract; less costly chain-operator investments in socializing and building a relationship with the new franchisee; and consequently less costly management infrastructure required to work with these franchisees. This mechanism also saved the substantial investment required to find new franchisees.

MANAGING FRANCHISEES: CONTROL OVER UNIT GROWTH

Control over growth was a potent source of influence that chain operators had over the franchisees. Ray Kroc, the founder of the McDonald's chain, recognized this fact early on and allowed virtually no territorial franchises. Love's excellent book on the history of McDonald's (1986) succinctly captures the logic of this strategy: "By retaining the right to determine whether a franchisee is to be granted a license to operate a second store and then another, McDonald's also retained the only carrot it could use to motivate a franchisee to follow the system's rules on quality, service, cleanliness, and value." Maureen Miller, a franchise consultant at Hardee's, concurred: "Growth is the real lever of control we have. Two of the franchisees I have [of eight] are not qualified to grow until they resolve some outstanding issues." The strong desire of most franchisees to grow provided chain operators with a powerful lever to influence their behavior.[15] This source of influence was extremely important in the management of franchisees, as formal contracts were of limited use.

Since most franchisees sought to add units, this strategy had broad applicability. However, it did have some limitations. First, along with forsaking a source of capital, when the chain operator halted a franchisee's growth it increased the likelihood the franchisee would invest in an outside business. As the CEO of one chain remarked, "We like to keep the hands of our franchisees tied to the wheel. Once they start doing other things they lose their focus on our business." The concern with outside investments was shared by other executives. On the other hand, Don Mucci, director of franchising at Hardee's, argued that growth sometimes created its own problems, distracting franchisees from operations: "As a franchisee grows they of course lose some of the local entrepreneurship—mainly because they spend so much time on development and financial issues." Second, the strategy was also limited when a franchisee possessed an exclusive territory. In that case, restricting growth left the territory unavailable for development by either the franchisee or the chain operator. Even in this circumstance, however, chain operators sometimes used this strategy. For example, one chain prevented its second largest franchisee, who possessed restricted territories, from adding any units due to the chain operator's dissatisfaction with the franchisee's performance.

The idea that control can be exercised through growth leads to several testable propositions. One might compare performance of franchisees that are adding units to those that are not within the same chain. Another way to evaluate the relationship between growth and performance would be to compare the average uniformity scores of chains that are growing at different rates. An important implication of this "growth as control" argument should be noted: when the growth disappears, so too does the lever of control. The potential for a cycle of decline is easy to imagine: growth slows, the chain operator's control is weakened, uniformity among units falls, the value of the trademark erodes, franchisees shift their investment elsewhere, which slows growth further, and so on. The slowing growth of the chain industry described in Chapter 2 may make the management of franchisees a more challenging task in the future.

This discussion has focused exclusively on how the growth process affects the management of franchisees. But keep in mind that the growth process, by determining the mix of units in each market, has a powerful indirect influence on performance. In the next chapter we will see how the performance comparisons between company and franchise units in a market offered chain operators a way to persuade franchisees to change their behavior. In line with that logic, one division of KFC was pursuing a strategy of placing company units in every market to serve as a model of how a unit should be managed. The influence of the mix of company and franchise units on uniformity, local responsiveness, and systemwide adaptation will be discussed in detail in each of the following chapters.

CONCLUSION

The analysis presented in this chapter makes two points clear. First, growth is a central management challenge facing chains. In past research a chain's need to add units has been either ignored (agency cost theory) or viewed as an important issue only in the infancy of a chain (ownership redirection theory). Both views are mistaken. Unit growth is a distinct and important challenge and displays unique dynamics that help explain the use of each arrangement.

Second, the plural form strengthened a chain's ability to grow. The assumption that chains choose between company and franchise units ignores the simple fact that the simultaneous development of both types may enable faster growth. Moreover, the use of company people as franchisees helped chains overcome one of the main constraints facing the franchise arrangement: finding capable franchisees. This constraint was also overcome by multi-unit franchising, since the chain operator selected only well-performing franchisees to add units. Indirect support for the proposition that plural forms grow faster than pure forms can be found in the fact that virtually all large restaurant chains are plural forms.

One of the keys to understanding how franchisees are managed is to understand the role played by multi-unit franchisees. They enabled these chains to grow faster than was the case with either adding new franchisees or company units. Moreover, the growth process itself was a critical factor in a chain's ability to manage franchisees. And, as we will see, multi-unit franchisees played a critical role in a chain's ability to meet the challenge of uniformity. Some scholars puzzle over the use of multi-unit franchisees (Rubin 1978; Brickley and Dark 1987; Hadfield 1991), and even try to wish them away, but their contribution to growth and their implications for management must be incorporated in any theory that hopes to explain the operation of chain organizations.[16]

The focus of this chapter has been on the growth process itself. However, the accomplishment of the other management challenges—uniformity, local responsiveness, and systemwide adaptation—was affected by the growth process, as well as by the resulting mix of company and franchise units. If the growth process alone determined the mix, we might predict that we would see more pure franchise chains since the constraints on franchise growth (especially with multi-unit franchisees) were less binding than the constraints on company growth. However, once we examine how the dynamics of the mix itself helps the chain operator accomplish its other management objectives, we get a more balanced picture of the benefits of having company units along with franchise units.

Chapter 5

Uniformity

COMPANY AND franchise arrangements displayed similar levels of uniformity. Data from two chains that used third-party evaluators to assess uniformity displayed equal performance levels. Using a 100-point scale to assess adherence to the uniform standards, in one chain the franchise units averaged 94.6 and the company units 93.9; in the other chain, franchisees averaged 89.7 and the company units 90.6. These data were supported in my interviews with company managers and franchisees, most of whom agreed that the two arrangements exhibited similar levels of uniformity. This chapter describes the different mechanisms used by company and franchise arrangements to accomplish uniformity and explores how and why the two approaches led to equivalent levels of performance.

Company and franchise arrangements presented contrasting strategies for achieving uniformity. Company arrangements displayed more mechanisms related to managing uniformity and used them more frequently than did franchise arrangements. For example, "mystery shoppers" who anonymously evaluated restaurants and automated MIS that helped ensure uniformity were central features of the company arrangement but were rarely used by the chain operator to manage the uniformity of franchisees. This difference in management strategy can be attributable in part to other elements of the organizational design like the differing incentive structures. Ken Williams, chief operating officer of Jack in the Box, offered an explanation for the contrasting strategies that I heard repeatedly: "The franchisee's concern about the business is far greater than the company restaurant manager's. The company manager is in a bureaucracy; they believe in and obey the procedures. Therefore, you see a lot more rules in the company arrangement. The franchisee focuses on what is important on their own." Echoing Williams's point, one company area manager in another chain said, "My biggest problem is getting people to do things right. We need these tools to ensure that." In contrast, a franchise consultant suggested the tools played a smaller role in the franchise arrangement: "Ignorance is bliss. What you don't know doesn't hurt you. Franchisees usually take care of things themselves."

Along with the differing constellation of management elements, the simplicity of the tasks involved in operating a restaurant help to account for how the two strategies lead to the same outcome. On the one hand, all of the cause-effect relationships could be specified and monitored, as indeed they were in the company arrangement. On the other hand, that same specificity and simplicity enabled local operators with the right incentives to undertake these activities themselves, which was what occurred in the franchise arrangement. These different strategies help to explain the seemingly contradictory comments of industry participants. They sometimes said, "There are a million details you have to get right"; other times they observed, "This is a really simple business—making and selling chicken." Within the context of company and franchise arrangements, respectively, each of these perspectives was true.

The two strategies did influence each other through two plural processes I identified that equalized and raised the level of uniformity in the chain. By "equalize," I mean that the same level of uniformity was achieved by all the units across the chain; by "raise," I mean that the units reached a higher level of uniformity. The first plural dynamic was the "ratcheting process," which used the performance in one arrangement to set the standard for the other one. The ratcheting process was an inherent feature of plural-form chains since the management of franchisees depended in several ways on the relative performance of company units; at the same time, chain operators used the performance of franchisees to benchmark company units. The second plural dynamic was discussed briefly in Chapter 3: the replication of company practices by multi-unit franchisees. This "modeling process" tended to equalize the levels of uniformity in each arrangement since the same practices led to the same levels of performance.

This chapter begins by examining how company and franchise arrangements achieved uniformity, highlighting how the different types and number of performance measures influenced performance. It then explores how two such contrasting approaches could produce similar performance outcomes, highlighting some of the underlying patterns of behavior evoked by the different control strategies. In the company units, the gaming of the system by managers and a neverending cycle of shifting priorities I label "rotations of control" are common. In franchise units, "proportional response" is the key pattern, reflecting the chain operators' need to focus only on issues that truly affected the business; otherwise, the broader relationship with franchisees might be jeopardized. The final section of the chapter lays out the two plural processes, ratcheting and modeling, and speculates about how they affect performance.

MAINTAINING UNIFORMITY IN THE COMPANY ARRANGEMENT

Certainty about what needed to be accomplished and how to accomplish it permeated the management practices in the company arrangement. Indeed, at the heart of a business-format chain was the codification of this knowledge, which facilitated the cloning of units. The relationship between certainty and bureaucratic structures is extensively documented in the organizational literature, and business-format chains with their well-specified procedures exemplified this pattern.[1] Rich Bachman, a KFC division director of operations, vividly described the challenge of managing company units:

> We are running thousands of identical factories. They need to be the same because customers need to get what they expect. Since customers can see the plant [the production process] and the process is in real time, the details of the business are crucial. There are forty-five steps to setting up a cooker—and if we do that right, we're still no better than the competition. This isn't brain surgery but you have to get the details right. Details are like a cancer: they start to grow out of control if you don't constantly monitor them.

Paying constant and explicit attention to the details of the business was how the chain operator established uniformity in the company arrangement; the cancer analogy expressed how seriously chain operators viewed this challenge. This approach to achieving uniformity was reflected in the type and number of the formal mechanisms used to monitor and manage uniform standards. As we will see, the company arrangement was built on a management philosophy of close and redundant control aimed at maintaining uniformity.

Systems for Maintaining Uniformity in the Company Arrangement

Procedures existed for virtually every activity in a restaurant, and standards were established that defined acceptable execution of the procedures. Chain operators used three main mechanisms for measuring and evaluating whether procedures were being followed and uniformity was being maintained. First, QSC field audits (which stands for "quality," "service," and "cleanliness") were conducted regularly to assess whether standards on these three dimensions were being met. Second, chains often used mystery shoppers, people (typically third-party contractors) who anonymously visited restaurants and evaluated the dining experience from the perspective of "the typical customer." Third, on a continuous basis MIS measured financial and operating performance to ensure that the appropriate ratio of inputs to outputs was maintained.

Field Audits. Every chain utilized field audits to evaluate the "front of the house and the back of the house." The front-of-the-house field audit evaluated the business from the perspective of the customer: for example, the physical product, service, and dining experience. The back-of-the-house audit assessed the procedures involved in producing the product: for example, the temperature of ovens, the holding time of products, and the cleanliness of equipment. All five chains evaluated three broad categories of activity during a field audit: quality, service, and cleanliness. Depending on the chain's focus, the audit was variously referred to as a QSC audit (Pizza Hut), SQC audit (Hardee's), and QSC&F audit (Jack in the Box—the "F" is for friendliness). KFC and Fishermen's Landing measured essentially the same things but called the audits the Operations and Facility Review (KFC) and the Product Service Analysis (Fishermen's Landing).

All of the companies used a detailed field-audit form. The Hardee's form consisted of 295 items. Among the items evaluated were the temperature of products, service times, visual appearance of products, and bathroom cleanliness. The following description of the appropriate preparation of bacon was representative of the level of operational detail that was evaluated during the field audit:

> FLAT GRILL—Cooked from frozen state at 325 degrees; cook up to 3 layers; time set for 2 minutes after all bacon is on grill; timer set for 1 minute and then bacon turned; cooked additional 30 seconds if needed; bacon not piled in middle of insert; maximum of 120 strips per holding pan; held uncovered; 4-hour holding time observed.

The behavior of employees was also part of the field audit. Do they follow the sales script? Do they "suggestively sell" other items on the menu? Do they display a "sense of urgency"? District managers at Hardee's estimated that a field audit took between two and four hours. The audit ended with the district manager sharing the scores with the restaurant manager and identifying issues that needed improvement. The completed audit form was posted in the kitchen and a copy was sent to the regional office. In all chains a detailed evaluation instrument of this sort was filled out regularly. Pizza Hut, Hardee's, KFC, and Jack in the Box did field audits once a month, and Fishermen's Landing did a mini-inspection once a week and a major inspection once a quarter.

The Fishermen's Landing Product Service Analysis (PSA) audit was probably the most comprehensive audit I observed. It was done by the division manager from behind a one-way window that was located in the door of the manager's office and looked out directly on the food preparation area. Robert Brown, executive vice-president, noted, "Since the division manager is often in the office making phone calls anyway, the audits are essentially unannounced." The PSA audit started with timing everything that occurred from when the customers "hit the door to when the door swings closed behind them." The division manager used a stopwatch and sampled fifteen to twenty customers to measure when the customer entered, was seated, ordered, received the food, was given the check, received change, and left. Brown said that this inspection gave the company a "true picture of what is happening in the unit. People may say that a certain cook is really good, but let's look at the numbers and see. Let's not be fooled by flashiness."

At KFC, Pizza Hut, and Hardee's, area managers conducted the field audits of their restaurants. Jack in the Box was the only chain I studied that specialized the audit activity in a separate department—the Quality Assurance Systems & Training (QAS&T) department, which reported directly to the president. A primary reason for specializing the activity, said chief operating officer Ken Williams, was "to obtain valid feedback about how we are doing. Having people evaluate their own restaurants doesn't make sense." Moreover, the field audits were unannounced at Jack in the Box, which was usually not the case in the other chains. Area managers at Jack in the Box sometimes conducted audits for management purposes, but the performance-evaluation and compensation system was based on the field-audit results from the QAS&T department.

Williams's concern about the integrity of the data was shared by executives in other chains. The problem with this measurement technique was that essentially area managers were evaluating themselves since the numbers were used for their own performance evaluations, a circumstance that might predictably lead to biased scores. In fact, almost all the area managers I interviewed said that they announced their field audits beforehand, which certainly made the numbers unrepresentative of a typical day in the restaurant. Accordingly, a Pizza Hut regional manager said, "I don't take the QSC scores too seriously unless there is a real problem. They are too subject to playing. Being in the restaurant every day is what makes a big difference, and that is where I want my area managers." Tony Deluca, division director of operations at KFC, expressed a similar concern: "Often the area manager is too close to the unit and listens to the excuses. But the fact is that the customer doesn't care about excuses." Jack in the Box solved this problem by specializing the audit function in a separate department. Another strategy used to "control the controllers" was mystery shopping.

Mystery Shopping. The word "mystery" refers to the fact that an evaluator makes an anonymous, unannounced visit—a "shop"—to a restaurant and rates the eating experience from the perspective of the customer. The mystery-shopping evaluation was similar to the QSC evaluation, except that data were gathered without the knowledge of the restaurant manager, fewer items were assessed, and the items focused only on the dining experience. Jack in the Box and KFC had companywide mystery-shopping programs that were managed by the QAS&T and Quality Assurance Departments, respectively. At Hardee's and Pizza Hut, no corporate program existed but many divisions contracted with outside vendors to provide mystery-shopping services. Fishermen's Landing did not use this management tool, although its PSA program allowed for the anonymity typically associated with a mystery-shopping program.

A training videotape for restaurant managers described what mystery shoppers did at KFC. The tape began with the mystery shopper dressed in casual attire entering a restaurant and ordering a "three-piece meal" with all the side dishes and a large Pepsi to go. This two-minute transaction on the videotape was then followed by a replay of the entire visit with a voice-over indicating the places where the mystery shopper took points off for violations. One employee was not wearing a hat—minus 2 points. There was trash in the parking lot—minus 2 points. The wait in line was over two minutes (the shopper carried a stopwatch in his pocket)—minus 2 points. The tape then showed the mystery shopper driving out of the parking lot and stopping at the "nearest safe place to park" to take the temperature of the chicken (the shopper carried a meat thermometer in the car). The chicken was not hot enough, a major violation—minus 5 points. The restaurant scored 89 points out of a possible 100, which was below the company minimum of 90. The video went on to say that a week later copies of the evaluation were sent to the restaurant, the district office, and the headquarters.[2]

Chain operators routinely used mystery shopping to evaluate units because they believed it offered an undistorted picture of the business. Bob Price, an area director of operations at Hardee's, claimed, "The element of surprise gives us a real picture of how the business is doing." Robert Nugent, CEO at Jack in the Box, concurred: "The mystery-shopper report gives us enough information to isolate the key problem facing each unit. It is not a full [QSC] report but it is from the perspective of a guest which in the end is who we have to satisfy. It is the best measure of execution we have." In some chains, the data from the mystery-shopping program was used to counteract some of the organizational pathologies provoked by the other control mechanisms. One vice-president said he used the scores to ensure the integrity of the QSC audits: "I compare the mystery-guest score with the district manager's QSC score to see if the DM has been honest about what is going on."[3] Similarly, Gary McCain, a division vice-president at KFC, argued that mystery shoppers counteracted some of the deleterious behavior caused by slavish adherence to budgets: mystery shoppers "protect against the short-term results created by budget pressures such as selling old product that otherwise would have to be written off. Running a restaurant is not like stocking shelves; instead, we are delivering a service and we need to know that we are doing it right." In part, mystery shopping was a mechanism that compensated for the limitations of the other control mechanisms.

Not everyone was so sanguine about the benefits of mystery-shopping programs. The CEO of Pizza Hut, which left it to the discretion of its divisions to use the program, warned that mystery shopping "can end up usurping the power of the managers; it can end up substituting for management." Jim Jordan, a division manager at Pizza Hut who opted not to use mystery shoppers, agreed: "I don't think it is the way to manage QSC. The AM and DM need to be in restaurants as much as possible and instill pride in their people. If the DM is successful in getting people fired up, the issues go away. Pride is better than fear as a way of motivating people." Several people echoed Jordan's association of mystery shopping with fear. In part, the mention of fear related to some people's belief that it was unfair to judge a unit based on one transaction out of the thousands that occurred each month. Debbie Stewart, a district manager at Hardee's, remarked, "If an employee doesn't show up that day or is late, and that is when the shopper comes, you are going to fail. It just scares and worries people and is of little value."

The "panoptical" nature of this control mechanism—being constantly watched and judged without knowing when or by whom (Foucault 1979)—contributed to the fear some people felt. "You never know," said one restaurant manager during an interview I conducted, "they could be in here right now and I could be failing!" In the chains that used this technique the scores weighed heavily on performance evaluations, which is not surprising since the expressed reason for using the technique was to provide an "accurate picture" of the business. The decor of one area manager's office suggested the importance of this program: the walls were ringed with graphs charting the mystery-guest scores for his six restaurants.

Management Information System. MIS helped maintain uniformity by measuring in detail the ratio of inputs to outputs. MIS indicators, both automated and manual, highlighted both waste, which imposed financial costs (reflected in a high ratio of inputs to outputs), and "under-serving," which compromised uniformity (reflected in a low ratio of inputs to outputs). For example, I attended a budget-planning meeting of company managers that discussed the damaging consequences of a low labor-to-revenue ratio because it indicated diminished service, and of a low food waste-to-revenue ratio, which suggested that restaurants might be holding and selling food that was beyond its proper "hold time." The MIS measured and assessed performance on indicators that were to be met—not necessarily exceeded.

KFC, Pizza Hut, Hardee's, and Jack in the Box had point-of-sale (POS) systems that recorded the details of each customer transaction; Fishermen's Landing did virtually the same thing manually. The important aspect of these systems in terms of maintaining uniformity was their capacity to track food and labor costs through inventory and time-keeping functions. For example, every night the restaurant manager at KFC counted the number of "chicken heads" (whole chickens), Chicken Littles (small patties of chicken), and Kentucky Nuggets in the freezer, and entered those numbers into the computer. By comparing inventory and the day's sales figure, a "chicken variance" number was generated each day. Similarly, by tracking the labor each day and comparing it to the budget and to sales, the MIS produced a "labor variance" number. These detailed data on costs, coupled with the automatic recording of sales data by product category, enabled chain operators to construct a profit-and-loss statement each day for each restaurant.

A restaurant's performance on individual line items was available to managers throughout the chain on an almost real-time basis. The MIS thus made the operational detail of its local restaurants transparent. Not only was everyone's superior immediately able to view their performance, but these data were usually accompanied with a comparison to a budget, to the previous year's performance, or to averages for the district, region, or company. Variances from expected performance could be identified at a glance. The management technique that accompanied these data in one chain was referred to as "management by red pen": senior managers circled in red ink the numbers that were out of bounds and asked subordinates for explanations and action plans.

At Hardee's (not the "red pen" company), Debbie Stewart employed a variant of this management strategy that was also mentioned by managers in two other chains. Each week she received a "mini-P&L," which measured the performance of her restaurants on key items. "If a restaurant's food variance is more than 1.8 percent for a week," Stewart said, "the following week the manager has to call me each day and tell me what his or her variance is running. If the variances are within range, I don't see daily numbers." She used this same management practice for labor variances. During the average week, she estimated that 30 percent of the restaurants reported to her on a daily basis about either food or labor variances.

Pizza Hut's new MIS formalized this process of "managing by exception." Alan Feldman, senior vice-president for operations, stated that one of the virtues of the new system was that "you will be able to push a button and see exactly what things need attention. We will set tolerance limits for each item, and if those limits are exceeded the computer screen will highlight the number." Feldman noted that the benefit of this system resided not only with enhancing and simplifying control over operations but also with the free time managers could then devote to "the two most important parts of our business: our customers and our people." Specific applications of Pizza Hut's new MIS included automating some of the reporting tasks, making a restaurant's operation visible through technology, and programming the computer with the heuristic rules of thumb used by managers to spot trouble areas.

Performance Evaluation and Management

The three mechanisms for maintaining uniformity described above were the primary measures the chain operators used to evaluate managers in the operations department. The operations department "delivers on our promise to consumers," said Bob Haberkamp, a Hardee's area vice-president, "and they have to get things right." Managers in the operations department, from restaurant manager to regional manager, had two major responsibilities: maintaining the uniformity of the business format and managing the financial elements of the business. In practice, the balance between these responsibilities tilted heavily in the direction of maintaining uniformity since managers in these chains had little discretion to act in ways that directly boosted sales. Additionally, the financial measures of performance tended to be directed toward maintaining uniformity. A restaurant manager offered a characteristic description of his job: "Mainly, I make sure that everything is at standards, like opening on time."

The job description for the restaurant manager in one chain, which was similar for other chains, encapsulated the relative importance of uniformity over financial measures: the restaurant manager "effectively and efficiently manages the restaurant within the policies and guidelines of the company and with emphasis on profit maximization and customer service." "Profit maximization" followed "manag[ing] the restaurant within the policies and guidelines." Indeed, several company executives worried that placing too great an emphasis on financial measures would compromise uniformity. As the senior vice-president of human resources at Pizza Hut, Dan Paxton, put it, "We might lose control over operations if we get too fancy with compensation and encourage people to focus on financial measures." Financial measures played a role in the management of the company arrangement, but as the next chapter shows, restaurant managers had little discretion over decisions that might alter those numbers except for "running the restaurant right."

The management emphasis on meeting the chain's standards and maintaining uniformity existed from the bottom to the top of the company hierarchy. The performance-evaluation measures for senior managers in the company arrangement almost always were aggregations of the numbers from the lower levels. Dan Fassbender's description of his position as a regional manager at Pizza Hut illustrated this pattern: "After rolling up the numbers from below [related to both uniformity and the budget], I work hard with the poor performing units—troubleshooting, trying to get them on track. That is most of my time. Also I have two new area managers so part of my job is to nurture them and help them along." The primary management difference between the top and bottom of the hierarchy was the number of units rolled-up in the performance review; the actual tasks undertaken by managers at different levels were quite similar. An area director of operations at Hardee's gave a description of his job, which highlighted the fundamental similarity of the top and bottom positions in the hierarchy: "I am the last quality-control person. While I pay close attention to facilities and capital-related issues, I also emphasize operations. This business is about doing simple things right, so when I visit I try to teach people some of the basics: how to wash windows right, how to organize the stock room, and things like that." The tight link between uniformity and performance evaluation led executives to become highly involved in the management of local units—and the minute details of those units.

In my field interviews, I witnessed several examples of the extent to which superiors in essence did the work of their subordinates. On one field visit I observed, a restaurant manager greeted the area manager with the words "You better go get your shoes." The area manager told me that she always had a pair of comfortable shoes in the car in case she needed to work, which happened, she estimated, several days a month. Another area manager carried a beeper with him. On a half-day tour of restaurants I made with him he was paged three times. One call was from a restaurant manager who needed help straightening out an employee's paycheck. Another call was from a restaurant manager who had been visited by the area manager and district manager the previous day. During the visit the district manager told the restaurant manager he needed to pull out some of the dead plants in front of the restaurant and the manager wanted to know which ones. On another field visit an area manager signed the cash-deposit receipts for each day of the previous week and reprimanded the manager for not making two deposits each day. He then proceeded to sign off on each miscellaneous cash outlay—like a $2.46 bottle of Lysol. Although field managers could not be in all their restaurants at once, the relatively narrow spans of control enabled them, and the performance-evaluation system encouraged them, to become highly involved in the management of the levels below them.

One chain I visited, which was not in my main sample, exemplified the similarity of positions in the hierarchy. In this chain, field audits were conducted on every restaurant once a month by an area manager, once a quarter by a district manager, and semiannually by a regional vice-president. The average of the scores generated by each level was weighed equally in the evaluation of the restaurant manager's annual performance. The difference in the tasks of hierarchical superiors was mainly one of geographic scope of audits rather than scope of decision-making authority.[4] The vast majority of the time spent by all company managers was in the field either formally or informally auditing units. Most senior managers I interviewed said that they spent at least three days a week in the field. This depiction of hierarchy as a mechanism for redundant and personal control contrasts with other scholarly conceptions that view hierarchical superiors as integrators of interdependent functions (Perrow 1986) or as managers associated with decisions focusing on different time horizons (Jacques 1990).

Performance Measures in Action: Gaming and Rotations

While the company's performance-management system focused attention on uniformity, it produced some unintended effects that actually may have compromised uniformity. Nohria and Eccles (1992, 214) suggest the conundrum created by performance measurement in organizations: "[A]ny attempt to measure performance 'feeds back' into the organization and becomes a powerful *influence* on action itself." In this case, the emphasis on the measures and their sheer quantity led to two notable effects: first, gaming the system and second, a continuous cycle of shifting priorities that I call "rotations of control."

Gaming the System. "Gaming the system" occurred when people directed their efforts toward affecting the evaluation measures rather than the actual performance being evaluated. In essence, the reliance on the measures produced a reversal of means and ends: the means of evaluating performance (field audits, mystery shopping, and budgets) became the ends. While this dynamic is not unique to restaurant chains, the management and evaluation of details in chains may amplify its effect.[5] Not only does this dynamic create distortions in the measures, which influence decisions and resource allocation, but the gaming consumes time and energy that might otherwise have been put to better use. Moreover, the investment in "controlling the controllers" noted earlier—for example, using mystery shopping to ensure the integrity of the field audits—were primarily responses to the gaming of the measures. Bob Jones, senior vice-president of human resources at Jack in the Box, described this aspect of the company arrangement: "This is the old story of bureaucracy at work. There is clipboard after clipboard in the restaurants, checklists to make sure checklists are being done right."

The most extraordinary example of gaming I observed was one district manager's five-year computer analysis of the dates that mystery shoppers had previously visited his restaurants. He showed me a chart (pinned to the wall next to a trend analysis of the scores) that reported which week of the month the visits had occurred the past five years. "There does seem to be a pattern, and on those weeks I tell my restaurant managers to be prepared," said the district manager. The district manager acknowledged that his strategy might bias the data, but he said, "The fact is that if I have the choice of knowing or not knowing, I'd rather know. I've seen job actions [dismissals] taken on the basis of these scores."

While this example might be viewed as extreme, virtually everyone I talked to discussed how they tried to identify the mystery shopper. Bob Price, an executive at Hardee's, asked rhetorically: "How many average customers ask for a receipt? How many customers order in the restaurant at the counter and then go to their car and go through the drive-through? Often you can figure out who they [the mystery guests] are." KFC's Ken Tyler noted that the mystery guest usually ordered one of everything. He said that a few weeks earlier the crew noticed the "order," and when they saw that the customer was in a rental car they knew that he was a mystery shopper. They immediately called the nearby restaurants and said, "Watch for the guy in shorts driving a Thunderbird." Jack in the Box's strategy of using short-term hires to serve as QSC&F specialists was in part a response to this problem. The company went even further, sending a memorandum to all employees stating that calling another unit about a mystery guest in the area was grounds for termination. The strong emphasis on this evaluation measure led to behaviors that in the end compromised the value of the measure and may have even diverted people's attention away from achieving the desired performance.[6]

The extent to which performance was dependent on the evaluation measures was indicated in one chain when it stopped using the mystery-shopping program. In that chain, the scores dropped precipitously in one year from 93.9 to 87.0.[7] An executive offered an explanation for this finding: "People do what we measure." Indeed, that is the point of the measurement system! Nohria and Eccles (1992, 215) note, "Since to measure something is to direct attention to it as important, most people in organizations cleverly direct their actions to optimize known measures to the best of their ability." Consequently, it is not surprising that we observe the gaming of the measurement system and the tight link between specific measures and performance outcomes.

Rotations of Control. Managers reported that the management of the company arrangement had a circular quality, with management rotating its emphasis from one issue to the another until the cycle repeated itself. As one executive observed, "Whenever we focus on something it is almost always the case that something else gets worse. People can only juggle so many balls without dropping one and that is usually what happens." As one ball dropped (for example, service times declined in a region) management focused on it, which set in motion the next ball to drop (for example, restaurant cleanliness worsened), which then received attention, and so on. This pattern reproduced itself, with each cycle sowing the seeds for the next cycle. This led to a dynamic that managers at Hardee's called WIN: "What's Important Now."

Robert Brown remarked on the same pattern at Fishermen's Landing: "What we pay attention to gets better; what we ignore gets worse. Folks will do a better job on things if you pay attention to what you want to get done." Brad Johnson, another senior executive at Fishermen's Landing, offered an interesting analogy: "It is like sweeping a beach: there are so many things to get right that there is always something to do." Johnson labeled this the "Law of Selective Negligence," the logic of which he went on to describe: "If we did everything we need to do, then we would never sleep. We just have to not get caught short." In all the chains I visited, managers made reference to the cyclical rotation of control in maintaining uniformity.

The rotations of control were not usually a product of a chain's changing strategy or of attempts to adapt to new market conditions. They tended to be a natural consequence of the management of multiple detailed performance measures. The range of tasks individuals must do right, as defined by the assorted control mechanisms, may either overwhelm their cognitive capacity or overwhelm the capacity of controllers to monitor the tasks (Simon 1976); this limitation may set in motion the rotation of control. While managers repeatedly told me that managing a chain "is not brain surgery," the panoply of control mechanisms the chain operators have instituted may have created a level of complexity that extends beyond the capacity of mere mortals. This line of reasoning suggests a management paradox: the easier it is to break the task into component pieces and the more specific and fine-grained the performance-evaluation mechanisms, the more likely it is for that task to move through rotations of control—making, in the end, a relatively simple task difficult to accomplish.

An alternative explanation for the rotations of control is suggested by White's interesting analysis of principal-agent relationships (1985). White argues that control often slips from the hands of the principal (the superior) to the agent (the subordinate) when the agent develops specialized expertise. One strategy principals use to curtail the autonomy of agents that may emerge from this situation is "the continuing realignment of boundaries" (White 1985, 209). In the case of chains, where the simple uniform format virtually guarantees that everyone in the hierarchy shares the same expertise, the key lever of control available to superiors may be the setting and shifting of the agenda that was reflected in rotations of control I observed. Along these same lines, Nohria and Eccles (1992) argue that one way that managers may prevent the gaming of the measurement system is by constantly changing the measures the organization uses.

Factors Amplifying the Two Effects. The two effects of the performance-measurement system were amplified by two other factors: the wide availability of performance data to people in the hierarchy and the inherent comparability of data across units. These two features of the system were beneficial insofar as they highlighted areas where a unit was above or below an average; the disadvantage was that they created conditions that exacerbated the gaming and rotations of control by focusing even more attention on the measures. These features often led managers to know their percentile ranking or their absolute ranking compared to other units on a variety of performance measures—for example, QSC scores, sales, profits, labor ratios, or mystery-guest scores. One manager told me how he had transformed a unit ranked 269th in the company on QSC to the rank of 84th in just eight months. "We want people to compete with each other to be the best," said one CEO, "so we make sure everyone knows where they stand."

By emphasizing the data generated by the performance measures—and making them public—subordinates focused almost exclusively on them, which sometimes led to the gaming of the measures. Read how one executive used the scores to manage his subordinates:

> When the [mystery-shopping] numbers for the month come in on who ranks where—for both restaurant managers and area managers—it is either hero or zero. A score of 90 is passing. This month we got 87 percent of the units over 90; only four of thirty-two failed. Those four units fell in two areas and the area managers feel terrible. The report is seen throughout the company—from the EVP for operations on down. It is quite motivational.

Subordinates confirmed to me that they devoted almost all of their time to achieving the necessary performance as defined by the standards. This dynamic sometimes led to gaming (and later to rotations), which affected the performance measure but not necessarily the underlying performance.

MAINTAINING UNIFORMITY IN THE FRANCHISE ARRANGEMENT

The mechanisms for monitoring and managing uniformity in the franchise arrangement were less extensive than in the company arrangement. Except for Jack in the Box, where the mechanisms were nearly identical, the other chains used fewer mechanisms, used them less frequently, and exercised less direct managerial control than their company counterparts. A major reason for the difference can be traced to franchisees' motivation to operate their restaurants effectively. The key performance measure of franchisees, profit, created an incentive at the local level that reduced the chain operator's need to manage the details of the franchisee's business. In essence, self-control replaced external control. "Every dime goes into the pocket of the franchisee," said Ron Rehahn, regional general manager at Hardee's. Additionally, multi-unit franchisees utilized many of the same systems as the chain operator, which effectively substituted for the chain operator's systems. This approach to accomplishing uniformity did not generate the gaming and rotations of control observed in the company arrangement; rather, the chain operator exercised "proportional response" to problems with uniformity in the franchise arrangement.

Mechanisms for Maintaining Uniformity

Chain operators used two main formal mechanisms to assess the uniformity of franchise units: field audits and mystery-shopping audits. A third mechanism was information provided by franchisees to the chain operator, but such information was not routinely available to the chain operator. In addition, peer monitoring was an informal but important means of maintaining uniformity in the franchise arrangement. Franchisees often let the chain operator know if a nearby franchisee (or company unit) was doing something that compromised the trademark and hurt their business.

Field Audits. Four of the chains used identical evaluation forms for both company and franchise arrangements; Fishermen's Landing did not conduct formal field audits on its franchisees. In all the chains except Jack in the Box, field audits were less frequent in the franchise than in the company arrangement. At Pizza Hut, Hardee's, and KFC, audits were done in company units every month or quarter (depending on the region), while in franchise units they were conducted annually. Aside from these formal aspects of the audit, the conduct of a visit by the chain operator to franchisees was entirely different than a visit to company units. Appendix C describes the typical visit by a field representative to each type of unit, highlighting the sharply contrasting relationships and control strategies.

Jack in the Box used identical mechanisms for both company and franchise units and visited both with the same frequency. The absence of a difference can be attributed to several factors. First, the franchisees signed a more stringent contract compared to other companies. Franchising was in its relatively early stages at Jack in the Box, and the chain operator included a strict provision about auditing in the contract. Second, the large number of former company personnel who were franchisees made them more tolerant of the chain operator's exercise of control. By virtue of their experience in the company, these people accepted that these mechanisms were an integral part of the business. Third, Jack in the Box had relatively few large multi-unit franchisees, so in most cases there was not an intermediate structure simultaneously conducting audits along with the chain operator.

Fishermen's Landing did not formally audit franchisees. Brad Johnson, who was responsible for two of the chain's biggest and most experienced franchisees, said, "Everything is pretty informal. I take notes during a trip and afterward talk to the franchisee and compare what we saw, but there is no score or anything." With the less experienced franchisees, Jordan Brant, who also had responsibility for several franchisees, noted, "I have to make sure they follow the rules, but only if the place is like a pig sty do I suggest to the manager that we do an actual inspection." The majority of franchisees had been with the chain for over two decades and were personally involved with the business, which reduced the need for close control by the chain operator and, in any case, made it difficult for the chain operator to exercise such control.

Mystery Shopping. Mystery shopping was used much less frequently in the franchise arrangement, and was done only with franchisees' concurrence. (Jack in the Box was the exception to this pattern for the reasons discussed earlier.) Fishermen's Landing, Hardee's, and Pizza Hut did not do mystery shops on franchisees. KFC used mystery shoppers, but only if the franchisee signed an agreement permitting it. The infrequent use of this mechanism stands in contrast to its common use in company units. Most people I asked about the disparity were stymied by the question; they simply took for granted that chain operators did not mystery-shop franchisees. When I asked a Pizza Hut executive to speculate on why the difference existed, he replied, "Franchisees probably wouldn't want us checking up on them."

The way KFC implemented and utilized mystery shopping exemplified some of the differences between company and franchise mechanisms. KFC encouraged franchisees to participate in a mystery-shopping program, conducted by a third party, and 85 percent of the franchisees agreed. It was clear from the high rate of participation that franchisees regarded the program as an aid to their business. This perception was fostered by the fact that the chain operator was not permitted to use the scores in its evaluation of franchisees when it was time to terminate or renew a franchisee's contract. Moreover, the data was made available only to the franchisee being evaluated and his or her franchise consultant; otherwise, the data was aggregated in ways that made an individual franchisee's performance anonymous to other people. The KFC example suggests that franchisees were not opposed to mystery shopping per se, but were opposed to its use as an evaluation mechanism.[8]

Management Information Systems. Chain operators received little operating data from franchisees on a regular basis. Ed Jacob of Pizza Hut said, "At some point I might get a P&L from a franchisee but that is usually a function of personal contacts. Usually I just get a monthly revenue number." Even when data was obtained, "we really can't be sure they are counting things like us," said Dennis Hill, a Hardee's division director of finance. This situation limited the chain operator's ability to monitor directly the relationship between the costs and revenue that might indicate problems with uniformity.[9] While the sharing of data aided in the maintenance of uniformity, its relatively infrequent occurrence also limited its use in this way.

Peer Monitoring. Franchisees were always alert to other units that might be providing poor quality or service. In three of the chains, I observed meetings when a franchisee told a representative of the chain operator about the poor performance of a fellow franchisee. In one case, the franchisee put the issue quite bluntly: "When are you going to get the three meatheads in my market out of the system?" Franchisees were motivated to tell the chain operator about poor performers because, as one franchisee put it, "If someone is running a poor operation it hurts the chain and it hurts my business." Also, franchisees viewed it as part of the chain operator's role to police the system and protect the integrity of the trademark: "It is the job of the chain operator to get on the people running a shoddy operation," said one franchisee. To some extent, peer monitoring substituted for the monitoring conducted by hierarchical superiors in the company arrangement.

Performance Measures in Action: Proportional Response

Chain operators used the data generated by the monitoring mechanisms in the franchise arrangement in a different way than was observed in the company arrangement. Most significantly, the chain operator, and specifically the franchise consultant, did not manage every detail of the franchisee's business. Indeed, the spans of control and the infrequency of field audits made this kind of intensive oversight virtually impossible. Instead, chain operators responded in proportion to the issue at stake; minor deviations did not preoccupy the chain operator. Brad Johnson of Fishermen's Landing put it this way: "I watch for trends. I can't worry too much about single occurrences. The goal posts are wider with franchisees. There are things we would get on a company manager for that aren't worth arguing about with a franchisee." Steven Reinemund of Pizza Hut said, "It is important to figure out what is important to control versus what is not when it comes to franchisees. Otherwise everything becomes a crisis."

The chain operator's use of the data on uniformity in the franchise arrangement exhibited proportional response. To begin with, the data were not public as in the company arrangement, so there was not the incessant pressure to achieve relative success. In most chains, the chain operator used "threshold scores" to establish whether a franchisee was in compliance with the chain's standards and could add units or renew the franchise contract. Additionally, the chain operator paid close attention to the uniformity scores on a punctuated basis, not continuously—typically during contract renewal and when considering proposals to add new units. For example, when a contract was up for renewal the chain operator would require that a unit be brought "up to the prevailing standard." Thomas Dolan, a Hardee's franchisee, recalled that the contract renewal of one of his units was contingent on his "updating to the current concept. I would have rather not invested here—I would have rather opened a new unit—but if you want to renew you have to keep up the image." In all the chains, the chain operator conducted an inspection of the unit under consideration before renewing the contract. Finally, franchise consultants were not rewarded based on the "roll-up" of the supervised franchisees' uniformity scores, which made them less focused on intervening in the local operation. These three factors made the franchise arrangement less likely to exhibit the ends-means reversal observed in the company arrangement and reflected the strategy of proportional response.

Proportional response was also apparent in the day-to-day management of uniformity. For example, during an interview a Pizza Hut franchisee asked me if the vice-president of franchising (whom I had interviewed earlier that day) mentioned anything about the nonstandard window shades the franchisee had recently installed. He said that the franchise consultant "has been after me for awhile, and I wondered how big a deal they were going to make of this." Later, when I talked to the vice-president of franchising again, he said, "I might send him a letter, but it isn't a giant issue. As long as it doesn't affect the consumer on a day-to-day basis, we just keep up the pressure but we don't push it." Chain operators' tolerance of deviations from uniformity and their reliance on proportional response to address lapses in standards contrasted sharply with the management patterns observed in company units. It was highly improbable that the following incident ever could have occurred in a company restaurant. Dave Hoban, an area director of franchising at Hardee's, recounted the story:

> Occasionally franchisees try things they are not supposed to. Just last week I received a customer complaint about our pecan pie. The problem is that we don't sell pecan pie! I called the franchisee and said, "How is the pecan pie doing?" He said he just wanted to see what consumers thought of it—just kind of experiment with it—and that he sold a little bit. I asked him to get rid of it and he did. The guy runs good restaurants, but has a tendency to break some of the rules. I'm sure it will be something else in a few months.

In cases of this sort, the chain operator exercised discretion about whether to force a franchisee to remedy the performance issue at stake. It was noted earlier that if a performance problem was significant enough the chain operator sometimes would take a franchisee to court, but this was rare.

The proportional response of the chain operator was driven in part by the economics of the arrangement, which caused franchisees to internalize the costs of their behavior. Quite simply, the internalization of these costs substituted for the use of external mechanisms to achieve uniformity;

franchisees were, to some extent, self-monitoring. While scholars have argued that economic self-interest may lead franchisees to free-ride on the trademark or deviate locally at the expense of uniformity across the system (Caves and Murphy 1976; Brickley and Dark 1987; Kaufmann 1989), the former problem was reduced by the high rate of repeat customers at chain restaurants, which made franchisees bear the costs of their actions. The marketing executives I interviewed estimated that on average between 65 percent and 90 percent of a unit's customers were repeat visitors. The second problem, local variations, was relatively easy to monitor, since it usually took the form of variations on the menu and could be openly observed. The use of profit as a control mechanism may lead to some free-riding, but my data suggest it produces more productive than unproductive behavior.

To some extent, proportional response was simply a necessity: the contract limited the chain operator's ability to tell a franchisee what to do, and the argument that a "rule is a rule" carried little weight. Gary McCain's description of how he dealt with deviations from the uniform format at KFC illustrated this point: "Either their deviation is a good idea, in which case we want to learn from it, or it is a bad idea and we need to show them why." The emphasis was on *why* it was a bad idea. (The next two chapters reveal that sometimes the deviations were the source of ideas for system-wide adaptations.) Since the chain operator did not have authority over franchisees and only rarely could compel them to act, proportional response was almost the only way to get things done. Many people told me that franchisees had little tolerance for nit-picking by the chain operator. Hoban of Hardee's noted, "You don't want to burn up your goodwill bothering franchisees with little things. There are too many big issues that we have to deal with—like convincing them to install new ovens—to get caught up in the little ones." The chain operator was constantly modulating its response in the franchise arrangement, acting in proportion to the issue at stake in its attempts to maintain uniformity.

The franchise arrangement's reliance, or perhaps dependence, on proportional response was reinforced by several subtle factors as well. Ouchi (1980) argued that when performance is difficult to observe, organizations often develop "clan" systems that socialize people into the desired patterns of behavior. Units in a chain were often plagued by a lack of observability, especially on the franchise side of the business, given that franchise units are often located in remote areas and the architecture of information does not routinely offer insight into the business. Although Ouchi viewed clans as being embedded within organizations, the franchise arrangement suggests that clanlike properties may develop across organizational boundaries among franchisees and between the chain operator and franchisees. In fact, practitioners almost universally referred to the franchise arrangement as the "franchise community." The careful selection of franchisees, their long tenure with the chain, and the constant group meetings built and sustained that community. These elements of the social context may be necessary conditions for the exercise of proportional response.

CONTRASTING STRATEGIES FOR MAINTAINING UNIFORMITY

The company and franchise arrangements exhibited contrasting strategies for achieving uniformity. In the company arrangement, uniformity was maintained through multiple performance-measurement mechanisms tied to the evaluations of managers throughout the company hierarchy. In the franchise arrangement, uniformity was maintained mainly by the reward system for franchisees—profit—with specific measures related to uniformity used less frequently and intensively, and serving primarily as boundaries within which the franchisee was expected to act. Table 5-1 summarizes some of the key differences between the two strategies. Despite the different characteristics, each strategy resulted in virtually equal levels of uniformity.

The simplest explanation for the similarity in results is that local incentives and external controls substituted for each other to produce an equilavent performance level (Brickley and Dark 1987). The franchise arrangement utilized more incentives and internalized controls, and the company arrangement relied more on external controls. While the equivalence of the two strategies offered chain operators the appearance of choice, these choices also reflected other elements of each arrangement. For example, the incentive-based control strategy may have been enabled by the background, tenure, and clanlike features embedded in the franchise arrangement, since these features constrained potentially deleterious behaviors that might have otherwise emerged (for example, free-riding). On the other hand, in the company arrangement the turnover of personnel, their relative inexperience, and the extensive specialization of tasks (which made accountability difficult) may have forced chain operators to specify required behaviors and use external controls (Ouchi 1979; Schlesinger and Heskett 1991). For example, the necessity of external control in the company arrangement was suggested by the performance decay accompanying the halt of mystery shopping discussed earlier. Each of these strategies for control therefore must be understood within their distinctive organizational context.[10]

At a deeper level, the two approaches to accomplishing uniformity represented alternative ways to induce people to think about the business and make necessary tradeoffs. The discussion of performance measurement offered by Nohria and Eccles (1992) loosely describes the company arrangement:

> [Multiple performance measures force managers] to think hard about the tradeoffs between objectives and how to achieve an appropriate balance among the different performance measures being employed. When a variety of measures are being used, managers have no choice but to exercise their judgment constantly about what to focus on at any particular moment.

The company arrangement, though, does not quite fit this pattern. Despite the use of multiple measures, the array of dimensions on which performance was evaluated was in practice relatively narrow: meeting the standards and maintaining uniformity, not boosting financial performance. The existing measures may have forced managers to make tradeoffs among the standards, but the rotations of control indicated that, in fact, well-conceived tradeoffs were not being made—the organization was trying to

Table 5-1   Contrasting Strategies for Accomplishing Uniformity

Feature of Strategy	Company	Franchise
Type of performance measures	Behaviors/specific/external	Results/general/internalized
Number of measures	Many	Few
Frequency of use	Often	Seldom
Performance standards	Relative	Threshold
Response to weak performance	Poor evaluation/lower reward	Discussion/slow growth
Secondary organizational effects	Gaming of system/rotations of control	Proportional response

do everything, overextending itself and setting in motion more problems and yet more rotations of control. The specialization of tasks and responsibilities in conjunction with the steep hierarchy also diffused local responsibility for making tradeoffs: the priorities of different managers reverberated down the hierarchy, which made it virtually impossible for anyone to implement their tradeoffs, even if they recognized the need for them.

An alternative approach to making managers think and take action is suggested by Morgan's description of control (1986, 102) based on "minimum critical specification." He proposed that less specification may be what provokes managers to make consistently appropriate decisions: with minimum critical specification "the basic idea is to create a situation where inquiry rather than predesign provides the main driving force. This helps to keep organization flexible and diversified, while capable of evolving structure sufficient and appropriate to deal with the problems that arise." In this model, which loosely reflects the franchise arrangement, the avoidance of detailed predesign such as multiple measures enables a form of organizational self-regulation. The use of profit as the key performance measure forced franchisees to think about the tradeoffs they were making and develop a model of the business that guided their actions. The other performance measures were used as thresholds that had to be met before the franchisee could exercise choice and make tradeoffs, rather than serving directly as performance-evaluation measures.[11] (It is important to keep in mind that this argument refers to the relationship between the chain operator and franchisee, not to the management practices that occurred within a multi-unit franchisee's organization.)

The major reason both of these strategies were feasible was the well-specified nature of the tasks associated with operating a restaurant. The chain operator had the ability to either specify the behaviors it wanted and the appropriate results would follow (company arrangement), or specify the results it expected and allow the appropriate means-end relationship to ensue (franchise arrangement). Merchant's discussion of control (1982) emphasizes that organizations have this latitude of choice when both the results are measurable and the required actions are well-specified. Both of these conditions existed in restaurant chains. The choice of approach, then, may be determined by other characteristics of the arrangements.

RATCHETING AND MODELING PROCESSES

The main point of this chapter is to show that company and franchise arrangements accomplished uniformity in widely differing ways and to suggest why these contrasting approaches may have produced similar re-sults. In the final part of the chapter, I want to discuss how two plural processes increased the level of uniformity across the chain: ratcheting and modeling.

Ratcheting Process

A ratcheting process occurred between company and franchise arrange-ments because the chain operator's ability to legally or informally impose the standards on franchisees was in part based on the level of uniformity in company units. Conversely, the higher the level of performance in company units, the higher the standards that could be set for franchisees. The high performance of each side set a benchmark for the other to pursue, and as one overcame the other on a performance dimension, it then became the new benchmark. In virtually every interview, respondents re-ferred to the relative performance of company and franchise units.

Pizza Hut vividly illustrated the ratcheting process at work. Its franchisees historically outperformed company units in terms of sales and field audit scores, but during my research the company arrangement's performance on both dimensions moved ahead of franchisees. This shift was mentioned to me within the first five minutes of my initial interview with Steven Reinemund, the CEO. He remarked that he was using these results to influence the behavior of franchisees: "They need to get on board and improve their operations. We've shown them what kind of opportunity there is in this business." Two Pizza Hut franchisees I interviewed agreed that the change forced franchisees to pay more attention to the chain operator. One franchisee said, "For years the company units were terrible compared to us. Now when they tell us to do something we listen a bit more."

In other cases, the ratcheting process worked in the other direction: the relatively strong performance of franchisees put pressure on company units. On a field visit I made with a franchise consultant, the franchisee we met suggested I return to the company units I had visited in the morning: "Those guys think you won't come back, and you won't get the dog-and-pony show. I guarantee you, Jeff, you'll see a bunch of violations." The franchisee wanted to remind the franchise consultant (and me) that he "way outperform[ed] the company units" and was not interested in hearing a critique of his business from a representative of the company whose units performed less well than his. The franchise consultant acknowledged that this dynamic led him to call the company district manager and tell him to keep his units in order. The chairman of KFC, John Cranor, noted the significance of this process: "To be the leader of a chain, you have to operate excellent units. It is a top priority of ours."

Performance differences between the two arrangements had legal implications that reinforced the ratcheting process. One chain executive remarked, "Whenever we confront a franchisee on his performance he lists all the company units that are worse. And often he is right." Unfavorable comparisons such as these limited a chain operator's legal options because it was difficult to take a franchisee to court for poor performance when there were even weaker performers in the ranks of the company arrangement. This dynamic adds to Walker and Weber's argument (1984) that the information generated by a company's experience in making a part, for example, enhances its capacity to contract with and monitor an outside vendor. The pressure on performance runs the other direction too: from the outside vendor to the company's internal activities.

A second-order effect of the ratcheting process was felt on the performance measures themselves. At Jack in the Box, franchisees demanded that if their performance was to be compared to company units, then the gaming of the anonymous field audits in the company arrangement would have to stop. Stated Chuck Stouffer, a Jack in the Box franchisee: "People want the process to be fair. If scores are part of the equation for us to add units, then it isn't fair that we're compared to company managers who call each other and know when the QCS&F auditor is coming." Executives in the chain said that this problem was only a minor factor in their decision to redesign the field audit and mystery-shopping programs, but nonetheless company managers were informed by the chain's executives that calling other managers to warn them of an auditor in the area was grounds for dismissal. More generally, this case suggests that to manage franchisees effectively the company arrangement had to be a high performer, which likely led to the more thoughtful design of performance-measurement systems.

Two factors helped make the ratcheting process important to controlling the behavior of company and franchise personnel. First, people often identified strongly with their side, that is, with the "company" or the "franchise community." This sharp distinction—inherent in the plural form—was fertile ground for intergroup dynamics, including intense competition between groups (see Sherif and Sherif 1953; Alderfer 1983). The intergroup competition was often organized around common measures of performance.

Second, the similarity of units in a chain enabled performance comparisons that were perceived to be legitimate by both company people and franchisees. While people often cited differences in markets and customers as explanations for performance differences, no one disagreed that the comparisons were relevant, since in both arrangements people were doing essentially the same tasks. At the same time, the different ownership arrangements and management practices associated with each arrangement—which tended to emphasize rules in company units and the achievement of revenue and profit in franchise units—provided the chain operator with different sources of ideas from which to identify opportunities to improve overall performance.

Modeling Process

One of the most interesting findings in this research is that multi-unit franchisees emulated the policies and practices used in the company arrangement, a process I label "modeling." Judy Ross, a Fishermen's Landing franchisee who owned thirteen units, summed up why she copied the company: "It works there, so why change it." The modeling effect is a variant of the ratcheting process in that, if the company arrangement is successful, then the franchisees have an incentive to emulate the designs that produced that performance. In addition, the modeling process offered franchisees a proven solution to managing multiple units (a very different management problem than managing one unit) and enabled them to avoid the costs of experimenting with new organizational designs (Stinchcombe 1965; Rubin 1978). Consistent with Dimaggio and Powell's argument (1983) for why firms mimic each other—to signal to key stakeholders that they are operating in legitimate, widely accepted ways—one franchisee explained that he copied the company model because "I don't want to spend my time justifying to [the chain operator] how I manage my place. It's easier to follow their lead."

The modeling process accounted in part for the equal levels of uniformity displayed by company and franchise units: the same designs, we might predict, would lead to similar levels of uniformity. An intriguing puzzle presented by Jack in the Box was the fact that the uniformity displayed by franchisees was the same regardless of how many units the franchisee owned. The modeling process suggests that larger franchisees would display greater uniformity (and/or less variance in it) than small franchisees, but the data did not support this proposition. Jack in the Box may not be the best test of this hypothesis since its multi-unit franchisees were relatively small and its auditing program was strict and uniformly applied to all franchisees, but these data are suggestive. Furthermore, interviews with managers and franchisees in other chains supported the notion that performance did not vary based on a franchisee's size.

What might explain this pattern? The most obvious answer is that the same dynamics accounting for the equal performance between company and franchise arrangements hold true *within* the franchise arrangement. The internalized control of the single-unit franchisee is the functional equivalent of the hierarchical control exercised in multi-unit franchises.

Another possibility is suggested by Kaufmann (1991, 1), who argues that "an individual franchisee managing two outlets will not be able to manage the provision of service as closely as two franchisees operating one each, and the level of service provided to the customer can be assumed to decline." This line of argument, consistent with agency theory (Brickley and Dark 1987; Rubin 1978), implies that performance will decay as a franchisee adds units to a chain. However, the modeling process may counteract this effect. The data showing no relationship between the size of a franchisee's mini-chain and uniformity may be the product of both dynamics: the modeling process may counteract a natural decay in performance that would otherwise accompany the addition of new units. Another factor moderating the possible performance decay associated with adding units is that the chain operator permitted only franchisees that were solid performers to grow. What may be occurring is that above-average small operators are adding units and, due to the performance decay, they ultimately become average large operators.[12]

CONCLUSION

Two factors related to my sample may moderate the findings reported in this chapter. First, the chains I studied were large and established organizations, and four of the five advertised extensively in the television markets where they competed. These chains had strong trademarks; consumers expected certain patterns of behavior and products to exist when they visited a restaurant in the chain. This meant that consumers served as a powerful force pushing units toward uniformity, because they could judge whether their experience conformed to their expectations. This created a market-based feedback mechanism that probably had its greatest impact on franchisees since they personally incurred the costs associated with not meeting the expectations of customers; but it also created a form of monitoring and direct feedback that also likely influenced the behavior of company employees. In smaller and less well-known chains, deviations from uniformity may be greater since this market dynamic does not exist. At the

same time, the very absence of consumer expectation suggests that deviations may have a minimal impact on the performance of a unit.

The second factor is the quality of the business concept. Again, I studied
chains that clearly had successful business concepts and well-codified standards for implementing them. The ratcheting and modeling were predicated on an effective baseline of performance, especially in company units.
It is easy to imagine that uniformity would be difficult to manage if the
concept was unproven, which is often the case early in the life of a chain,
or if the business concept was losing its effectiveness, which can happen
when competitive circumstances change.

Chapter 6

Local Responsiveness

THE GEOGRAPHIC reach of the chains I studied dictated that individual restaurants had to compete in diverse local markets. This chapter reports that the franchise arrangement generated more effective, more numerous, and more fine-grained local responses than the company arrangement. George Kelsey at Hardee's summed up the difference: "In a company market, coffee would be the same price in all units. In a franchise market with five franchisees, there easily could be five different prices of coffee." The way each arrangement produced local responses helps to explain the different performance outcomes. In the company arrangement, local responses were mainly formulated *centrally* by superiors or specialists: company managers in the operations department played a peripheral role in meeting this challenge. By contrast, in the franchise arrangement local responses were primarily created *locally* by individual franchisees, who were rewarded directly for their ability to sell products in their particular markets. This chapter argues that the local generation of responses led to greater local responsiveness than the central creation of local responses.[1]

The differing capacities of the two arrangements to accomplish local responsiveness hinges on the challenges associated with transferring information about idiosyncratic circumstances as well as the inherent nature of the two arrangements. Local responsiveness in the franchise arrangement was enhanced by the co-location of local knowledge and the prerogative to make decisions on local responses, which clearly worked more effectively than the process of moving local knowledge to centralized and specialized decision makers in the company arrangement (see Jensen and Meckling 1991). The company's bureaucratic structures were relatively blunt instruments for responding to the often idiosyncratic conditions faced by individual units or local markets. Furthermore, in both cases, characteristics of the arrangements created and constrained their capacity to be locally responsive (see Chapter 3). For example, local responsiveness was influenced by the contractual relationship, the economics of the relationship, the local operator's rewards and orientation, and the tenure of individuals in local markets, all of which reinforced local responsiveness in franchise units and inhibited it in company units.

A key task of the chain operator was to find a balance between local responsiveness and uniformity. Too much local responsiveness could damage uniformity and ultimately dilute the value of the trademark.[2] In the company units, this equilibrium was maintained by having superiors or specialists involved in decisions about both tactical and strategic local responses.[*] The use of specialists reflected the need to create mechanisms to *generate* local responsiveness in the company units; as described in the last chapter, the arrangement was largely organized to maintain uniformity. Conversely, the main challenge in the franchise arrangement was to *constrain* local responsiveness when it might unduly erode uniformity. While tactical local responses were largely the province of the franchisee, strategic local responses were initiated by franchisees but approved by the chain operator. This approval process was not administrative fiat as in the company arrangement but instead involved proposing, testing, and reviewing ideas for local responses, with a bias toward exploring reasonable ideas. While every chain engaged in tactical local responses, a chain operator's strategy affected the role played by strategic local responses. Fishermen's Landing and Jack in the Box allowed few strategic local responses; the other three chains permitted more latitude.

Beneath the surface of the arrangements were plural dynamics that affected the local responsiveness of each one, although the relative strength of the franchise arrangement remained constant. First, the presence of franchisees in a chain organization helped the company arrangement increase its local responsiveness, because company units sometimes copied the local responses of nearby franchise units. I call this the "local learning process." Second, the effectiveness of the chain operator's staff personnel, in overseeing local responsiveness, was increased by the existence of both company and franchise arrangements in a chain. Not only was the expertise gleaned from the operation of company units valuable to company personnel but the right of franchisees to choose whether to use the chain

---

[*] Tactical local responses are grounded in local circumstances but do not affect the uniformity of the business format. For example, hiring personnel and selecting suppliers involve being responsive to local conditions but do not necessarily affect uniformity. Strategic local responses entail adapting individual restaurants to local contexts in a way that diminishes the uniformity of the business format. The most common example of a strategic local response is a variation in the menu, where a unit offers an item not available to other units of the chain. See Chapter 2 for a detailed discussion of these two types of local responses.

operator's staff provided additional incentive to overcome bureaucratic sluggishness. I refer to this as the "market pressure process," which made the chain operator's staff more effective than they would be in either arrangement alone.

COMPANY ARRANGEMENTS:

CENTRALIZED AND SPECIALIZED LOCAL RESPONSES

The organization and management of the company arrangement emphasized uniformity rather than local responsiveness. The previous chapter revealed the hesitancy of chain operators to employ financial performance-based compensation to company managers, lest such policies lead to actions that would compromise the uniformity of the company arrangement. Because the chain operator could not (and did not want to) rely on company managers for local responsiveness, these activities were pursued through centralized and specialized administration. One executive explained the logic of this organizational design as it applied to local marketing decisions: "The best marketing a restaurant manager can do is to operate the restaurant effectively. The marketing department's job is to bring in the customer; it is the restaurant manager's job to deliver on the promise. We don't want to burden the restaurant manager with outside projects." Throughout my interviews, variations on this quote were applied to other business functions like purchasing, pricing, menu planning, and labor management. The job of the company restaurant manager was to operate the restaurant according to the standards, not to respond to particular market conditions. While this approach helped preserve uniformity, it limited the company arrangement's capacity to generate local responses.

Centralization

The centralization of local responses shifted the locus of decision making from the local level to more senior levels in the company hierarchy. Centralization was most evident in four areas that depended in part on the circumstances of local markets: (1) pricing, (2) menu, (3) suppliers, and (4) labor. In all of these key areas of business policy, senior personnel made or approved the decisions.

Pricing. In all five chains, the prices found on the menu in company units were set in the headquarters. The Hardee's process for setting prices was representative. Area managers gathered data on competitors' prices on a monthly basis and sent it to headquarters. On a quarterly basis, the headquarters delivered to local restaurants the new menus with the new prices. A marketing manager at Pizza Hut, which used a similar process, estimated that the company used fifty different menus for its three thousand company units; that is, the company had fifty different pricing schemes for its units. (At Pizza Hut, all the company units in a *local* market used the same prices, however.) Although the details of the pricing policies varied across chains—for example, the frequency of price changes, the factors on which prices were based, and the means by which data on these factors were gathered—in all the company arrangements new prices were determined at the headquarters and set for local markets, not individual units.

Menu Variation. There was no element of a chain's business format more inviolate from the perspective of chain executives than the menu. It is not surprising, then, that decisions about menu variations were carefully weighed and were made by corporate executives. Menu variations were very uncommon in the company arrangement.[3] Steve Honeycut, director of new concept implementation at Hardee's, observed: "We vary in only minor ways compared to the franchisees. For example, when we roll a new product out to the system like crispy curls or pancakes, franchisees decide whether to introduce them or not while all company units provide the product." Virtually every company restaurant at Jack in the Box and Fishermen's Landing had an identical menu. At KFC, Pizza Hut, and Hardee's, the menu occasionally varied by region: Hardee's served a pork sandwich in Iowa, home of most of America's pork producers, for example, and KFC served "Hot and Spicy Chicken" in urban markets. Bruce Frazer, director of marketing research at Jack in the Box, explained why local variations were uncommon: "It is extremely difficult to tailor ideas to units or markets. Our goal is to find product ideas that work in all the units."

KFC's approach was unusual in that it varied its menu in a significant way depending on the clientele of its company restaurants. Every KFC restaurant was required to carry "Original Recipe" chicken. Along with this a unit also carried either "Extra-Crispy" or "Hot and Spicy" chicken depending on which was more popular in that market. The marketing department periodically reviewed the product mix of its restaurants—measuring the ratio of Original Recipe to the other two options—and if the Hot and Spicy or Extra-Crispy was underperforming, then the menu was switched to offer the other one. Marion Jones, a division director of marketing, said, "Other than the different chickens, everything else in company units is standard across the chain."

Company arrangements displayed few menu variations, and when variations occurred they were usually at the local market or division level and not targeted to individual restaurants. The marketing department typically initiated these ideas, as seen in the KFC example above. Rarely were local variations initiated by personnel in the operation's hierarchy. As one company executive put it, "The job of the restaurant manager is to focus on a sparkling clean restaurant, not figuring out the next generation of products." In fact, when I asked a division vice-president for an example of a company manager–originated menu variation, he offered a case where a manager had asked to serve toast with a breakfast meal. That this was the only example he could think of confirmed that restaurant managers were rarely the source of menu variations.

Suppliers. The chain operator usually had established relationships with suppliers—or had its own internal capabilities as a supplier—that dictated the selection of suppliers to local restaurants. For example, all the company units at Hardee's used FFM, Fast Food Merchandisers, a wholly owned subsidiary of Imasco, the parent corporation of Hardee's. Similarly, all company units at KFC and Pizza Hut utilized PFSI, Pepsi Food Services International, which was owned by Pepsico, the corporate parent of the two chains. Company units did not select the suppliers; rather, they were required to use the suppliers provided by the corporate office. Restaurant managers made some decisions at Pizza Hut, where they chose whom to use as carpet cleaners, maintenance people, and grass cutters. These decisions, though, accounted for only between 1 percent and 2 percent of a unit's costs, as estimated by an area manager at one of the chains.

Labor. Throughout the company hierarchy, no manager had the direct authority to hire his or her own personnel. Assistant managers were hired by area managers (two organizational levels separated these two positions), restaurant managers were hired by division managers, area managers were hired by regional managers, and so forth. Pizza Hut and Hardee's were both revamping this pattern and trying to get restaurant managers more involved in selecting their assistant managers, but even under this new arrangement, area supervisors and human-resource personnel would still be active participants in the selection process. As with hiring decisions, local managers had little say over the amount and deployment of labor in the restaurants.

Specialization

Along with the centralization of local responses, most chains used specialized people and departments to respond to local conditions. In the company arrangement, the operations department was charged with meeting the standards while specialized departments were responsible for generating many of the local responses. The division marketing department developed local marketing programs; the division human-resource department tailored its recruitment of crew and managerial personnel to the exigencies of local markets; the division real-estate department selected sites and managed contractors during the development of a site; the maintenance department often approved and did capital improvements on restaurants; and the corporate purchasing department often selected and managed local vendors. While these departments were the locus of local responsiveness, it should be kept in mind that the dotted-line relationships between the functional directors in the each division and their corporate counterparts constrained the range of local responses available to these managers.[4]

The regional marketing department provides a good example of how these specialized departments produced local responses. "Field marketing managers" in each division formulated and implemented the local marketing plans for local markets and individual units. The typical field marketing manager had responsibility for between seventy-five and three hundred company units. Mike Sick, director of field marketing and promotion at Jack in the Box, who had thirteen field marketing people reporting to him, described his department's function: "The key objective is executing on the system marketing plan, which is done centrally. Their job is to get compliance and commitment at the local level; to try and get restaurant people enthused; to try and create religious fervor and get everyone together." Chris Carpenter, a KFC marketing manager, described his job this way: "We send a communication to the unit managers to let them know what is being done on radio or in print, and we let them know when we are dropping coupons." These comments indicated that along with being the responsibility of a specialized function, the development of a local marketing plan was typically a variation on a chainwide plan. At KFC, for example, the marketing manager would occasionally adjust the timing of a product promotion campaign, but only rarely were different or original programs developed for a local market or restaurant.

Even when regional plans were being developed, the primary unit of analysis and implementation was the designated marketing area (DMA), which was defined by the reach of television stations. The nature of television advertising, which communicated the same message to all the consumers in a DMA, accounted in part for this emphasis since many marketing programs were built around television. Yet even if television was not the dominant advertising medium, the emphasis on markets likely would remain since field marketing personnel had such wide spans of control. Sick noted that many marketing managers did not even visit all the restaurants under their jurisdiction because of the large number of them. Jeff Lawson, director of marketing research at Pizza Hut, traced the implications of this approach to accomplishing local responses. He stated that sixteen marketing managers covered the chain's 6,000 units (3,000 company, 3,000 franchise) and 208 DMAs, although their primary responsibility was to assist company units. (Keep in mind that multi-unit franchisees often had their own marketing specialists that did local marketing for them. At Pizza Hut, for example, 57 of the nearly 140 franchisees had a full-time dedicated marketing specialist serving their organization.) Lawson observed that with such broad spans the marketing plans could only occasionally be customized to the level of DMA and almost never down to the level of the restaurant. "You have to manage the exceptions," he said, "and essentially go with the corporate recommendation for the rest of the DMAs, which usually involves adding 'top-spin' to the national program." The coarse-grained management approach in the previous chapter for the operations department—for example, managing the performance of aggregates and troubleshooting the units or DMAs that deviated from average—was mirrored in the management of local responsiveness.

One solution to this coarse-grained approach would be to add more specialists to analyze local markets and adapt units to them. But the logic of specialization itself made this strategy impractical: the narrow issues around which the specialized departments were organized did not have the potential to increase revenue enough to justify narrower spans and the heavier involvement of specialists. The specialization of local responsiveness created an organizational dilemma: its economic logic prevented the narrow spans necessary to produce effective local responses, but at the same time local responsiveness was dependent on precisely the knowledge gleaned from the intimate familiarity of local markets enabled by narrow spans. The lack of familiarity may have been compensated for somewhat by having the specialized expertise of the staff department applied to the problem of local responsiveness. In essence, specialists with wide spans were substituted for generalists with narrower spans. While perhaps not capable of identifying needs quickly, a staff department may generate better solutions than the nonspecialists once the needs are identified. In the context of the company arrangement, where company managers could not be counted on to respond effectively to local conditions, the use of specialists was a necessity.

The marketing function was a particularly good example of the specialization of local responses, but it existed for other functions, too. For example, at Fishermen's Landing all purchasing activities—even ones involving local vendors—were managed through the purchasing department. At KFC, all maintenance requests and capital improvements had to be approved by the maintenance department. Real-estate selection and development fell under the purview of the development department, which had its own "real-estate specialists" in each market who were experts on local trends and opportunities. In the area of human resources, compensation policies were standardized throughout the chain, although the specific salary levels were established by division human-resource departments and varied by region. The responsibility for many types of local responses resided with functional specialists.

Conclusion: Local Responsiveness in the Company Arrangement

Centralization and specialization were the primary organizational mechanisms through which company arrangements generated local responses. This organizational design may have been a necessity given the nature of the operations hierarchy, but it limited the amount of local responsiveness displayed by a chain and led to local responses at the level of the region and local market rather than at individual restaurants. The limitation on local responsiveness imposed by this design was due to the mismatch that existed between the right to make decisions and the knowledge important to those decisions. Jensen and Meckling (1991) argue that in situations where the transfer of knowledge is costly, the most efficient organizational structure co-locates the right to make decisions in the hands of people with the information relevant to those decisions.[5] In restaurant chains, the transfer of local knowledge to centralized and specialized decision makers was costly, as it entailed conveying the often idiosyncratic details of hundreds or even thousands of local markets. Evidence of the costliness of this transfer was abundant: limiting the local responses of company units, "managing by exception," and responding at the market rather than unit level.

Why did chain operators centralize and specialize local responsiveness given the apparent loss in effectiveness? The characteristics of the company arrangement offer a partial answer. To begin with, salaried company managers were not viewed as sufficiently motivated to make efficient local responses or for that matter to even attend to the external market environment. This was reflected in the comment of a division vice-president: "We don't want restaurant managers doing local store marketing. A bad decision can kill you. You don't have to give away much product before you destroy the profits." Given the relative low experience of people in the company hierarchy and their weak performance-based incentives, local responses had to be generated by someone other than the local manager.

Second, most company managers were experienced only in the operation of the restaurant and the maintenance of the standards. They often lacked the knowledge required to analyze and generate local responses in disparate functional areas like marketing, purchasing, or pricing. The executive vice-president of marketing in one chain pointed to one implication of this system: "We want managers to keep their eyes and ears open to the world, but really we want them to keep their arms and legs moving." Aside from whether managers had the motivation or knowledge needed to generate local responses, the relatively short tenure of managers—especially good ones—in local markets prevented them from accumulating detailed knowledge on the local market. To compensate for these elements of the company arrangement, chain operators used specialized and centralized structures to obtain local responses—despite the fact that they were not perfect solutions.

Centralization and specialization may limit the local responsiveness of the company arrangement, but on the positive side, they may lead to the cultivation of economies of scale and a base of accumulated expertise. This logic holds most clearly in the case of purchasing, where requiring units to buy from a single supplier may yield economies of scale. Another benefit of centralization and specialization may be a better understanding of the repertoire of effective local responses, drawn from the cumulative experience of working with scores and even hundreds of diverse markets. For example, the construction department may identify the most effective local strategy for selecting and managing contractors and building units, because of its experience in building fifty units a year. This knowledge may be very useful to a local operator who builds only one or two units a year. A similar logic may hold for marketing, pricing, suppliers, and labor: the experience of operating in many diverse markets may produce learning and knowledge—and make it easily accumulated and accessible due to the responsibilities of the specialists—that would be unavailable to a system where individual operators made their own local decisions. The economies of scale and the opportunities for learning created by centralizing or specializing local responses may compensate for the loss in fine-grained responsiveness caused by the wide spans of control as well as for the high costs associated with transferring the local knowledge to the decision makers. Future studies will need to analyze these different factors affecting local responsiveness.

In summary, a theme that runs through all the arguments in this chapter is that company restaurant managers were not responsible for local responsiveness. Whether this was a cause or a consequence of specialization and centralization is difficult to say. Regardless, chain operators did not expect and rarely wanted managers to vary from the standards associated with the uniform format. A regional vice-president in one chain reflected this emphasis: "In company units it is the exception when a manager asks, 'How can I build my business?' In fact, when people start doing that they are perceived as mavericks. You succeed in the company organization by performing exactly as the company expects." The extent of resistance to local managers making decisions was revealed in the hyperbole used by executives at Pizza Hut and KFC when they discussed involving managers more in local responsiveness:

> Of course, we don't want to have people paint the roofs blue [all Pizza Hut roofs are red], but they should have more local freedom.

> We can't have people screwing around with the eleven herbs and spices, the recipe for our chicken. We have to be careful about what we allow them to do.

The exaggerated fear that local managers would make inappropriate decisions showed the entrenched resistance facing executives who tried to change the existing approach to local responsiveness.

FRANCHISE ARRANGEMENT: DECENTRALIZED LOCAL RESPONSES

Local responses were generated and executed in franchise arrangements through decentralization. Franchisees, acting in their local markets, served as the locus of initiative for both tactical and strategic local responses. In the latter case, however, chains established mechanisms that essentially gave them the power to ratify any strategic local response proposed by a franchisee. These mechanisms served as an arena for negotiating the line between uniformity and local responsiveness, like the dotted-line relationship linking the division and corporate functions in the company arrangement. These mechanisms sometimes were also the conduit through which a franchisee's local response became an idea for a systemwide adaptation. The local production of local responses led to a greater number and variety of local responses than the company arrangement. The franchisees' right to exercise choice, their incentive to meet the demands of the local market, and their long tenure in their market provided them with the motivation and information to generate a stream of productive local responses. At the same time, some franchisees copied the local responses of company units.

Tactical Local Responses: Decentralization

The franchise contract granted franchisees the right to make a variety of decisions concerning tactical local responses. The previous chapter showed that franchisees were required to meet the standards specified by the chain operator, but that the means by which the franchisees met those objectives were in large part left to them. As long as the integrity of the business format was maintained—which the chain operator monitored through field audits, occasional mystery shops, and informal field visits—the franchisees could make decisions regarding prices, selecting suppliers, hiring and deploying labor, and local marketing.

Pricing. Franchisees set their own prices. In fact, antitrust laws prevent chain operators from dictating prices to franchisees, although local advertising cooperatives (composed of company and franchise representatives) are permitted to agree on price points for advertising.[6] Franchisees employed several pricing strategies, the result of which was a high degree of local responsiveness. In a KFC market I visited, one franchisee sold the two-piece chicken dinner for $2.39; another franchisee sold it for $2.89; and the company price was $2.19. And as mentioned earlier in this chapter, each Hardee's franchisee had a different price for coffee. Every franchisee had a different rationale for setting prices, ranging from the actions of nearby competitors to their own local marketing strategy. Greg Collins, a Fishermen's Landing franchisee, showed me a Lotus model he used for determining prices in his units, which considered variations in the volume, price, and product mix of the menu.

The most common pricing strategy reported by franchisees was to copy the company's prices, especially if company units were located nearby. As Spike Erhardt of Hardee's noted, "When there are nearby company units, I pretty much follow them. It is all pretty well thought out." Referring to the chain operator's corporate staff, a Fishermen's Landing franchisee said, "They've got a whole building of people studying that stuff, so I pretty much go with what they're doing." Another Fishermen's Landing franchisee concurred: "They have all the stuff figured out. I just buy the new menus from them." A variation on this strategy was to use the company's prices as a benchmark. "I follow the company, but I try to get my royalty back," said one franchisee, which meant his prices were approximately 4 percent to 5 percent higher than the company's.

Suppliers. Except for proprietary supplies that were integral to the identity of the product—for example, the famous recipe of "eleven herbs and spices" at KFC—franchisees were free to purchase goods from outside suppliers. While the suppliers had to be approved by the chain operator, the chain operator was legally obligated to provide franchisees with a list of approved suppliers. A chain operator could not say that it was the only supplier: agreements that force franchisees to purchase nonproprietary material from the chain operator are illegal (Klein and Saft 1985). All chains maintained a list of approved suppliers, and franchisees were usually able to add to the list if the proposed supplier met the required specifications. In no chain did I hear the franchisees complain about being constrained in their choice of suppliers. The term "suppliers" encompassed a wide array of products and services, ranging from food suppliers to air-conditioner maintenance people. In all these cases, the franchisees had choices over which vendors to use.

Interestingly, franchisees reported that they often used the chain operator's internal distribution operation. Franchisees said that usually the prices and service were better than other vendors. Said Tom Dolan, a Hardee's franchisee, "I believe that the company has the best quality for the lowest price. It takes time and effort for me to do this on my own. It's much easier to call them and they respond to us fairly quickly." A Pizza Hut franchisee, Bill Walsh, said, "Some products are high [on price] but overall they [Pepsico Food Services International] are the best deal. We stick with them." In four of the chains, executives reported that franchisees purchased the vast majority of the supplies offered by the chain operator. (At KFC, franchisees owned and operated an independent purchasing cooperative through which most franchisees bought their supplies.) This finding is not too surprising when one considers the firm-specific expertise and economies of scale an internal supplier offered due to its relationship with company units. A subtle benefit of having franchisees use the internal supplier was that problems with uniformity were somewhat diminished since the chain operator knew what inputs the franchisee was using.[7]

Labor. The deployment of labor was largely dictated by the nature of the business concept. For example, a certain number of people were needed to prepare the food, to serve the drive-through window, and to take orders. While company managers followed a fixed "labor grid," franchisees were free to deploy labor at their discretion. For the most part, franchisees deployed labor in very similar ways to the company. "These restaurants run on a tight schedule," said Ken Williams, COO at Jack in the Box. "If you start tinkering with things, you can get yourself into trouble."

Occasionally, franchisees altered the deployment of labor. For example, one Hardee's franchisee had a hostess who worked in the dining room greeting customers and clearing tables. The company had no such position. Several people I interviewed said that some franchisees utilized more labor than the company. Tony Deluca, a KFC senior manager with experience on both the company and franchise sides of the business, said, "We really push our company people hard. Franchisees are able to provide a little more of a cushion for themselves."[8] On a more individual basis, the deployment of labor sometimes reflected a franchisee's particular competitive emphasis. For example, a Hardee's franchisee who believed strongly in the importance of fast service times re-engineered the amount and allocation of labor serving the drive-through to increase the speed of service.

Local Marketing. Franchisees were free to conduct local marketing campaigns with the provision that any printed material had to be approved by the chain operator. This process ensured that the trademark was not being compromised by the local responses of franchisees. In most cases, the in-store marketing activities done by a franchisee duplicated the company programs: for example, the printed point-of-purchase material was identical in both arrangements. The chain operator's field marketing specialists were responsible for assisting franchisees in this area, but almost everyone I interviewed agreed that these people focused mainly on company units and simply served as a conduit of information and material to franchisees. As noted, though, large franchisees often had their own marketing specialists that essentially served the same function.

Franchisees occasionally promoted items in their local markets. Bill MacDonald, the senior vice-president for marketing at KFC, said, "Franchisees usually know their trade area better than company managers." George Kelsey indicated that franchisees at Hardee's often did promotions, such as selling coffee for ten cents a cup for a limited time. Some franchisees were more aggressive and introduced two-for-one pricing programs. Pizza Hut's "Pairs" program was created by Mike Dart and Dan Taylor, franchisees in Florida, who were responding to the competitive threat of a local pizza chain's two-for-one campaign. Several people agreed with the following observation of a Jack in the Box executive: "Franchisees are always doing more things in the community, like belonging to the Chamber of Commerce or supporting the local Little League team."

Strategic Local Responses: Local Initiative, Central Ratification

Unlike the tactical local responses, which usually did not directly affect the standard format, strategic local responses altered the format and thereby potentially changed the chain's identity. These types of responses covered a variety of circumstances and included instances when the franchisee sought to do something locally that violated the franchise contract. The most common strategic local response, and the one deemed by all parties to be most significant, was introducing items that were not part of the standard menu. The menu was a sacrosanct part of the business format, and the chain operator protected the menu from franchisees who added unapproved items. The choices on the menu, however, represented the vehicle by which the franchisee made money, so not surprisingly, franchisees often sought to adapt the menu to their particular market. Jack in the Box franchisees in Hawaii sold a "Hawaiian Burger," Hardee's franchisees in Texas and Louisiana sold chicken-fried steaks, and Pizza Hut franchisees in Nebraska offered a prime-rib sandwich. Roger Townley, director of research and development at Hardee's, observed, "It is an issue of survival for franchisees. When they are hurting financially, they look for ways to increase revenue." Such initiatives, though, potentially compromised the uniformity of the format.

It is important to distinguish between local responses that were within versus outside the bounds of the contract. Franchisees were often able to develop a customized menu by selecting from several specifically designated "optional products." KFC franchisees typically offered a much wider array of side dishes along with the systemwide requirement of serving cole slaw in all restaurants. In contrast, company units almost all sold just two side dishes. Similarly, Hardee's franchisees often offered more than the two standard sandwiches that were sold in company units. Pizza Hut exhibited the same pattern, as franchisees sometimes kept items on the menu that the company withdrew. These items were approved products, so the formal processes described below were not invoked. In many cases, these preapproved optional items were former mandatory items (at least in the company arrangement) that had been withdrawn from the menu; hence, they already had been considered acceptable in terms of being consistent with the business format. It is clear that chain operators believed franchisees had a greater capacity to manage local responsiveness than the company management.

In cases where the local initiative led to a local response that was not preapproved, the corporate staff at KFC, Pizza Hut, and Hardee's used a formal process to determine whether it would approve the local response. The chain operator essentially decided whether to ratify the franchisee's local response. In all three chains, franchisees submitted proposals that described the change, analyzed the financial impact of the idea, and specified an implementation plan. The proposals had to be approved at the division level by the division vice-president, after which the corporation office reviewed them. At KFC and Hardee's the marketing department was responsible for approving a proposed change to the menu. Jack in the Box and Fishermen's Landing, the two chains that exhibited the fewest strategic local responses, used an informal process to deal with proposed local strategic responses: the franchisee and chain executives negotiated over whether the deviation would be allowed. The feasibility of using this informal approach in these two chains was a function of the relatively few franchisees and the explicit corporate strategy of permitting few strategic local responses.

Pizza Hut had the most elaborate process for ratifying strategic local responses, the "Standard Exception Test" (SET) process. A SET committee met monthly and was composed of corporate staff personnel from the departments of research and development, marketing, operations, franchise services, purchasing, and legal affairs. After reviewing a SET request from a franchisee, the committee either approved, opposed, or deferred its decision. In the case of a new product, the committee often would sample it. The minutes from each meeting were disseminated to each member, who then had to sign off on each proposal. After the committee approved an idea, the president of the chain reviewed the idea and gave his final approval. The involvement of senior people reflected the importance the chain operator attached to managing the tension between uniformity and local responsiveness. Many SET requests involved items not related to the menu, like the decor of the restaurant or using an unapproved supplier, which also accounted for the composition of the committee. Pizza Hut's SET process highlights the two most important aspects of the strategic local responses in the franchise arrangement: first, they were generated locally, and second, they were then evaluated and approved centrally by the chain operator.

The criteria by which the chain operator deemed an exception test acceptable varied across and within the chains and were often ambiguous. Chains judged the tests on the basis of whether the proposed local response was a viable business proposition, adversely affected the integrity of the trademark, and/or was a possible candidate to be a systemwide adaptation. This ambiguity reflected the chain operator's occasional uncertainty about which core elements of the trademark should remain inviolate as well as its recognition that in the absence of authority over franchisees, an ironclad set of identifiable criteria would not be feasible.[9]

The formal processes for judging proposed exceptions served two subtle but important functions that affected the management of the franchise arrangement. First, the mechanisms provided a forum where proposals would be openly and fairly judged. A less formal process, said one executive who reflected on his past experience, "sometimes led to no one knowing who was approving what." Steve Honeycut, director of new concept implementation at Hardee's, noted that nearly half the tests proposed by franchisees had been previously undertaken, and once the franchisees saw the data they withdrew their proposal. Even when proposals were pursued, though, Honeycut said, "With the voluminous information generated, a clear answer usually emerges." An additional problem the informal process created was that different people used varying criteria to evaluate a proposal for a deviation.

Both these factors directly weakened uniformity, and also indirectly did so by making franchisees wary of asking for permission before implementing an idea. Several people told me, "It is easier to ask for forgiveness than to ask for permission." The SET process at Pizza Hut, argued Ed Jacob, made franchisees believe that their proposals would be treated fairly: "Now franchisees are in the habit of filing the SET." It is important to recognize that this was not an issue pitting franchisees against the chain operator; franchisees wanted the integrity of the business format to be maintained, too. A franchisee at Hardee's, Tom Dolan, put it this way: "I don't have control over the product and I don't want any other franchisee selling their own items either. The company and I are in line on this."

The second effect of formalizing the evaluation of strategic local responses was to create a learning opportunity for the chain operator and the franchisee. Frank Puthoff, Pizza Hut's director of franchise relations, explained that one reason the functional areas were involved in the SET process was because "sometimes the franchisee builds a better mousetrap and one of the departments might benefit from that." The next chapter highlights several examples of how generating an idea for a systemwide adaptation in this way created a learning opportunity for the chain operator. At the same time, by making the proposal for a strategic local response a "test," the process often created an opportunity for franchisee learning, too. Hardee's and Pizza Hut both incorporated into the testing process the criteria by which a test would be conducted and evaluated. The process made a rigorous learning opportunity out of what might have been a less well-conceived decision to undertake a given proposal.[10]

Conclusion: Local Responsiveness in the Franchise Arrangement

The business success of franchisees depended on their ability to meet the demands of their local markets. Consequently, it was not surprising that they were the ones who usually initiated actions aimed at meeting local circumstances. Ed Jacob explained the perspective of a franchisee: "The franchisee is a better street fighter. They understand the competition better. It is their life." Hardee's Steve Honeycut drew a sharp distinction between the mindsets of company managers and franchisees toward local responsiveness:

> In most cases it is the franchisees who really stoke the fires and put pressure on the company. They sing the loudest because their dollars are tied up. If they see competitors doing something, they will want to do it quickly. The company manager is not trying to generate sales; he is just trying to run a good clean restaurant. The franchisee is more in tune with local markets and customers.

Reinforcing the incentives that motivated franchisees to attend to local competitors and customers was the fact that these people often had lived in the local markets for a long time and had intimate knowledge of the dynamics of those markets.[11]

These findings suggest that the franchise arrangement produces more effective, more fine-grained, and faster local responses than the company arrangement. By more effective I mean that franchisees will better match their units to local conditions than will company managers. This outcome is based on the principle that decentralization (the franchise arrangement) is more effective than centralization and specialization (the company arrangement) for generating local responsiveness. Second, with scores and sometimes hundreds of franchisees implementing different tactical and strategic local responses, franchise arrangements exhibit a more diverse set of responses to local circumstances. In my research, this heterogeneity was a valuable source of ideas for systemwide adaptation, as we shall see in the next chapter. Moreover, local responsiveness is likely to be more fine-grained in franchise arrangements because it often occurs at the restaurant level, or at the level of the franchisee's minichain. In contrast, responses in the company arrangement were typically at the market, division, or system level. Finally, franchisees adapt more quickly to changing market conditions than the company hierarchy. Jim Winter, a Pizza Hut franchisee who had worked for several years in the company arrangement, stated this clearly: "Franchisees have a faster reaction time. With all the layers in the company, it takes a long time to get things done."

The use of multi-unit franchisees, who typically duplicated the company's practices, narrowed the gap between the two arrangements in terms of local responsiveness. However, the largest franchisee in my sample—432 units at Hardee's—was still smaller than the smallest division in any of the company arrangements, and the average size of a franchisee was far smaller than the size of a unit in the company organization that might undertake local responses. The franchise arrangement was composed of smaller "subassemblies" than the company arrangement, which suggests that the basic relationship between the two arrangements in terms of the quality, "fine-grainedness," and speed of the local responses remains solid. Moreover, the economic incentives and relative autonomy of franchisees will tend to make the franchise arrangement more fertile ground for local responses than a unit in the company arrangement of similar size.

The observation that franchisees often copied practices in the company arrangement would seem to contradict these findings. Indeed, it was precisely this process that helped ensure uniformity in the franchise arrangement. As noted, in the areas of pricing, suppliers, and local marketing, franchisees sometimes simply followed the lead of the chain operator. The most obvious reason for this pattern of behavior was that it economized on a franchisee's time and resources. A franchisee had the option to undertake a multitude of local responses—pricing, suppliers, hiring, marketing, menu variations—yet some lacked the experience and background to make well-informed decisions in all these areas. The company arrangement may therefore provide franchisees with satisfactory solutions for certain local responses and free them up to focus on a narrower set of concerns.[12] And even if the franchisee focused only on one issue, it still would be more locally responsive than a comparable company unit. The advantages of franchisee-generated local responses may also be especially strong in certain business situations, such as when a unit is remote or located in a sparsely populated market. The use of centralized and specialized structures to deal with a few units in idiosyncratic markets may be prohibitively costly, which may help explain the disproportionate use of franchisees in those situations (Brickley and Dark 1987; Norton 1988a).

PROCESSES OF THE PLURAL FORM

The plural processes related to local responsiveness did not equalize the performance of the two arrangements as was the case with uniformity, but they did have a generally beneficial effect. First, the company arrangement often benefited directly from the local responses of franchisees by simply copying them. As noted, franchisees sometimes copied company responses, but this actually led to greater uniformity rather than greater local responsiveness. Second, the effectiveness of the chain operator's staff was greater in the plural form than in the pure forms. The presence of franchisees who could choose whether to use the staff resources or develop their own responses added market pressure to the organization, while the ability of the chain operator to require the use of internal resources in the company arrangement helped to sustain economies of scale and the accumulation of expertise. Bringing together these two features—each of which was difficult to replicate in the other arrangement—led to a stronger corporate staff, which benefited both company and franchise arrangements.

The Local Learning Process: Adopting the Local Responses of Franchisees

Company units often adopted the local responses of nearby or comparable franchisees. The pork sandwich at Hardee's, for example, was initiated by a franchisee for his market and then was adopted by the company units in that market. In this way, franchisees made the company's local responses more closely tailored to local markets. It appeared that company units in markets composed of both company and franchise units displayed higher levels of local responsiveness than company units in pure markets. Jim Lowdermilk, a field marketing specialist at Hardee's, offered anecdotal support for this hypothesis. With reference to the local marketing cooperatives that made decisions about advertising on local television, where each unit had one vote, he said, "I have been in a position to win because there are more company units, but have backed down because franchisees disagree. When I have three franchisees disagreeing—even if they have just a few units—I'd better listen." Of course, in cases where franchisees controlled the local cooperative, the decisions more fully incorporated the exigencies of local conditions than was the case in pure company markets.

The Market Pressure Process: Strengthening the Chain Operator's Staff

The plural dynamic occurred when company and franchise arrangements utilized the same corporate functions like marketing, purchasing, and training. As we have seen, the effectiveness of the chain operator's staff was integral to the accomplishment of local responsiveness in the company arrangement. The chain operator's staff had an indirect yet often significant impact on local responsiveness in the franchise arrangement, since franchisees commonly emulated the local responses of the chain operator and drew on its resources. The basic difference between the two arrangements was that company managers were *required* to use the corporate resources, while franchisees had the *choice* of whether to adopt them. The mixture of these two structures led to a more effective corporate staff than either one would have created by itself. The introduction of market forces to the chain put pressure on the providers of corporate resources to be competitive with the local market in price and service; in the absence of that pressure, the providers of those services would likely be less responsive to the consumers—that is, to the local operators (Eccles 1985). Therefore, the services staff functions provided in plural forms are more likely to be effective than staff functions in pure company arrangements, where company managers are mandated to use internal resources.

The role played by the chain operator's supplier for products highlighted this dynamic. As mentioned, most franchisees utilized the chain operator's in-house distribution system, although they were free at any time to use an outside source. Tony Deluca, a KFC divisional director of operations, outlined the implications of franchisee choice on the operation of the supply division:

> The supply division knows that if it screws around with franchisees they will switch to other suppliers. In contrast, we [the company units] have a guy in the headquarters who we can call and he does a pretty good job of solving problems. But there is nothing better than being able to say, "We're going to take our business somewhere else."

This plural dynamic could be observed when Pepsico bought KFC. Among the incentives for the acquisition was that Pepsico would be able to serve Pepsi in KFC restaurants. In accordance with that strategy, the company restaurants converted from Coke to Pepsi immediately after the change in ownership. Franchisees, however, had the right to choose their soft drink supplier, and initially many of them did not make the switch. Some of the franchisees who did convert complained that they were being treated like "house accounts" and were receiving worse service from Pepsi than from Coke. Their persistent "rumbling," as one executive put it, and the hesitancy of some of them to convert led to changes in the services and prices provided by Pepsi's soft-drink division to KFC units. These changes benefited all company units, although they were precipitated mainly by the actions of franchisees.

While it may appear that the benefits of this plural dynamic run in one direction—from the franchise to the company arrangement—my findings suggest that the advantages may be symmetrical. On the one hand, the franchisees introduced market pressure into the management of company departments; on the other hand, the company units provided a stable base of demand for services, which enabled the chain (and its franchisees) to take advantage of economies of scale in critical areas such as purchasing. This cost advantage gave the chain operator's suppliers of services a competitive edge in obtaining the business of franchisees. Along with placing greater pressure on performance, franchisees also provided a natural incremental source of revenue and profit to the in-house supplier. The required use of such services in the company arrangement combined with the market pressure from franchisees for the best price, service, and product yielded advantages to both arrangements and made the plural form more efficient than either arrangement by itself.[13]

The expertise of personnel in the staff departments may have also been affected by whether the chain operator owned units. In my interviews, it was clear that people in the chain operator's departments honed their expertise in company units. From this perspective, the expertise provided to franchisees by the chain operator was in part contingent on the presence of company units. If this is the case, then the services provided by staff functions in plural forms are more effective than pure franchise arrangements. In a pure franchise chain, the sharp boundary dividing the chain operator and franchisees—and the concomitant inability of the staff departments to easily implement their ideas—may impede the functional experts' ability to "learn by doing" (Levitt and March 1990). Furthermore, although this is even more speculative, the best people in the industry would likely be less interested in jobs with pure franchise chains, where they might not be able to execute their plans and see the outcomes of their efforts. Even if the departments in a pure franchise and plural form were the same, the quantity of data derived from the MIS coupled with the sheer number of units in the company arrangement give the chain operator's staff a base from which to learn and develop expertise. This base would be more difficult to build in a pure franchise arrangement.

CONCLUSION

The different structures used by company and franchise arrangements produced different levels of local responsiveness. In general, the company arrangements were organized to maintain strict uniformity, while the franchise arrangement provided more latitude and generated greater local responsiveness. The plural processes leveraged these strengths and helped to compensate for the weaknesses of each one: franchisees maintained greater uniformity through the influence of the company arrangement, and company arrangements achieved greater local responsiveness due to franchisees' involvement.

The findings presented in this chapter confirm the basic assumptions of agency-cost theory (Rubin 1978; Brickley and Dark 1987; Norton 1988a, 1988b). The agency-cost argument assumes that the franchise arrangement motivates local operators to make efficient local decisions, an attribute that is especially important when units are remote from monitoring offices. The company arrangement is viewed differently. The theory argues that the company arrangement's reliance on salaries makes local responsiveness more costly and difficult to achieve because local operators do not make appropriate decisions by themselves (Williamson 1991; Brickley and Dark 1987). This chapter adds to this line of reasoning by explaining *how* the company arrangement generates local responses, which it still must do for tactical local responses and may do with strategic ones. It also offers insight into how the chain operator prevents too much local responsiveness in the franchise arrangement. While agency theorists contend that the chain operator simply terminates the contract to stop unwanted deviations from the standard, in practice a more complex governance process exists, exemplified by the SET process at Pizza Hut and the persuasion processes that guided the franchisee relationship.

It is important to recognize that generating more local responsiveness was not always the objective in a chain. Too much local responsiveness could compromise the integrity of the trademark and the shared identity of the chain's units. Chain operators were constantly working to balance the need for uniformity with the need for local responsiveness. But local responsiveness affected more than uniformity; it was also the source of ideas for many systemwide adaptations.

Chapter 7

Systemwide Adaptation

THE CHANGING dynamics of the chain-restaurant industry have magnified the importance of systemwide adaptation. As noted in Chapter 2, with the saturation of units in many markets, the key to growth has become a chain's capacity to respond to threats and take advantage of opportunities on a systemwide basis. Along with being seen as a critical factor in the industry's increasingly competitive environment, systemwide adaptation was also viewed by practitioners as the most complex management challenge that chain organizations faced. The particularities of diverse local markets, the difficulty of implementing a new activity in hundreds or thousands of units, the potential conflicts of interest between franchisees and chain operators, and the absence of authority in the franchise arrangement were but a few of the problems that made systemwide adaptation a major challenge.

Company and franchise units played a complementary role in accomplishing systemwide adaptations. The plural form enabled a "mutual learning process" that leveraged the distinctive strengths of each arrangement. Based on my research, I found that the systemwide-adaptation process falls into four distinct stages: (1) generating ideas, (2) testing and evaluating them, (3) decision making, and (4) implementation. Most theories of organizational decision making and adaptation encompass these four stages (Scott 1987), which match closely the variation-selection-retention framework used in the literature on strategy making (Burgelman 1991). By blending the company arrangement (with its expertise located in the company's functional departments) with the franchise arrangement (with its people with long experience in local markets who advocate their positions with top executives) the plural form produces greater variety of ideas and a more rigorous evaluation of them than either arrangement could by itself. In the last two stages of the process, each side ameliorated some of the weaknesses of the other. For example, the hierarchical authority in the company arrangement led to the rapid implementation of ideas in company units, which was critical to the chain's efforts to persuade franchisees to adopt. At the same time, the need to persuade franchisees introduced an internal discipline on decision making that was sometimes absent in company arrangements. Hence, the benefits of the plural form existed at each stage of the adaptation process.[1]

This chapter explicates the mutual learning process by describing in detail how company and franchise arrangements functioned at each stage of systemwide adaptation. It concludes by demonstrating how the plural form may outperform pure company and pure franchise chains based on three dimensions of the systemwide-adaptation process: the quality of adaptations, the speed of identifying opportunities for adaptations, and the speed of implementation.

THE ROLE OF THE CHAIN OPERATOR

While both company and franchise arrangements contributed to the systemwide-adaptation process, the chain operator usually took the lead in meeting this management challenge. Stern (1971, 309) argued that an interorganizational channel needs a "center of influence and/or power." He stated that the function of the central position—in this case, the chain operator—is "to provide the system of communication, to promote the securing of essential efforts, and to formulate and define purpose." Robert Nugent, president of Jack in the Box, described the chain operator's role in similar terms: "I don't want to patronize the franchisees, but it is our job to do strategic planning. You need a strong center guiding the company or else things will get out of control." For example, given that the development of commercials required specialized expertise and coordination with advertising agencies, the chain operator's marketing department typically proposed ideas to franchisees, which they then ratified with occasional modifications. The new-product development process displayed a similar pattern.[2]

Most franchisees agreed that the chain operator should lead in the area of systemwide adaptation, although they added the qualification that franchisees should play a significant role. Bill Walsh, a Pizza Hut franchisee, expressed the perspective of many franchisees: "The franchisees don't want to be the head of marketing. Franchisees want to be led, but in a fashion where they are listened to and have input. As long as the company has the data to support something, then the franchisees will go along. But we should be serious players in the process." Other franchisees offered a more direct explanation for why the chain operator should initiate product development and marketing: as one KFC franchisee put it, "New products are what I pay my royalty for—that is the job of the franchisor." Tom Dolan, a franchisee at Hardee's, concurred: "They have an office full of people testing new products—that's their job." Most franchisees agreed that adaptation was the province of the chain operator, although they wanted to be involved in the process.

The leadership role of the chain operator was reinforced by fundamental economics. If a chain operator owns units, then it is motivated to introduce adaptations that grow the business and enhance profitability. And if the chain operator franchises units, then it is motivated to search for adaptations that improve performance so that revenue increases, which in turn leads to more royalties. In either case, adaptation is in the chain operator's interest. The nature of the adaptations in each case may vary, however, since the chain operator's economic objectives differ in each one: revenue increases are more important in the franchise case, and income increases in the company arrangement. It is conceivable, for example, that the chain operator might propose a high-priced, low-margin product in a pure franchise chain that would benefit the chain in general but hurt particular franchisees. Such potential conflicts are mitigated if the chain operator owns units, in which case the economics of the chain operator and the franchisee converge. This obvious and crucial advantage of the plural form has been overlooked.[3]

The chain operator therefore has an overarching interest in investing in corporate resources related to systemwide adaptation, including a corporate marketing staff, research and development laboratories, and model test units. These resources are most visible in the early stages of the process. The chain operator's motivation to engage in systemwide adaptation overcomes what otherwise might be a classic collective-action problem: no individual franchisee would invest in these resources despite the net benefits they yielded to the system as a whole. The economics of the franchise contract solve this problem by providing the chain operator with the royalty stream, which motivates it to make such an investment. In addition, a hidden aspect of the plural form may encourage the chain operator to invest in specialized resources. In the chains I studied, the chain operators owned between 2.4 (Hardee's) and 21 (Jack in the Box) times more units than did the largest franchisee in the chain. From this perspective, the number of company units alone may have justified the investment in resources devoted to systemwide issues—with the franchisees, in essence, benefiting from the externality provided by this investment.

The analysis that follows attempts to discriminate carefully between the chain operator's activities that were solely the creation of a staff department and those that were linked to owning company units. The distinction is important in terms of trying to understand the dynamics of the plural form because in pure franchise chains the chain operator had staff departments as well. We should not confuse the contribution of a staff department with the contributions contingent on the ownership of company or franchise units. Only the latter situations involve dynamics of the plural form.[4]

MUTUAL LEARNING IN THE SYSTEMWIDE-ADAPTATION PROCESS

This section analyzes how each arrangement functioned at every stage of the adaptation process. I draw on a variety of existing theories to account for the data and to illuminate how and why each arrangement contributed to the adaptation process. The advantages of the plural form, I argue, are a result of these distinctive contributions, which I later contend cannot be generated in either a pure company or pure franchise chain. Product adaptations illustrate the dynamics of the plural form and most of the data in this chapter come from that type of adaptation. However, the process is similar for other types of adaptations (for example, new equipment or process changes) and where relevant I discuss those cases as well.

The pattern of activities described here could be observed with only slight variations in all five chains. KFC, Pizza Hut, and Hardee's, the three largest chains in my sample, followed this pattern almost exactly. Even Jack in the Box, whose franchise contract placed the most strict limits on the participation of franchisees in the adaptation process, followed the basic outline offered below. While its franchise contract repeatedly stated that the chain operator had sole control over decisions related to new products and advertising, Jack in the Box franchisees nonetheless played an active role in all the stages. Mo Iqbal, executive vice-president of marketing, noted, "We don't try and force things with franchisees. We take the lead and ultimately we make the decisions, but there isn't a case where we did something they did not sign off on." Fishermen's Landing was the exception, rarely engaging in systemwide adaptation.

Figure 7-1 identifies the distinctive contribution of each arrangement to the process at each stage. The left-hand side of the figure highlights the company arrangement's contribution; the right-hand side identifies the franchise arrangement's contribution. In the first two stages, the complementary plural dynamics were grounded in the different ways that ideas were generated and evaluated in company and franchise arrangements. It should be noted that the plural dynamics usually did not change the

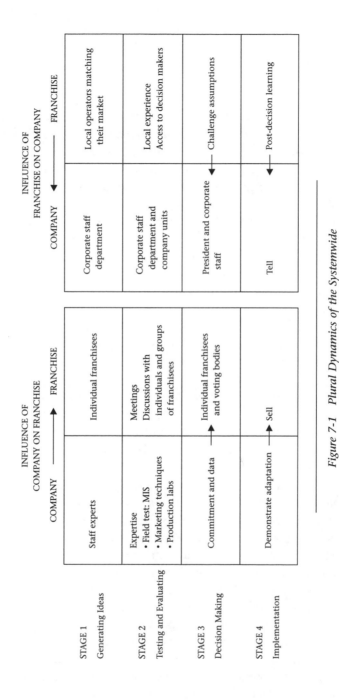

*Figure 7-1 Plural Dynamics of the Systemwide
Adaptation Process*

performance of the other arrangement but rather added something that other arrangement lacked. In the latter two stages, the activities in each arrangement directly affected the adaptation process in the other arrangement, and the arrows show the direction of that influence.

Generating Ideas

Ideas for new products were developed in two ways: by the chain operator's corporate staff, usually the marketing department, or by franchisees' ongoing attempts to meet the demands of their local markets. On the company side, a corporate staff department was charged with the job of identifying opportunities for new products. These departments were under the sole administrative control of the chain operator. As discussed in previous chapters, local managers in the company arrangement were rarely a source of innovation. By contrast, in the franchise arrangement ideas for systemwide adaptations were generated by individual franchisees. These ideas, which usually began as local responses, were motivated by the external market orientation of franchisees. Whenever a franchisee adjusted a unit to better meet the demands of the local market, an idea for a potential systemwide adaptation was born. The architecture of information in the franchise arrangement facilitated the flow of ideas from franchisees to the chain operator.

Generating Ideas: The Company Arrangement. The chains that I studied dedicated corporate personnel to the development of new products. For example, the New Products Group at Hardee's, a group composed of personnel from marketing, operations, and quality assurance, met several times and generated forty-seven ideas that were eventually tested over the course of one year. Similarly, Jack in the Box convened its Product Development Group on a monthly basis, since a central element of its strategy was product innovation. These brainstorming groups were made up entirely of company people, as were the corporate departments in charge of product development. Franchisees had the opportunity to express their opinions later in the process, but the chain operator worked autonomously on its own ideas in the initial stages.[5]

The chain operator was especially active in new-product development when its strategy depended on product introductions. As Robert Nugent, Jack in the Box's president, said, "Our system is based on constant innovation. When franchisees join the system, that is the capability they are buying. That is our job." Also, some marketing strategies like "in and out" product promotions (which lasted only a few weeks) were formulated by a chain operator's marketing department. This marketing tactic was used to generate customer traffic in restaurants. Short-term promotions were usually simple variations on existing products, like new sandwich combinations at Hardee's, or were products with seasonal appeal, like a Thanksgiving stuffing promotion at KFC. These promotions were usually tied to an advertising campaign that was also orchestrated by the marketing department.

In addition, the chain operator invariably took the lead in generating ideas when a product need was widely acknowledged. When a product problem was identified it was the job of the chain operator to find solutions. This pattern was exemplified by KFC, where, in the words of Gregg Reynolds, executive vice-president for public affairs, "Everyone knows— company people, franchisees, Wall Street analysts, and competitors—that we must introduce a chicken sandwich to strengthen our lunch business. Our people are working hard to find the right product." Similarly, the demand for healthy food by today's consumers—a phenomenon recognized by everyone—led Hardee's to invest corporate resources in developing a broiled-chicken sandwich, which later became a standard menu item.

In the chain-operator organization, responsibility for generating ideas was assigned to specialists. In 1990, Pizza Hut implemented an incentive-award program for field marketing specialists who generated the best new ideas; people in the operation's hierarchy were not included in the program because they were not viewed as a source of ideas. This was the common perception in all five chains. The reliance on specialists for innovation was built into the company arrangement: not only were company managers not given an incentive to innovate due to their salaried status but they were explicitly told to focus on operating the unit in accordance with uniform standards and to leave marketing to the specialists.

Generating Ideas: The Franchise Arrangement. Franchisees generated ideas for new products by proposing innovations for their local restaurants that sometimes resulted in profitable systemwide product introductions. A franchisee's local responsiveness was an important source of innovation for chains. Jack Laughery, chairman and CEO at Hardee's, contended, "Most good ideas that come out of chains had their genesis in the franchise community; the franchise community is inherently more flexible and open to new ideas" (Van Warner 1987). Laughery's assessment that "most good ideas" were generated by franchisees was not shared by all the executives in other chains, although the disagreement centered on the word "most." Everyone agreed that franchisees were an important source of ideas.

Several examples illustrate the contributions made by franchisees at this stage. In one of the most notable cases, a Jack in the Box franchisee led the company to an entirely new pricing strategy. After purchasing several restaurants from the company, the franchisee immediately raised prices. The company expected the franchisee's sales to decline, but instead they remained steady. Robert Nugent, the CEO, recalled, "The franchisee's experiment led us to study the pricing issue and ultimately we shifted to a premium pricing strategy." Similarly, the "Pairs" promotion strategy at Pizza Hut (discounting the second pizza a customer bought) was created by a franchisee. A Pizza Hut franchisee in Florida began a "2 Pizzas for 1 Low Price" promotion to meet the growing threat of a local competitor's two-for-one pizza campaign in his market. He then visited the corporate headquarters and explained to company executives the economics of the Pairs promotion, which was eventually tested and adopted by the chain as a centerpiece of its national marketing strategy.[6]

In 1990 breakfast accounted for over 30 percent of sales at Hardee's and biscuits were the core breakfast item. The biscuits were an adaptation created by a franchisee: Boeddie-Noell, the second largest franchisee in the chain, had added a homemade biscuit to its menu in the mid-1970s against the advice of Laughery, who believed "it wouldn't work north of the Mason-Dixon line." After its success in Boeddie-Noell restaurants, however, the chain decided to test it. The test process itself was a source of conflict because Hardee's wanted to sell preprepared biscuits while the franchisee insisted on homemade biscuits, which were much more labor-intensive. After testing and experimenting with different types of biscuits, the chain operator decided that the franchisee's product was better, and it was implemented throughout the chain.

These examples of major franchisee innovations should not overshadow the multitude of minor variations of existing products that also emerged from this process. When Pizza Hut created its "standard exception test" (SET) process (see Chapter 6), it received over eight hundred SET requests from franchisees in the first year and a half. A number of requests related to small but useful variations in products such as alternative salad-bar configurations, different suppliers, and new sauces to accompany the bread sticks. George Kelsey, an area vice-president at Hardee's, stressed the positive contribution of the chain's franchisees: "We learn a lot from the franchise side of the business. We bring those ideas in, analyze them, and try to duplicate them. One of the benefits of franchisees is that there often is not just one best way to do things."

Franchisees provided local variation and experimentation, which served as a natural laboratory for identifying and testing ideas for a systemwide adaptation. The rigid adherence to the uniform format in the company arrangement prevented such experimentation. What were in the end viewed as good ideas, however, often began as deviations from the uniform business format. The line distinguishing deviations that needed to be corrected from ideas that ought to be tested was not always obvious. Gary McCain at KFC made this point: "Rather than focus on whether it is approved or disapproved, I ask the franchisees what it is doing for their business. Usually the numbers don't justify the effort, and they agree to take it out. They are just experimenting. Of course, if it does make sense then we want to learn about it." This approach to deviations—which existed in some form in all chains—in effect gave franchisees the latitude to experiment. Throughout my interviews I heard stories of franchisees' experimenting with new products that violated existing standards: pecan pie and bottled water at Hardee's, milk shakes at KFC, fried steaks at Fishermen's Landing, cheese bread sticks at Pizza Hut. Strict adherence to the franchise contract prohibited all deviations of this sort, yet chain operators did not fully enforce these provisions. In return for not too tightly enforcing the contract, the chain operator benefited from the franchisees' ideas and local experiments.[7]

The preceding discussion has emphasized the specific innovations proposed by franchisees, but their effect on the first stage of the adaptation process was deeper and more subtle. First, franchisees served as early sensors of changing local-market conditions. Steve Honeycut at Hardee's observed, "If franchisees see a competitor doing something, they will quickly call us and want to do it themselves." John Cranor, the president and CEO of KFC, argued that franchisees accelerated the process of identifying opportunities for adaptation: "Ultimately we [the company] would identify these issues, but franchisees sometimes enable us to see things earlier." The architecture of information that linked the local operator to the top executives in the franchise arrangement facilitated this dynamic.

The second way franchisees affected the generation of ideas was by applying pressure on the chain operator to develop new products. Franchisees were a constituency within the company whose livelihood depended on what occurred at the interface of the restaurant chain and the external market. This factor, coupled with the access of franchisees to corporate decision makers, kept chain operators focused on the key issues. As Bill MacDonald, executive vice-president of marketing at KFC, noted, "In the corporate bureaucracy we can sometimes get caught up in hundreds of projects, of which only a few really impact the business. Franchisees are good at focusing on the few things that really hit the bottom line." This internal pressure was especially strong when the business suffered from a decline and franchisees wanted to know what the chain operator was going to do about it. According to the director of market research at Jack in the Box, Bruce Frazer, "Franchisees sometimes amplify an issue that we might not give our full attention to."

Generating Ideas: Dynamics of the Plural Form. The plural form provided a chain with two distinct sources of new ideas: one grounded in the expertise of the corporate staff and one emanating from the experience of franchisees trying to meet the demands of their local markets. Barabba and Zaltman (1991, 19), in their book *Hearing the Voice of the Market,* contend that one of the competencies required to "hear the market" is "competent curiosity," which they define as a firm's "inquisitiveness about the happenings in its markets that are of current and future importance, coupled with the ability to satisfy that curiosity with timely, relevant, accurate, and cost effective information." The locus of competent curiosity was different in franchise and company arrangements—individual franchisees in the former, and the marketing department dedicated to adaptation in the latter. These different sites of "competent curiosity," when combined, generated more (and more varied) new ideas than either one did alone.

An important question to consider when analyzing the contribution of each arrangement is whether the benefits derived from the corporate staff depended on the existence of company units. Put another way, does a franchise arrangement receive the same benefits regardless of whether it is part of a plural or pure form? If the answer is yes, then the plural benefits run in one direction—the franchise arrangement adds to the company arrangement in this first stage, but not vice versa. This question is difficult to answer with my data since I studied only plural forms, although I suspect that the MIS plays a major role in identifying trends, threats, and opportunities that bear on the generation of ideas by the corporate staff.

This provides an intriguing question for future research: Do the kinds of ideas generated by each arrangement substantially differ? One chain executive remarked, "Franchisees usually come up with the small variations on existing things; we [the chain operator] usually come up with the big ideas." An executive in another chain concurred: "Franchisees usually play the role of gatekeeper. They change the mechanics of programs like price points and timing." However, the president of another chain claimed that 60 percent of his chain's revenue was directly attributable to product ideas generated by franchisees. "We are spending way too much on corporate staff," he concluded. Each chain had examples of franchisees contributing important new ideas to the organization.[8] Clearly, both arrangements contributed to the process, and it would be well worth studying whether local knowledge and centralized expertise systematically produce different types of ideas.

Testing and Evaluating Ideas

The focal point of formal testing and evaluation activity resided with the chain operator and company units. The same company staff personnel dedicated to generating ideas often were also responsible for testing and evaluating them. The chain operator conducted market research and tested ideas in the laboratory and in company units. The latter form of testing and evaluating—"field testing"—generated data that were central to the decision of whether to pursue an adaptation and was conducted almost exclusively in company units. The characteristics of the company arrangement facilitated effective field testing: the architecture of information included an integrated and automated MIS that enabled the rapid and thorough analysis of field tests; authority over company managers made tests easy to implement; and rewards based on salaries made company managers less resistant than franchisees to experiments proposed for their units. However, franchisees still play a major role in the process. During this stage, franchisees were told of the new ideas under consideration and were asked for their feedback. These discussions were not superficial interactions but detailed examinations of the substance of a proposed adaptation. Chain operators often modified an idea based on feedback from these discussions. The participation of franchisees at this stage of the process also facilitated the chain operator's later efforts to persuade franchisees to implement the systemwide adaptation.

Before discussing the role of each arrangement in the testing and evaluating of ideas, it is important to recognize that the key criterion for evaluating a product was its fit to the chain's markets. The director of marketing research at Jack in the Box, Bruce Frazer, described the challenge he faced in developing new products: "It is a constant struggle to find new products that fit all our markets. Tacos sell well in our southwest markets, but do only fair in our northwest markets. The goal with a new product is to try and fit it in as many markets as possible without watering it down too much." Frazer's description was echoed by Steve Honeycut at Hardee's: "The basic idea is to meet the needs of the most customers possible in different markets. Only one thing is certain: you can't satisfy everyone. If you try, you'll end up needing a psychiatrist." Chains struggled to find products that were viable in as many markets as possible. Thus, Hardee's biscuits initially performed so poorly in northern states that one franchisee stopped selling them; people in the North simply were not familiar with and not interested in biscuits. Eventually that changed and biscuits were served throughout the system. Similarly, KFC's Thanksgiving promotion in 1989 was plagued by complaints from Florida franchisees that the name of the promoted product, "stuffing," was more commonly referred to as "dressing" in their part of the country. In both examples, after marketing testing and extensive communication with franchisees, the uniform standard was preserved.

The Frazer and Honeycut quotes imply that while a product may be optimal in terms of the overall profile of a chain's markets, a product may be poorly matched to any given market. In a pure company-owned chain that is not a problem, because the "average" product maximizes the value of the chain, which benefits the single owner. However, when different owners are involved, each competing in different markets, the trial results of a new product may produce conflicting perspectives on its economic feasibility. In these cases, systemwide and local rationality may conflict. For example, Pizza Hut and KFC franchisees were quick to point out that the differing demographics of company and franchise units—typically, urban versus rural, respectively—sometimes led to different economics and different preferences for new products.[9]

Testing and Evaluating Ideas: The Company Arrangement. Field testing was a central element in evaluating a product in the company arrangement. In all five chains, new products first were tested in a few company units and then tested in pure company or company-dominated markets. Marion Jones, divisional director of marketing at KFC, noted that the key reason why chain operators tested products in company units was the accessibility of information: the automated MIS produced detailed data about the performance of proposed products. Jack in the Box's Bruce Frazer agreed: "On a daily basis we are able to see how the product is doing, what effect it has on sales, and how it's changing the mix [of products sold]." This kind of information was extremely difficult to obtain from franchisees. "Not only are their MIS systems sometimes different," said Frazer, "but they also sometimes don't want to share the results." These data played a crucial role in the decision-making process for new products.

Jones highlighted another reason for testing products in company units: "We need to be able to ensure that the product is implemented the way we want." The chain operator exercised authority and compelled company managers to test new products in well-specified ways. Since their compensation was little affected by financial-performance measures, company managers typically did not balk at conducting field tests of new products in their units. In fact, the tests often provided local managers with visibility to senior managers, and some company people were eager to have their units selected as test sites. John Chidester, an area director of marketing at Hardee's, stated that company data from tests were "cleaner" because company managers adhered to the standards on all products and processes, while franchisees might have variations (approved and unapproved) that could affect the test: "It is easier to see what the impact of a product change will be by testing in company units."

Control over advertising was another important reason why chain operators tested new products in company units and company-dominated markets. Once a product proved its viability at the unit level, it was then tested in a market with advertising support. Operators were usually able to exercise control over advertising wherever they held the majority of units in a local market. "We test in company-dominated markets because we have to control the advertising," said one chain's marketing director. "We also want, if possible, the entire market to offer the product, and that is easier to accomplish if we own the units." In practice, the test market did not need to be entirely company-owned because the few franchisees in the test market—and under that market's advertising umbrella—usually followed the lead of the company and provided the product being tested. Franchisees did not want to disappoint customers who visited their restaurants asking for a new product they had seen in television commercials.

The field test was just one of several techniques the chain operator used to evaluate a new idea. Marketing personnel also conducted focus groups with consumers, who tasted and evaluated different products. They "intercepted" people at malls, showed them pictures of products, and asked them questions. Some chains conducted telephone surveys to profile the eating habits and preferences of consumers in particular markets. KFC regularly brought consumers to its headquarters facility for blind taste tests. Four chains had research and development facilities and personnel dedicated to menu development. When marketing people or franchisees came up with product ideas, the research and development people developed the recipes and assessed their commercial viability. A product's viability was a function of its cost (labor and other inputs) and its ease of manufacture. "A new product can disrupt the entire flow of activity in a restaurant," said John Chidester, an area director of marketing at Hardee's. "And that is something we have to consider." As part of their research and development facilities, the four chains had dedicated restaurants where prototype products could be made and tested.

Testing and Evaluating Ideas: The Franchise Arrangement. Franchisees rarely participated in the formal testing-and-evaluation process, mainly because the characteristics of the franchise arrangement were inhospitable to field testing. Scott Mackey, director of franchise operations at Pizza Hut, identified several of those characteristics: "Getting a test in a franchise unit, getting the data back, and making the franchisee 'whole' if the test fails is tough. It's easier to simply avoid it and work with company units." This division of labor was acceptable to most franchisees, since most believed that it was the role of the chain operator to provide and test innovations. Few franchisees felt they should bear the risk of testing new ideas in their units.

Still, franchisees did play a major role in testing and evaluating new products. The CEO of Pizza Hut described this role: "There is a tendency for company people to tell me what they think I want to hear. In contrast, franchisees tell me exactly what they think—whether they like something or they don't. The independent thinking of the franchisee brings a check and balance to the system that is very valuable." Virtually every person I interviewed expressed the belief that franchisees provided input into the process that might otherwise be overlooked. Company managers remarked on franchisees' ability to state their opinions directly and forcefully to company executives. "They are not afraid to say exactly what they think," said Kelsey of Hardee's. "In fact, one of the reasons they became franchisees was because they were tired of people telling them what to do." A KFC franchise manager recounted how a franchisee who owned a few units sent a letter to the chairman of the board of Pepsico—KFC's parent company—stating that he refused to implement a new packaging system for KFC products. When franchisees expressed their opinions openly to chain executives, they provided what one Pizza Hut executive referred to as "push-back." Since new products affected the economics of a restaurant, it is clear why franchisees were interested in the testing and evaluation of new ideas.

Each chain had examples of how franchisees influenced product development. In one meeting I attended, KFC franchisees raised concerns about freezer space during a proposed promotion of a new product. This problem was ultimately resolved by deciding to order smaller quantities of the product. The Hardee's biscuit episode also illustrated the nature of the contribution made by franchisees. At Jack in the Box, franchisees hesitated to implement a new promotion that involved a sandwich using lettuce and tomatoes during a time when these items were particularly high priced. "Franchisees are very sensitive to food costs," noted Frazer. Finally, Pizza Hut franchisees temporarily halted their "Cheese Lovers" promotion because of production problems: the middle of the pizza would not cook through due to the additional cheese. Later in the year, the production problems were resolved and the chain resumed the promotion. There were many examples from every chain of franchisees making decisive contributions at this stage of the adaptation process.

Franchisees and chain operators communicated through a variety of formal and informal forums. KFC had a standing committee called the "New Product Development Committee" composed of franchisees from different regions that met with the chain operator's marketing people regularly to discuss products being considered. Pizza Hut often convened a Joint Advisory Committee (JAC), an ad hoc committee of franchisees that assisted the chain operator in testing and evaluating specific ideas. Hardee's used a Business Planning Council (BPC), where franchisees elected by their peers met with the chain operator. Four chains had franchise advisory councils, which met on a quarterly or semiannual basis to discuss new products. (Fishermen's Landing did not have an advisory council.) The chain operator used these venues both to convey information to the franchisees and to obtain ideas and reactions from them. As one director of marketing said, "We really need the input of franchisees. They're the actual operators—they're the ones that really know the business." A KFC franchise manager, who had previous experience as a company manager, contrasted the company and franchise sides of the organization: "You don't screw around with franchisees. You better be prepared when you meet with them, because they will make you prove your argument." Scott Mackey, director of franchise operations at Pizza Hut, perhaps made the most telling observation when he said, "Presenting to the president of the company is one thing, but presenting at the franchise meeting is another. You better be ready."

The involvement of franchisees in product development was seen as vital, because they ultimately had the right to choose whether to implement the product. Mackey said:

> Selling these ideas is the whole game. If there is a key franchise that I need to have in my pocket, I better have them involved in the process. This is Organizational Change 101. This doesn't guarantee success because some people think that the JAC people are company lackeys. Furthermore everyone's situation is unique. The goal is to make the decision process clear to a good cross-section of franchisees so they will go out and sell the rest of the franchisees.

Jim Jaffrey, a former Hardee's executive, concurred with this approach: "It is very common to seek the counsel of key individual franchisees before really pushing ideas." Paul Headley, a franchise consultant at KFC, took a similar view: "If they are not part of the process, you get only a half-hearted commitment or no commitment." Jim Baxter, vice-president of franchising at Pizza Hut, argued, "As long as people have been heard and feel they affected the process, then they usually come along."

The need for early franchisee involvement, however, had to be balanced against the costs of possibly diminishing the company's reputation for expertise. Chain operators were deeply concerned with harming their credibility by considering product ideas that ultimately might fail. The following quotes from executives in three chains make the point:

> Franchisees will never let you forget a failed product. You don't want to have to hear about it forever.

> We can't afford errors on the franchise side of business.

> If the meat will stick to the bone [that is, if it is viable], then you start to get franchisees involved.

As a result of this concern, the solicitation of franchisees' input lagged a little behind the testing and analysis of new products by the chain operator, so that obviously flawed ideas could be screened before being shared with franchisees. In one chain, I observed a meeting between franchisees and chain executives that showed why this step was important. The franchisees aggressively questioned the division vice-president about how the product would fit into their operation, and the division vice-president did not have solid answers to several questions. One franchise summed up the sentiment of all those in attendance: "When you guys get it right, call me."[10]

In summary, three factors accounted for the contribution made by franchisees during this stage of the adaptation process. First, franchisees had a different perspective from company people based on their local market orientation, tenure in the chain, and business background. As Pizza Hut's Mackey pointed out, "These people have been in the system longer than almost anyone in the corporate headquarters and they know the restaurant business. They often have insights that we might not notice." Second, franchisees were motivated to share their perspective due to their incentives. They were affected directly by the decisions about new products, since they received the profits of the unit. Accordingly, they had an interest in ensuring that sound decisions—from their perspective—were made.

Third, franchisees had direct access to executives on the company side of the chain due to the federal structure and the architecture of information. The distortions often caused by the serial reproduction of information in a hierarchy and by the political dynamics associated with "not rocking the boat," as one manager put it, were avoided in the franchise arrangement.

Testing and Evaluating Ideas: The Plural Dynamic. Company and franchise arrangements provided the chain operator with different flows and kinds of information during the second stage of the adaptation process. The MIS linking all company units provided data, which enabled the detailed analysis of proposed changes. This feature of the company arrangement, along with the ease of implementing tests, caused chain operators to rely almost exclusively on company units for field tests. At the same time, franchisees added valuable data and insights into the process in the course of regular discussions with the chain operator. Their local perspective and their capacity to access decision makers directly gave this source of information immediacy and impact. In fact, I twice heard anecdotes about company managers who had called franchisees and urged them to speak *against* an idea proposed by the chain operator. The clear implication was that these company managers viewed franchisees as a more efficient way to communicate with corporate superiors than through their own company hierarchy. A chain's evaluation process was thus enhanced by the existence of both arrangements, each of which produced different kinds of information and communication.

The different and complementary architectures of information used in each arrangement were exhibited at this stage of the process. As was discussed in Chapter 3, the plural form enabled a chain organization to obtain both specific and general information (Jensen and Meckling 1991), rich and less rich information (Daft and Lengel 1984), and face-to-face and electronically mediated information (Nohria and Eccles 1992). Drawing on these eclectic types of information was especially important in the systemwide adaptation process, where the needs of local markets had to be balanced against the needs of the system.

Jim Winter, a Pizza Hut franchisee, pointed out that the plural form was a potent organizational design for testing and evaluating new ideas: "The best way to analyze a problem is to apply the wisdom of the franchisees and the good mental horsepower of the MBAs in the company." Bill MacDonald, executive vice-president of marketing at KFC, offered a similar assessment of the contribution of each arrangement: "The franchisees have good intuition based on their experience, and we have a lot of expertise to draw on."[11] The relatively long tenure of franchisees in a chain, their focus on the local marketplace, their role as generalists, and their accessibility to decision makers provided a valuable evaluation of ideas. At the same time, the specialized expertise and resources available with the company arrangement—and the use of company units for market tests—allowed for a thorough and precise analysis of ideas.

Decision Making

Decisions were made in a centralized fashion in company arrangements and in a decentralized way in franchise arrangements. In the company, the president and corporate staff had the final say on all systemwide adaptations. In contrast, there was often no fixed decision point for franchisees as a collective: each franchisee usually made decisions independently. This right of franchisee choice required the use of persuasion as a source of influence by the chain operator. For some adaptations, formal voting mechanisms were used, but personal negotiations were almost always involved in the decision-making process. These different decision mechanisms were each associated with a potential weakness. In company arrangements, the nature of hierarchy and the architecture of information sometimes prevented decision makers from receiving the information they needed to make sound decisions. In franchise arrangements, local autonomy sometimes prevented a proposed adaptation from ever becoming systemwide. The plural form at least partially remedied both of these weaknesses. Franchisees provided an internal challenge to decisions that was missing in the company arrangement, and the implementation of ideas in company units was a crucial way that the chain operator persuaded franchisees to adopt an idea.

Implicit in this discussion is the fact that franchisees did not automatically follow the lead of the chain operator. As mentioned, differences of interest could emerge when an idea was good on average for the entire system but not for an individual franchisee. If a proposed product, for example, were high priced but low margin, the chain operator would benefit, but it would not be in the best interest of franchisees. The chain operator's ownership of units, however, aligned the interests of both parties more closely and was one of the major advantages of the plural form.

Still, even with apparently aligned economic interests, the chain operator and franchisees often disagreed on adaptations. Why? One explanation can be found in the tendency of company units to be located in metropolitan areas and franchisees to predominate in rural areas. While this pattern of demographics may enable faster growth and leverage the local responsiveness of the franchise arrangement, it can produce fundamental conflicts of interest between the two arrangements. For instance, franchisees resisted KFC's attempt to build its lunch business through special product introductions because there were fewer opportunities to generate a lunch business in rural locations. The returns on investment of equipment were therefore unequal, which led to a conflict over whether to pursue the opportunity. A similar conflict arose at Pizza Hut with the introduction of the "Pairs" promotion: franchisees whose rural restaurants were the sole purveyors of pizza in their areas often argued that discounting was nothing more than "giving pizza away." Furthermore, those rural units often ran closer to full capacity, which meant they could not benefit from an increase in volume. Real conflicts of interest, grounded in the disparate demographics of company and franchise units, sometimes led to pronounced disagreements over proposed adaptations.

Particularities of individual franchisees also sometimes led to disagreements about adaptations. In some cases, their economic circumstances prevented them from adding a new piece of equipment immediately. In other cases, franchisees' work-leisure tradeoff was different than that found in the company arrangement. For example, several Pizza Hut franchisees did not want to add delivery service to their units because "it is a giant pain in the ass to manage," as one put it. Similarly, some franchisees were satisfied with their income and did not want to take risks on new investments. Finally, franchisees sometimes simply had different philosophies about the business. In the case of the Pairs program at Pizza Hut, some franchisees worried that discounting would compromise the reputation of the chain. As one franchisee complained, "The company is trying to take a Cadillac product into the low end of the market." On occasions when individual franchisees were seriously at odds with the views of the chain operator, it wasn't always possible to reach an agreement. Consequently, rarely did 100 percent of franchisees participate in a systemwide adaptation. Ron Rehahn, a regional general manager of Hardee's, said, "There are always a few that don't come along, but usually most do."

Decision Making: The Company Arrangement. Decision making in company arrangements was highly centralized and specialized. "Bill Prather [the CEO] has the final say as to whether we introduce a new product," said Honeycut at Hardee's. At Hardee's the Menu Development Team, composed of the directors of each functional area, studied data generated during the second phase and made recommendations to the president. In all the chains, final decisions on whether to go ahead with new products were made by a few people in the headquarters.

It is important to recognize that the chain operator was making a decision for all the company units and was making a recommendation for the chain as a whole. While the process was centralized, it relied on data generated in test markets that represented different demographic segments of the chain. Input on the company side was sometimes solicited from division vice-presidents in the operations hierarchy. Notably, however, the executives I interviewed rarely mentioned these people as having an important role in the decision process. Marketing specialists were the experts, and they made the recommendations to the chief executive officer.

Decision Making: Franchise Arrangement. A chain's franchisees decided independently whether to implement an adaptation. Accordingly, there typically was no identifiable moment of decision when franchisees, as a collective, introduced a new product. The decision process in the franchise community was usually the aggregation of the decisions of individual franchisees. At any point in time, only a portion of the franchise units might have adopted an adaptation, which is why advertisements often say that a product is available at "participating locations." "We don't want to force things on the franchisees," said Jim Jaffrey, former executive vice-president at Hardee's. "If the [adaptation] process is working right—we tested it adequately in company units and involved franchisees throughout—then they will all introduce the product because it makes sense." The crucial point here is that franchisees exercised choice over whether to introduce a new product, which meant that the chain operator had to pursue systemwide changes through persuasion rather than by mandate.

The decision process at Jack in the Box was somewhat anomalous since franchisees were bound by a much stricter contract, which stipulated that franchisees had to comply with the chain operator's product-introduction decisions. While franchisees had a variety of forums within which to express their opinions about new ideas, they did not exercise local autonomy in deciding whether to introduce a product. As one Jack in the Box executive said, "We didn't begin franchising until 1982, so we were able to learn from everyone else's mistakes." In his mind, a key mistake of other chains was allowing franchisees any discretion over the menu. Whether such discretion is indeed a mistake may be debated, but it is true that franchisees in other chains appeared to have greater choice over adopting proposed systemwide adaptations in their units.

The Jack in the Box case is also important to consider because even in a context where formal control was granted to the chain operator, franchisees still played an important role in product development. Ira Fishbein, a Jack in the Box franchisee who owned multiple units, noted, "The franchise system may vote on some things and express that opinion to the franchisor. But it [the franchisor] can do what it wants. It is unlikely, though, that they would ignore the franchisees if it was a big issue." Like the other chains, Jack in the Box involved franchisees in the decision-making process from beginning to end, to a much greater extent than they did personnel associated with company units. Like the other chains, franchisees were informed of product ideas in Stage 2, and their own ideas were solicited. Frazer remarked that when a Jack in the Box franchisee offered a new idea, it was taken very seriously and a senior-level staffer would get back to the franchisee. He said that it was rarely the case that conflict arose because franchisee "buy-in" was carefully nurtured throughout the process.

The Decision-making Process for Advertising. The systemwide-adaptation process outlined above was modified for advertising decisions. Advertising was a form of systemwide adaptation because decisions in this realm affected the uniform identity of every unit. For advertising, authority and persuasion were often accompanied by voting schemes based on majority decision (votes were apportioned on the basis of units).[12] KFC, Pizza Hut, and Hardee's used formal voting arrangements for local advertising, and the first two chains used such arrangements for national advertising too (Hardee's did no national advertising). At Jack in the Box, the chain operator had the right to make advertising and product-related decisions for the entire chain, but recall that the chain operator owned a majority of the units.[13] Fishermen's Landing did not advertise on television and rarely changed its business format. For the chains that ran television commercials, the institutional mechanism was necessary because advertising is impossible to implement incrementally: once the advertisement is aired, it affects all the units in that television market. Formal voting procedures therefore were used to aggregate the individual preferences of franchisees into a collective decision.

The franchise contract specified that franchisees contribute a certain percentage of revenue to marketing, usually 4 percent or 5 percent, most of which was spent on advertising (this was in addition to the royalty payment). At a minimum, the chain operator contributed the same percentage for company units. KFC, Pizza Hut, and Hardee's used democratically organized "marketing cooperatives" to make local and regional marketing decisions. Local co-ops were organized by Designated Marketing

Areas (DMAs) or Areas of Dominant Influence (ADIs), marketing terms used by different media rating agencies to define the reach of television stations. At Pizza Hut, there were 250 local co-ops; KFC had 275; and Hardee's, 148. The composition of the local co-op reflected the mix of units in the local market and therefore often included both company personnel and franchisees. Interestingly, if the market was entirely company-owned, there was no local co-op; the division marketing department made decisions for pure company markets. What was lost in the pure company markets was the direct participation of local operators in the decision process. One result of voting was that franchisees controlled advertising in some markets, while the chain operator controlled others. For example, at Hardee's 79 percent of the markets were controlled by franchisees. KFC and Pizza Hut, the only two chains I studied that advertised nationally, also had a national advertising cooperative that made decisions based on the mix of company and franchise units in the chain.

The decision-making process for advertising was important. Advertising was a major discretionary investment by chains and it had a big influence on sales. More subtly, it gave franchisees veto power over new products because they could refuse to advertise them. Although this rarely happened, Scott Mackey at Pizza Hut noted, "Franchisee-controlled co-ops could vote not to support a new product, which would effectively kill it." The fact that majority voting ruled in most chains points to an obvious aspect of the plural form: the mix directly determined advertising decisions. In fact, chain operators sometimes shifted the mix of units in their chain at both the local and national level to obtain control of these decisions. Pat Williamson, a Pizza Hut executive vice-president, explained that his chain's shift from 48 percent to 52 percent company-owned units over the course of two years was motivated by "our desire to exercise more control over the system. Now we control national-advertising spending." Gerald McGuiness, executive vice-president of development at Hardee's, said that a similar factor influenced growth decisions at the local level: "To the greatest extent possible, we want to maintain control over our fate in local markets."

Decision Making: The Plural Dynamics. The company and franchise arrangements became intertwined during the decision stage of the process. Each arrangement had an effect on the functioning of the other arrangement. One of the main ways that the chain operator persuaded franchisees to adopt an innovation was to show its commitment to it by implementing it in company units. Tom Dolan, a franchisee who owned three units at

Hardee's, described how he thought about the decision process: "You have to have faith in the name on the sign. Our attitude is that they've done their homework. Unless something really doesn't make sense, the approach we take is to accept their lead." In each chain I visited, I heard comments like, "If the company felt strongly enough to roll this out in their units, then it probably is a reasonable idea." Geneva Thomas, a KFC franchisee who owned two units, echoed this proposition: "If it makes sense for them, then it more than likely makes sense for me. They've got a lot of smart people at corporate, plus they've got a lot to lose if they screw up. I pretty much do what they do." The company's implementation of an adaptation thus directly affected the decision-making process of franchisees. Thomas's quote suggests that along with signaling the chain operator's commitment, the convergence of interest created by the plural form also encouraged the franchisees' compliance.

At Pizza Hut, the role of company commitment was articulated explicitly in the franchise contract, which stated that the company could not compel a franchisee to adopt a product at a faster rate than the company units were adopting the product. (Remember, most franchisees owned multiple units.) Pizza Hut displayed its commitment to a product by adding it to the menus of company units; franchisees were then contractually obligated to follow. The company commitment to an idea often eliminated the potential schism of interests between the chain operator and the franchisee.[14] The number of units owned by the chain operator obviously affects the influence of this dynamic. If the chain operator owns only a few units, then the schism of interests might remain.

For the company commitment strategy to work effectively, franchisees must trust the chain operator's judgment. The firm's track record was the foundation for that trust. At a KFC meeting of franchisees, reactions to corporate proposals were often prefaced: "I hope this isn't another Chicken Littles fiasco." The previous year the chain operator had committed itself fully to Chicken Littles, and after much discussion persuaded the franchisees to implement it too. The product ended up having operational and marketing problems and was ultimately removed from the menus of most restaurants. This failed initiative cast doubt on the credibility of the chain operator, which diminished the impact of its commitment. Now the chain operator had to "prove" the benefits of a proposed adaptation in a much more rigorous fashion.

The plural dynamics also ran from the franchise to the company arrangement in the decision stage. Franchisees did not hesitate to challenge the assumptions and business logic of decisions proposed by the chain operator in Stage 3 (selecting a proposal). Compared to company managers, they were affected more directly by the outcomes of these decisions and hence were more motivated to speak. Their perspectives added new insights to the decision process. As one franchisee observed, "If things get screwed up, they [chain operator personnel] may have to find another job. I may end up losing my business, home, and car." He argued that this situation made him much more thorough and critical of business ideas. Additionally, as we have seen, the architecture of information ensured that the perspectives of franchisees were conveyed directly to decision makers. In essence, the franchise arrangement exhibited the conditions for "constructive conflict" outlined by Assael (1969). Among the conditions he identifies are constant communication, reliance on self-regulatory procedures to resolve conflict, and frequent interaction of actors. These conditions enabled the franchise arrangement to deal with conflict in a productive fashion that encouraged learning.

Chain operators listened to and acted on the feedback of franchisees at this stage. Steve Honeycut, charged with managing product introductions in the franchise community for Hardee's, said, "It wouldn't make sense for us to go forward with something franchisees oppose." Most of the executives I spoke with agreed that franchisees often made valid criticisms of proposals. "If they refuse to do something," said Ed Jacob, division director of franchising at Pizza Hut, "it is a sign we better make sure we are right. These are smart people." Of course, these comments also reflect the *necessity* of the chain operator to listen; as we have seen, franchisees had the ability to stop a systemwide adaptation by refusing to implement it. Consistent with this argument, Hirschman (1986) pointed out that the "voice" of an actor may be amplified if it is accompanied by the threat of "exit"—with the threat in this case being a franchisee's right to reject a proposal. A franchisee's refusal to implement a new product was therefore an important source of information about the viability of the idea.[15]

The franchisees' capacity to challenge decisions, however, was a double-edged sword, since it slowed the decision and implementation process. As one executive put it, "There is not time in today's environment to take a vote with franchisees whenever an issue arises. We must be able to act quickly if we are to survive." Bruce Frazer observed:

> Sometimes when you [the company] just want to "make a call" and give something a try, you immediately remember that you'll have to stand in front of one hundred franchisees and someone will surely ask, "Why?" The franchisees keep you honest and make you have reasons for everything. Sometimes this is helpful and sometimes it's not.

Sometimes decisions needed to be made on which good information did not exist; other times, before good information could be gathered. Franchisees created an impediment in both of these circumstances. John Cranor of KFC summarized this dynamic: "In terms of organizational change, with franchisees you do 'slow S's' not 'fast Z's.' They keep us from doing big swerves." He too concurred with Frazer's observation that this was sometimes helpful and sometimes a hindrance. Later, we will see that the desire to be able to act more quickly was leading some chains to shift their mix of units in the direction of company ownership.

The dynamics of the plural form are crucial to explaining how decisions were made in chain organizations. The franchisees' eagerness to challenge the reasoning of chain operators (if found lacking from the perspective of the franchisee) provided a flow of information and devil's advocacy (Janis 1983) that was important to the decision process.[16] More subtly, the presence of franchisees forced company managers to articulate fully the reasons behind decisions, which made the testing and evaluation stage more thorough. At the same time, the chain operator's capacity to decide and implement a proposal in company units demonstrated its commitment to an idea, which powerfully influenced the individual decisions of franchisees. In the area of advertising, the plural dynamics were not so subtle, since the voting majority had control of the decision-making process.

Implementation

One often-repeated industry adage captures the essence of the difference between company and franchise arrangements during this stage of the product-introduction process: "We tell company people; we sell franchisees." These two approaches reflect the prevailing method of influence integral to each arrangement: authority with company managers, and persuasion with franchisees. As in Stage 3, the complementary dynamics of the plural form pervaded the implementation stage of the adaptation process. By implementing changes in company units, the chain operator was able to demonstrate the viability of the idea to franchisees. The franchisees' ability to challenge decisions offered the chain an opportunity for post-decision learning, which often was not exhibited by the company arrangement.

Implementation: The Company Arrangement. The implementation of a new product in company arrangements entailed providing the supplies and equipment necessary for the product and training personnel to make the product. In most cases, a memorandum was sent out to all company field personnel that described in detail, step by step, how to prepare a new menu item. Typically, a period of hands-on training in the field preceded a product introduction to ensure that everyone understood what to do, and managers throughout the company operations hierarchy were required to attend the training. The week I visited the Detroit office of Hardee's, the vice-president of operations attended a training session on how to make Crispy Curls, a new type of french fry: "I have to know what is going on in the restaurants," he said. These training periods focused entirely on implementation: there was no discussion of whether the proposal would work since that decision had already been made. "After the decision is made, it is nonnegotiable," said a district manager at Hardee's. "Our job is to roll it out." A Pizza Hut manager made a similar statement: "Once the decision is made, the time for discussion is over—you better get on board."

The implementation phase in company arrangements had one objective: effective compliance with the standards set out for the new product. When I made this observation to company executives, they often vigorously disagreed and talked about how they spent time selling changes to company personnel. Company personnel cited several examples of how they thought they solicited employee commitment for new ideas. In one case, an executive vice-president made a videotape, distributed to all restaurants, that explained the importance of the new products and procedures. Most executives alluded to memos as an example of how they fostered commitment. However, in most of the memos, after a brief explanatory paragraph, the employees were simply told *how* to make the change. Another tactic used to stimulate "commitment" to new products was through contests: "Whoever sells the most in the next month, gets a $100 bonus." While all these approaches might increase a person's understanding of or interest in a new product or program, they did not invite a critique of the new product or provide any element of local choice or local voice. Once the decision was made, there was no more discussion: the local manager's job was to comply. One vice-president of marketing put the issue clearly: "With company units, selling is a stylistic thing. The fact is, that if you take the paycheck, you better get on board."

Implementation: Franchise Arrangement. The selling process of franchisees was sometimes obscured by the extensive involvement of franchisees during the earlier stages. Jim Jaffrey at Hardee's believed that "implementation is tied directly to how closely you listen to franchisees in the beginning. That is what makes the sell easy." John Chidester, a colleague of Jaffrey's, concurred: "Usually by the time we [the company] roll, they've talked enough, seen it, tasted it, and already have their orders in. The question they always ask is 'When do we get it?'" Ed Jacob of Pizza Hut made a similar comment: "Most of the time no vote is necessary because franchisees have been involved all along, and by the end every franchisee adds the product because it makes sense and is profitable." Several people made the point that if the process was working right, then there was no need to sell franchisees: "By the end, every franchisee adds the product because it makes sense and is profitable," said Dave Hoban, a divisional director of franchising at Hardee's. While the participation of franchisees slowed the decision process, it also was crucial to getting them to agree to adopt the idea.

The selling of franchisees may make the maintenance of uniformity easier since it enhances the prospect of eliciting solid commitment. When a franchisee agreed to do something, the chain operator's personnel were typically convinced that it would indeed happen; monitoring was superfluous. I observed Pizza Hut staffers selling franchisee Ken Staab on why he should put the Pairs promotion on his menu. After two days of intensive discussions he finally agreed to do it. When I asked the Pizza Hut franchise-operations representative what the follow-up would be, he said, "None. Once Kenny gets some numbers we'll take a look at them." It was never in doubt that he would do it: "He said he would." One benefit of having franchisees commit to adaptations was that it reduced the need for monitoring. In contrast, the use of authority to execute decisions in the company arrangement had to be supported by monitoring programs to ensure compliance.

Persuasion was at the heart of the implementation phase. The importance of selling franchisees was reflected in a key performance measure used to evaluate franchise consultants: the percentage of franchisees that have adopted a chain operator's initiatives. The importance of selling is also reinforced by previous research on the use of noncoercive power, defined as power based on expertise, identification, and rewards (French and Raven 1959). Noncoercive power has been found to be associated with franchisee satisfaction (Hunt and Nevin 1974; Lusch 1976), to reduce levels of channel conflict (Lusch 1976), and to produce a higher degree of channel cooperation (Sibley and Michie 1982; Frazier and Summers 1984). Aside from the legal prohibitions that often constrained a chain operator from forcing a franchisee to implement an adaptation, these dynamics made resorting to coercion an extremely costly strategy because it harmed the relationship and cast a shadow over future transactions between the franchisee and chain operator.[17] Nonetheless, the chain operator sometimes resorted to limiting a franchisee's growth or even pursuing litigation if the chain operator felt strongly about the issue at stake, although the latter course of action was unusual.

Implementation: Plural Dynamics. The plural dynamics in Stage 4 were an extension of the dynamics of Stage 3. The implementation of the adaptation in company units was used to demonstrate to franchisees the economic and operational viability of the adaptation—remember, the franchisees still need to be convinced at this stage. Pizza Hut used data from company units to construct a "business case" that laid out the rationale for a new product. The large number of company units involved made it easier for the chain operator to find comparable company units for any given franchise unit. KFC went so far as to pursue a strategy of locating company units in every major market in the United States. When I asked why a local presence was needed, the regional vice-president said, "We need to be able to show them the upside of running their restaurants correctly and also be able to show them the viability of corporate proposals in their markets." The presence of company restaurants in a market answered directly the question of whether company and franchise restaurants were facing comparable circumstances.

The use of company data to demonstrate the viability of proposed products existed in every chain. At a KFC meeting of franchisees that I attended, the company made a presentation that showed the economics of the "Hot Wings" product. The item had been introduced in some company markets, and the revenue, cost, and profit numbers shown to franchisees came from company units. Similarly, at Hardee's, where the company was implementing pancakes and Crispy Curls, the franchise consultants used data from company units to persuade franchisees to add these items to their menu. At Jack in the Box, franchisees did not have the individual choice that was visible in other chains, but still the chain operator's presentation of new products included extensive data on the economics of the product, which were generated from company units.[18]

In an elaboration of the original French and Raven (1959) typology of the bases of social power, Raven and Kruglanski (1970) identified another source of power, "informational influence." Information is used to persuade one actor to pursue a course of action that otherwise might not have been taken. Researchers in the marketing literature have highlighted the important role played by information in generating channel coordination, but they give little attention to what kind of information generates this dynamic and where the information comes from (Etgar 1978; Guiltinan,

Rejab, and Rodgers 1980; Sibley and Michie 1982; Frazier and Summers 1984). Even when these theories define the concept of information with phrases like "retail management assistance" (Etgar 1978) or the percentage of time the chain operator field person "discussed the overall strategy of dealership operation" (Frazier and Summers 1984), the antecedent question is overlooked: Where and how did the chain operator obtain this information? The answer in plural form was that it was generated by the operation of company units, both directly by the company MIS and indirectly through the use of former company people as franchise consultants.

Etgar (1978, 60) warns of the fragility of noncoercive power in contract relationships because as the franchisee "becomes more experienced they will be able to draw on their own expertise and rely less on their suppliers [chain operator] for retail management assistance." He speculates that companies may have to vertically integrate or engage in product development—in essence, to *produce* the expert power—to maintain control over the system. In my study, the information generated by company units provided the chain operator with a resource that was valuable to franchisees and enabled the effective exercise of noncoercive power. One of the reasons why the chain operator might not want MIS in the franchise arrangement is that it might diminish the chain operator's base of power— its sole control over these types of data.

Like the previous two stages, the franchisees provided a check on the company's decision-making process during Stage 4. Franchisees provided what I call "postdecision learning," because even if the company made a decision, the franchisees continued to study and evaluate it. In contrast, once the decision was made on the company side the discussion ended (if it ever took place), and data that might cast doubt on the decision was rarely sought or welcome. One executive observed that after a decision, "organizational momentum takes over. Everybody focuses on getting it out there and making it work. Once the company has committed to it publicly, you'd be crazy to stand up and say, 'I'm having second thoughts about this.'" While franchisees' opinions were usually integrated into the process at an earlier stage, several people remarked on how "organizational momentum" took over in the company arrangement, after which few discordant voices were heard. "We get so involved proving why it will work that we sometimes forget to be objective about whether it is working," said one executive.

In one chain, a senior executive recounted how "it took the franchisees to blow the whistle on a poor product" before the company reconsidered its decision:

Once the decision is made and implemented, my job is to make it work. We might throw more marketing dollars at it, promote it more, anything to make it work—particularly in this case because the top people were behind it. The franchisees, though, go after the toughest and most ambiguous variable that is the problem. Essentially, they'll stand up and tell the emperor he has no clothes!

In this case, the chain halted further implementation of the product until the chain analyzed the problems. The story in itself demonstrated the powerful effect franchisees can have on adaptations in the implementation stage. Moreover, the fact that the executive prefaced this story by saying "off the record, several of us agreed with the franchisees" showed how the company arrangement can inhibit the free flow of ideas.

THE ROLE OF MULTI-UNIT FRANCHISEES

An aspect of the franchise arrangement that we might speculate affected the systemwide adaptation process was the size of the franchisee. I say "speculate" because my data are not fine-grained enough to enable detailed analysis of this issue, but they do provide clues that suggest that the size of the franchisee affected the process. I previously showed the wide dispersion of sizes of franchise "minihierarchies" and argued that as franchisees added units their management structures looked more like the company arrangement. This pattern influenced both what the franchisee contributed to the systemwide-adaptation process and how the plural dynamics affected the behavior of franchisees. In the first category, larger franchisees probably contributed fewer local innovations (Stage 1) than small franchisees, as the management of local units was similar to that of company units. However, the contribution made by franchisees in the other stages likely stayed the same, since access to the chain operator's decision makers and individual choice remained regardless of a franchisee's size. While large franchisees may cost the chain operator in terms of new ideas, the concentration of franchises simplified the selling process for ideas that did emerge. The CEO of one chain captured the issue succinctly: "It is much easier to get things done if you only have to deal with a few big franchisees rather than hundreds of little franchisees." This perspective was shared by virtually all the executives I interviewed: the more highly concentrated the base of franchisees, the easier it would be to implement proposed adaptations.

It is worth considering the possibility that while large franchisees may reduce the cost of selling in terms of the number of people that need to be convinced, they may be more difficult to persuade than small franchisees.

First, chain operators commented that large franchisees often possessed a higher level of business acumen than small franchisees and were less likely to be swayed solely on the basis of the chain operator's commitment in its company units. (On the other hand, this attribute may enhance the quality of the constructive conflict provided by the franchisees.) Second, the large franchisees were likely to be less susceptible to the chain operator's threats to halt their growth since the chain operator's own growth depended heavily on the continued expansion of large franchisees. As such, the role of franchise size in instituting systemwide adaptations is clearly significant, with its effects both impeding and facilitating the process at different stages.

INFLUENCE OF THE PLURAL FORM ON THE SYSTEMWIDE-ADAPTATION PROCESS

The central argument of this chapter is that the plural form enhanced a chain's ability to accomplish systemwide adaptations. Underlying this argument is a comparative assessment of plural forms and pure forms, which I want to make explicit here. An organization's effectiveness at instituting a systemwide adaptation can be assessed in three ways: (1) quality of the adaptation, (2) speed of identifying opportunities and threats that require adaptation, and (3) speed of implementation. What follows is a hypothesis about the relative success of pure company, pure franchise, and plural forms on the three dimensions of effectiveness (see Table 7-1).

Table 7-1   Hypotheses: Systemwide Adaptation

	Pure Company	Pure Franchise	Plural
Quality of Adaptation	Low	Medium	High
Speed of Identifying Opportunities	Low	High	High
Speed of Implementation	High	Low	Medium

Quality of Adaptation

I predict that the quality of adaptation is "low" in pure company chains, "medium" in pure franchise chains, and "high" in the plural form. One measure of the quality of an adaptation is its sales performance over time. The relative weakness of the pure company arrangement is a function of few locally generated innovations, the relatively low level of local pressure on the corporate staff to develop new ideas, and the absence of a local screen to evaluate new ideas. For example, in one pure company chain that I visited (not in my main sample), the company recently had introduced a salad bar in all its restaurants. This labor-intensive component added so much to the work load of the restaurant manager that 40 percent of the restaurant managers turned over during the year, a dramatic increase from the previous year's turnover rate of 20 percent. The adaptation was described as the "pet project" of the president, which, people said, accounted for the lack of critical analysis that should have accompanied the proposal. We might reasonably conjecture that had franchisees been involved in this process, the difficulties involved in managing the salad bar likely would have been raised earlier and more forcefully.

The pure franchise chain provides three things lacking in the company arrangement. First, franchisees are an important source of local ideas. Second, the franchisees serve as a strong internal constituency pushing the chain operator to generate ideas. Finally, franchisees serve as a "check and balance" to the occasional tendency of managers in the company arrangement to rely too heavily on centralized expertise and to ignore information generated at the local level by subordinates. One possible drawback is that the pure franchise chain may not provide for the thorough market testing and evaluation of ideas that occurs naturally in the company arrangement. Even so, I believe that this limitation of the franchise arrangement is less consequential than the weaknesses associated with the company arrangement. My hypothesis is that in chain organizations the inclusion of the local perspective—which might be viewed as the "voice of the market"—is more important than the role played by the corporate staff in determining the quality of an adaptation. Accordingly, I rate pure franchise as "medium" and pure company as "low" on the quality of adaptation. My findings also show that the plural form overcomes at least some of the limitations of each component arrangement by coupling it with the other one, which has complementary characteristics. To some extent, one arrangement's weaknesses are the other one's strengths. Therefore, the plural form exhibits high-quality adaptations.[19]

Speed of Identifying Opportunities

I predict the speed of identifying opportunities to be "high" in pure franchise and plural forms and "medium" in the pure company arrangement. The economics underpinning the franchise arrangement make franchisees highly sensitive to opportunities for and threats to their business. Furthermore, identifying opportunities entails more than being sensitive to information; it also entails communicating that information to people who can act on it. Again, the federal structure and the architecture of information exhibited by the franchise arrangement made such communication more rapid and less subject to distortion. While the MIS provided the company arrangement with data from which trends might be discerned, this form of market intelligence lagged behind the information conveyed by franchisees to decision makers. On top of that, the information delivered by franchisees compared to the information acquired from the MIS was richer and accompanied by an interpretation, which also may accelerate the speed of identifying and understanding the implications of important market dynamics. As noted earlier, the size of a franchisee may affect its capacity to identify opportunities or threats to the business. Simply by incorporating franchisees into the management structure, the plural form obtains these benefits.

Speed of Implementation

Assessing the speed of implementation offers clear hypotheses: the authority structure present in the company arrangement and absent in the franchise arrangement leads to ranking the company arrangement "high"; the plural form, "medium"; and the pure franchise arrangement, "low." The crucial management challenge with franchisees is getting them to sign on to systemwide adaptation in a timely fashion. Jay Willoughby of Pizza Hut stated, "With voting [franchisees], it is like trying to steer an oil tanker away from an iceberg. By the time the vote is taken and the command goes down, the tanker is on the ice." This chapter makes the argument that the plural form enabled the chain operator to increase the speed of the decision and implementation processes in the franchise arrangement—mainly because those dynamics emanated from the decisions and implementation that *already* occurred in the company arrangement. Two chains, Pizza Hut and KFC, were gradually shifting the mix toward more company units in large part because they wanted, as one executive put it, "the capacity to act." The obvious danger that accompanies such a shift is that it may lead to lower quality adaptations.

Of the three dimensions of the systemwide-adaptation process, I would argue that the quality of the adaptation is probably the most important, and it is the dimension on which the plural form is clearly superior to both pure forms. But even if all three dimensions are viewed as equally important, simple addition down the columns indicates that the plural form is superior to the other types of chains. This analysis suggests that the plural form significantly outperforms other structures in terms of systemwide adaptation.

*The greatest problem with the company side of the business
is excessive bureaucracy and rigidity. On the other hand,
the biggest problem with franchisees is getting them to
move in the same direction. At the same time, the company arrangement gives us control and the franchisees
provide a spark of entrepreneurship. Each one to some
extent helps us deal with the other one's weaknesses.*

—John Cranor, Chief Executive Officer, KFC, Inc.

Chapter 8

Conclusion

THIS BOOK PROPOSES a new model for understanding the management of chain organizations: the plural form. I have argued that the
simultaneous use of company and franchise arrangements enables a set of
plural processes that positively affects a chain's ability to meet its four key
management challenges: unit growth, uniformity, local responsiveness,
and systemwide adaptation. This theory was developed by observing the
management practices in five major restaurant chains, identifying what was
similar and different in how company and franchise units met the challenges, and illuminating the patterns of behavior produced by the plural
form.

This detailed description of how one of the most important organizational forms of our times is managed can aid theorists as they attempt to
explain, for example, why a chain exhibits its mix of company and franchise units. To understand *why* chains are organized in this way, we need
a better understanding of *how* they function. At the same time, this model
helps practitioners by highlighting important, though often overlooked
and poorly understood, patterns of organizational behavior that influence
a chain's performance. Like John Cranor, many managers and franchisees
remarked on the benefits of using both company and franchise units, yet
they typically had a difficult time articulating just how and where those
advantages were produced. This book casts light on those underlying plural
processes.

In addition, this book argues that the plural form constitutes a new "ideal
type" organizational configuration. My research suggests that the benefits
of the plural form go beyond Weber's bureaucracy (1971) and Williamson's

market (1985) conceptualizations; the plural form has properties of its own that make the whole greater than the sum of its parts. The union of two different structures—built on internal and external relationships—to perform a similar set of activities helps an organization accomplish objectives that are unattainable by any single structure. But more than that, the plural form provides a context for processes that strengthen an organization's capacity for self-correction and self-renewal. The plural-form configuration can also be observed in a variety of other settings, which makes the implications of these findings especially important and interesting.

After reviewing the findings in the next section, this chapter traces the implications of the plural form in four directions. First, I explore how the mix of units in a chain might influence the processes of the plural form. There is reason to believe that some plural processes may be dependent on certain combinations of company and franchise units. Second, I highlighted the most important practical implication of this work, which is that managers must recognize and use the plural processes to strengthen performance. The subsequent section discusses the intriguing insights the plural form offers into two fundamental questions with which theorists have struggled—why organizations decide to make an activity or buy it and how a single organizational structure might support both control and innovation. The final section discusses alternative approaches to obtaining the benefits of the plural form: ambidextrous and hybrid organizations. Neither of these alternatives, however, provides an organization with the same vital properties as the plural form—its capacity for self- correction and self-renewal.

SUMMARY OF FINDINGS

The heart of the argument presented in this book is that the presence of franchisees solves some of the problems associated with the company arrangement, and the presence of the company arrangement helps ameliorate some of the weaknesses of the franchise arrangement. As a consequence, the plural form can do things that neither of the constituent arrangements could do by themselves.

Figure 8-1 (which we first encountered in Chapter 1) shows how this works. *Unit growth* was shaped by the additive process, which helped chain operators escape the constraints on growth associated with each form, and the socialization process, which led experienced company operators into the ranks of the franchise arrangement. *Uniformity* was deeply influenced by multi-unit franchisees' modeling the practices used in company units and by the ratcheting process, where each side set performance benchmarks for the other. *Local responsiveness* was positively influenced by the local-learning process, where company units learned from franchisees' local responses, and the market-pressure process, which strengthened the chain operator's corporate staff through the presence of franchisees, who could opt not to use corporate services. Finally, and most important given the trends in the industry, *systemwide adaptation* was enhanced by the mutual-learning process. Company and franchise units provided a chain with a more diverse set of ideas and a more thorough screening of those ideas than was available from either arrangement by itself. The decision-making and implementation phases of the systemwide-adaptation process also exhibited plural processes: franchisees were influenced by the commitment and demonstration of company units, and the company units benefited from the challenge and postdecision learning offered by franchise units.

Both sides of the plural form thus benefited from the other. The socialization and modeling processes enabled the company units to influence the franchise arrangement. The local learning and market pressure processes ran the other direction, from the franchise side to the company arrange-

Figure 8-1   The Model of Management in Restaurant Chains

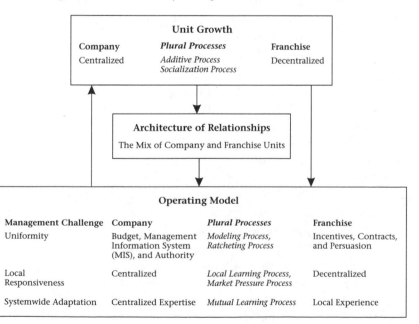

ment. The additive, ratcheting, and mutual-learning processes ran in both directions. Significantly, these processes were visible in all five chains I studied. An important extension of this work will be to examine whether these processes always exist in plural-form chains or only exist under certain conditions. Since I studied successful chains, I may be missing a key source of variance that might explain differences in performance: the development of effective plural processes.

While this research centered on the plural form, the conceptualization of company and franchise arrangements developed here also contributes to the literature. Most existing work conceives of company and franchise arrangements as a simple relationship between a local unit and chain operator (Brickley and Dark 1987; Hadfield 1991; Williamson 1991). The architecture of relationships within which the dyads operate is ignored, and more generally, the literature does not view each arrangement as a complex *organization*. But in my research, it was precisely the organizational aspects of each arrangement that strongly affected its performance. For example, each arrangement's architecture of information (which made the operations of local units either transparent or opaque to the chain operator) and structure (hierarchy or federation) affected their ability to meet the management challenges. These attributes profoundly shaped the organizational behavior of the units and influenced their performance.

The limitations of the literature are most evident when considering the franchise arrangement. This book has highlighted the important role played by specific aspects of the organization and the particular people used by the chain operator to manage franchisees. It has also illuminated the key method by which chains manage franchisees—through persuasion. The structure of the corporate field organization, the career paths of the franchise consultants, the desire of the franchisee to add units, and the nature of the face-to-face interactions all affect the chain operator's ability to influence franchisees in noncoercive ways. While the literature tends to focus on the formal provisions of the contract (Rubin 1978; Brickley and Dark 1987) or on the norms surrounding the relationship (Macneil 1980; Kaufmann and Stern 1988; Kaufmann and Dant 1991), almost no research exists on the organizational design of these relationships or on how the persuasion process is conducted.[1]

One of the most notable findings here is the pervasive use of, and managerial significance of, multi-unit franchising. Multi-unit franchising affects a chain's ability to meet every one of its management challenges: it increases the level of uniformity, it curtails the degree of local responsiveness, it makes the chain operator's "selling" process in terms of points of contact easier (though perhaps more difficult in terms of bargaining power), and it is crucial to the process of adding units. Yet, this aspect of these organizations has been almost entirely ignored (for exceptions, see ' Bradach 1995; Kaufmann and Dant 1996).

Although this research suggests that the advantages of the plural form outweigh the disadvantages, it is nonetheless important to be clear about the potential pitfalls. The most obvious drawback is that executives must be effective in operating two entirely different organizational designs. This dichotomy was summed up by the executive in one chain who noted, "The worst thing you can do is treat a franchisee like an employee." Executives in chains had to be comfortable with two sharply contrasting management styles: one that was directive (company), and one that was more participatory (franchise). Anecdotal evidence from the chains I studied suggested that it was difficult to find people good at both. In addition, a separate administrative structure may be required for each arrangement, which may, under some conditions, create prohibitively high costs.

The second potential disadvantage of the plural form is that along with the strengths company and franchise arrangements offer come their weaknesses. While the exercise of authority in the company arrangement enables the rapid implementation of strategies, for example, it also tends to inhibit potentially useful challenges to those decisions. Although the data presented here suggest that the plural form tilts toward providing chains with the best of both forms rather than the worst, this issue needs to be examined more closely in future research. I discuss this issue more fully below in the section on hybrid forms.

PLURAL PROCESSES AND THE MIX

Figure 8-2 shows the distribution of the mix of company and franchise arrangements used by the 100 largest restaurant chains in 1995. Several patterns are notable. First, pure franchise chains were relatively uncommon (eight out of the top one hundred chains). The plural processes emanating from the company arrangement—for example, the socialization, modeling, and demonstration processes—may be necessary for making the franchise arrangement a viable organizational form. Based on this research, we can hypothesize that in the absence of these processes, a pure franchise chain would exhibit less uniformity and have greater problems producing systemwide adaptations. A small number of company units may be all that is required to produce these effects, which may account for the large number of chains that are between 91 and 99 percent franchised.

Second, while pure company arrangements are more common, they were used primarily in small chains. Ten of the thirteen pure company chains contained fewer than five hundred units. In part, this was a by-product of the growth process: plural chains grow faster than pure company chains, which might account for large chains being plural forms. The pattern may also reflect a negative relationship between the size of the company arrangement and its ability to be effective—more specifically, its ability to meet the challenges of uniformity, local responsiveness, and systemwide adaptation. Large size also may be accompanied by increasingly elaborate and bureaucratic management structures that impede performance. Additionally, size widens the distance between decision makers and local markets, which in all likelihood affects the architecture of information, having negative consequences for local responsiveness and systemwide adaptation. While these limitations may be manageable in a small company arrangement, they may severely decay performance in a large arrangement. In this latter case, franchisees may provide the chain operator with some of the attributes that are lost in a large company arrangement.

The connection between the overall size of a chain and the presence of franchisees is suggested by comparing the size of pure company chains to the size of company arrangements within a plural chain. Friendly's, the largest pure company chain, operated 735 units in 1995 (see Table 8-1).

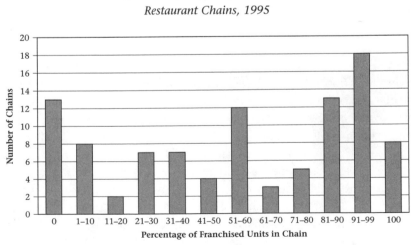

*Figure 8-2   The Mix of the Top 100
Restaurant Chains, 1995*

Source: Technomic, Inc.

There are ten plural-form chains that actually operated a larger number of company units than Friendly's, with Pizza Hut operating over five thousand company restaurants—almost seven times as many.[2] While the company hierarchy's size may correlate with "control loss" and a decay in efficiency (Williamson 1975), these data point to a variable that may mediate this

Table 8-1   The 25 Largest U.S. Restaurant Chains, 1995

Chain	U.S. Units Co-owned	U.S. Units Franchises	Total U.S. Units
1. McDonald's	1,796	9,572	11,368
2. Subway Sandwiches	0	10,093	10,093
3. Pizza Hut	5,078	3,615	8,693
4. Burger King (Pillsbury)	447	6,155	6,602
5. Taco Bell	3,022	3,247	6,269
6. KFC	2,031	3,111	5,142
7. Little Caesar's	1,240	3,550	4,790
8. Domino's Pizza	688	3,543	4,231
9. Wendy's Old Fashioned	1,200	2,997	4,197
10. Hardee's	864	2,530	3,394
11. Dunkin' Donuts	16	2,945	2,961
12. Arby's Restaurants	358	2,432	2,790
13. Denny's	933	596	1,529
14. Sonic Drive-Ins	186	1,305	1,491
15. Long John Silver's	982	492	1,474
16. Jack in the Box	863	368	1,231
17. Blimpie	0	1,197	1,197
18. Waffle House	500	475	975
19. Church's	589	363	952
20. Shoney's	356	526	882
21. Papa John's	217	661	878
22. Popeye's	117	761	878
23. Boston Market	3	826	829
24. Big Boy	87	733	820
25. Friendly's Ice Cream	735	0	735

Source: Technomic, Inc.

relationship: the presence of franchisees. The franchise arrangement may enable the company arrangement to grow larger for two reasons. First, franchisees may provide the chain operator with attributes lost as the company arrangement grows, such as face-to-face interactions between local units and the leaders of the chain, constructive conflict, and a local-market perspective. Second, the franchise arrangement may actually halt the decay in the company arrangement that would otherwise accompany large size through dynamics such as the ratcheting effect. Future research will need to examine how the plural processes are influenced by the size of these organizations.

PRACTICAL IMPLICATIONS: FROM MANAGING THE MIX TO
MANAGING THE PLURAL PROCESSES

The variety of mixes of company and franchise units displayed by the largest restaurant chains sends a warning that there may be no ideal mix between these arrangements. The answer indicated by my research is clear but general—chains need some of both. A multitude of factors might dictate whether a unit in a given site should be a company or franchise unit, or whether the next unit the chain builds should be one or the other. Geography, capital constraints, and territorial agreements with multi-unit franchisees are some of the factors highlighted in this book. In the end, though, the ownership of a given site may have little influence on the performance of a chain. What may matter most is how well the overall system functions: in particular, whether it is leveraging the strengths of both sides to the fullest to meet the management challenges. Managers, then, must assess the extent to which the chain is benefiting from the processes of the plural form.

As seen earlier in this chapter, even though executives intuitively believed that the combination of company and franchise units made a chain stronger, they had difficulty identifying precisely how those benefits emerged. The processes highlighted in Figure 8-1 illuminate the source of this advantage. One of the key elements affecting a chain's performance may be the simple recognition that *both* sides contribute importantly to the chain. While the chains studied here exhibited this characteristic, my interviews with executives from other chains suggested that they sometimes construed the benefits of franchisees much more narrowly, merely as a source of capital.

Once a chain recognizes the potential benefits of the plural form, management can actively ensure that the plural processes are in place to leverage its advantages. For example, Pizza Hut used the SET process to collect proposals from franchisees for local responses and used them as a source of ideas for systemwide innovations. Chains that view these local responses simply as deviations from the standards rather than ideas to be considered are missing an opportunity for learning. Similarly, chains that do not creatively and constructively share data on the performance of company and franchise units—and use that statistical information as a source of learning—are missing opportunities to strengthen the chain. Managers must proceed on the assumption that both sides have something to add to the chain, and then must create mechanisms that promote the interactions that improve performance.

THEORETICAL IMPLICATIONS: THE POWER OF PLURALITY

Many of the theoretical implications of these findings have been discussed throughout the book. There are two broad implications, however, that bear highlighting. First, these findings show the limitations of applying "make-or-buy" approaches to analyzing questions of institutional choice. Second, the plural form suggests one way managers have found to resolve the dilemma of sustaining control and innovation in a single structure.

Theories of Institutional Choice

The existing literature on chains has focused almost exclusively on the issue of whether chains should own or franchise their units, missing entirely the processes of the plural form. One reason for this oversight is the tendency to view that choice as a simple make-or-buy question (see Appendix A). Scholars examining this question typically frame it as an either-or proposition, that is, choosing among "discrete structural alternatives" (Williamson 1991). This way of thinking extends beyond franchising into other settings as well. For example, why do firms make or buy a part (Monteverde and Teece 1982); utilize a direct or third-party sales force (Anderson and Schmittlein 1984); or wholly own foreign enterprises or ally with foreign partners (Hennart 1991)? A common underlying assumption governing the analysis of such questions is that certain conditions lead to the use of certain institutions. For example, market arrangements are assumed to provide strong incentives, while hierarchies offer strong system-responsiveness properties (Williamson 1980). Then, the argument goes, depending on whether strong incentives or system responsiveness is more important, an organization chooses either a market or hierarchy form.

But what if an organization wants both (as indeed most do)? Or what if the institutional effects the organization seeks are contradictory (Cameron 1986), like tight control and local responsiveness? Or in the case of chain organizations, what if a chain wants local responsiveness and uniformity? In such situations, the choice of any one form may enable an organization to achieve one of its objectives but not the other. The plural form provides a partial solution to this apparent dilemma. Along with asking the question "make-or-buy?" scholars and practitioners need to ask a different question: "make-*or*-buy" or "make-*and*-buy"? Only by incorporating the processes of the plural form into theory will we be able to understand what configuration of arrangements is most effective.[3]

Recognizing the role of the plural form offers new insights into old problems. For example, it deepens our understanding of why tapered integration exists (that is, when firms conduct an activity internally *and* externally). Current theory suggests that the primary motivation for this arrangement is to enable easy switching from one source of supply to another, essentially ensuring against being exploited by a single source of supply (Scherer 1970; Porter 1980; Harrigan 1983). The plural form indicates that the reasons may be much more far-reaching. A recent study by Powell, Koput, and Smith-Doerr (1996), for instance, argues that a firm's capacity to learn hinges on engaging in the research process oneself—so as to appreciate the value of new knowledge—concurrent with being tied into networks of firms that are generating new ideas in similar fields of endeavor. Similarly, what researchers often view as a channel in transition from one form to another (Rangan, Corey, and Cespedes 1993) or a channel dominated by one form or the other (Monteverde and Teece 1982) may obscure a deeper underlying structure: the value of operating more than one structure. In all of these cases, what needs to be asked is whether the whole is greater than the sum of the parts.

Self-Correcting and Self-Renewing Organizations

The plural form highlights one way organizations may strengthen their capacity to correct and renew themselves. One of the most vexing challenges confronting managers is achieving control and innovation in a single structure. Burns and Stalker (1961) and Lawrence and Lorsch (1967) started a stream of research—contingency theory—predicated on the notion that certain organizational designs are effective for certain situations. Burns and Stalker argued, for example, that organic structures—characterized by informal webs of relationships, lateral communications, and fluid role structures—are required to generate new ideas, while mechanistic structures—embodied by task specialization, hierarchy, and vertical communication—are needed to ensure adherence to standards. The underlying premise is that these different activities can be specialized into different structures. But does that assumption hold true? Although company arrangements tend to be better at controlling units and franchise arrangements tend to be better at generating innovations (especially locally), even on those dimensions each benefits from the presence of the other—as we have seen, the effects of the additive, ratcheting, and mutual learning processes run in both directions. And in any event, the nature of the chain business requires that all units, company and franchise alike, have the capacity to maintain uniformity, respond locally, and be adaptable on a systemwide basis.

The plural form addresses this dilemma by using two different structures, doing roughly the same thing, to produce variety—the source of information for innovation and control—while providing mechanisms to ensure the adoption and maintenance of standard practices. Plurality keeps control processes fresh and enables an organization to correct itself and educate itself. Such capability depends on two primary features of the plural form: first, balancing the amount of similarity and difference between the two arrangements, and second, building processes that leverage the strengths of each arrangement. For a restaurant chain, the units obviously must be quite similar to preserve the trademark, but they also need to be similar so that valid performance comparisons can be made across units and structures. Indeed, the power of the plural form is derived from the built-in comparisons it makes possible. At the same time, there must be differences among units—in this case produced by the different ownership and management structures—so that variety is created. Rather than specialize innovation and control activities into entirely autonomous structures, the processes of the plural form capitalize on these similarities and differences to provide the organization with reinforcing sources of innovation and control.

Eccles and White (1986, 24) point out how these kinds of structures provide managers with potent indirect levers of control. Using the multidivisional firm as an example, they argue that the way profit centers are locked into a relationship with the market (the profit centers of other firms) and with hierarchies (the other profit centers within the firm) represents a powerful mode of control derived from the "enormous energies of self-reproducing social mechanisms such as interfaces." These interfaces, and the processes they enable, emerge as differently configured institutions that abut each other, constraining and influencing one another, much as we see in the plural form. These are areas where we rarely look to explain organizational performance (for an exception, see Padgett 1981). Yet if restaurant chains are any indication, it may be precisely at these interfaces, and in the configurations that produce them, that important outcomes are determined.

More broadly, the plural form offers an organization the kinds of contrasting perspectives that many scholars contend are critical to organizational effectiveness. Quinn and Cameron (1988, 302) have argued that "[h]aving multiple frameworks available is probably . . . the single most powerful attribute of self-renewing individuals and organizations." The multiple frameworks inherent in plural forms lead to a variety of differences in behavior and performance that encompass some of the fundamental dualities that organizations need to balance—stability and adaptability (Parsons 1951; Steers 1977), tight and loose control (Eccles and Crane 1988), goal-oriented rationality and "sensible foolishness" (March 1985), and single- and double-loop learning (Argyris and Schon 1978). Successful organizations, say these authors, embrace both attributes in each duality. By incorporating attributes from both sides, plural-form organizations may be able to escape the natural tendency of internal arrangements to ossify over time and external relationships to suffer from entropy by creating a built-in constructive tension between the parts. The plural form, then, may be integral to the long-term sustainability of these organizations.

ORGANIZATIONAL ALTERNATIVES:
AMBIDEXTROUS ORGANIZATIONS AND HYBRID FORMS

Ambidextrous and hybrid forms appear to offer similar attributes to the plural form. However, an ambidextrous organization—which involves switching from one form to another—is a quite different approach to obtaining both innovation and control. The hybrid form tries to create an arrangement that incorporates the best of the constituent arrangements, but I contend that such an effort is unlikely to be successful because it may dilute the strong elements of each form. In any case, creating hybrids may be impossible because elements of different forms may not fit together.

Ambidextrous Organizations

The common definition of ambidextrous organizations is that they possess the capacity to both maintain control and undertake revolutionary innovations (Wilson 1996; Duncan 1976; Tushman and O'Reilly 1997). Duncan argues that organic structures are needed to generate innovations, while mechanistic structures are required to implement them. This leads to a problem because no single arrangement can do both. Duncan suggests that organizations resolve this problem by becoming ambidextrous: adopting the form appropriate to where it is in the innovation process, switching when needed between organic and mechanistic structures. There is little evidence, though, that firms are able to do that (Daft 1982). Tushman and O'Reilly (1997) agree with this definition of ambidextrous organization but argue that firms may encompass both objectives by specializing structures for each purpose, with managers placing emphasis on one structure or the other at different points in time.

The underlying premise of ambidextrous organizations is that different structures are required for different circumstances. This line of argument builds directly on contingency theory, which argues that subunits of an organization need to be *differentiated* to fit their respective environments, and at the same time need to be *integrated* to achieve the organization's objectives (Lawrence and Lorsch 1967). The premise of the plural form is that different structures are used to do the same activities. Rather than being based on specialization, the plural form is predicated on the idea of redundancy and variety. Each of the constituent parts of the organization grapples with innovation and implementation, but they deal with them differently because each part embodies a different set of characteristics.

The plural form offers an intriguing alternative to the widely held view that the external variety in the environment needs to be matched with internal variety of structures and systems. In most theories of organization, internal variety is said to be achieved through specialization. My research shows that another way to obtain that variety is by having different kinds of structures in tension in the same organization, each generating different kinds of ideas.

Hybrid Forms

The increasingly competitive environment facing chain organizations has led chain operators to experiment with new organizational forms. Steven Reinemund, the CEO and president of Pizza Hut, described his vision of an ideal organization: "We want company people to be more like franchisees, and franchisees to be more like company people." When I probed what he meant by this comment, he illustrated his point: "We want a local perspective [a franchise characteristic], but when it comes time to make a decision we want to be able to go with it [a company characteristic]." Executives in several chains echoed Reinemund's comments, sometimes invoking other pairs of attributes such as combining "the control in the company unit with the effort of the franchisees." An executive vice-president in one chain stated that his long-range objective was to "have the exact same management structure on both the company and franchise sides of the business." To that end, company arrangements widened spans of control, installed more pay-for-performance compensation schemes, and preached the gospel of "empowerment." Franchise arrangements, on the other hand, re-wrote and tightened the franchise contract, routinized and formalized decision-making processes, and added more intensive monitoring mechanisms. In essence, people on both sides were proposing a hybrid form.

Like the Sirens of classical mythology, a hybrid form is an almost irresistible temptation, mainly because it seems so easy to achieve: combine the strengths and avoid the weaknesses of company and franchise arrangements, and the result—seemingly by simple addition and subtraction—will be a more effective organization. In practice, though, I contend that this approach will, at best, not work, and, at worst, may actually weaken the performance of a chain. First, efforts to hybridize an arrangement come at a cost: you dilute its distinctive strengths. Second, these forms may not be as malleable as they appear, so it may be impossible to obtain the benefits of one in combination with the other. In the following pages, I will discuss these drawbacks of hybrid arrangements in detail.

The Dilutive Effect of Hybrid Forms. Altering company and franchise arrangements to make them more like the other may have the deleterious effect of undermining each arrangement's original strengths. The potential loss in performance will be felt most critically if it compromises a chain's ability to meet the challenge of systemwide adaptation. A chain operator may relax its authority in the company arrangement to foster more local responsiveness, but that weaker central authority may inhibit its ability to field test, decide on, and implement an adaptation. Similarly, a chain operator may make the franchise contract more restrictive so as to implement adaptations more quickly, yet by doing so may prevent a franchisee from engaging in the constructive conflicts that strengthen the quality of decision making. Changing an arrangement to improve performance on one dimension may weaken an arrangement's performance on another.

Such tradeoffs are inevitable because the same organizational characteristic represents a strength on one dimension and a weakness on another. For example, the strong external market orientation of franchisees, coupled with their right to exercise choice over many systemwide adaptations, produces the constructive conflict that both improves decisions and slows the decision process. Similarly, the source of influence in the company arrangement—authority—enables the rapid execution of the decision and implementation stages while at the same time inhibiting challenges to decisions, which sometimes leads to the distortion of information. In an effort to avoid tradeoffs, firms may hedge the extent to which they alter the arrangements to avoid incurring the weaknesses of the other. But this strategy also makes it impossible to achieve the full benefits of both forms. For example, chain operators may increase the amount of a company manager's compensation that is based on financial performance to boost that manager's external market orientation. But the degree of incentive will still not be equivalent to a franchise situation, where the franchisee receives the full profit stream of the operation and can sell the business. And if more profound changes are made, then the result essentially recreates the other arrangement with both its strengths and weaknesses.

Along with prompting tradeoffs *within* each arrangement, changing an arrangement to a hybrid form may affect the performance of the *other* arrangement by altering the plural processes that shape its behavior and performance. Consider the systemwide-adaptation process. Assume that the chain operator shifted its source of influence from authority to persuasion in the company arrangement and permitted company managers more choice over whether to adopt a systemwide adaptation. This would change the demonstration and commitment effects that were central to persuading franchisees to implement a proposed adaptation. In the absence of these plural dynamics, the pace of implementation would almost surely slow (and chain executives already complained that it was too slow). Similarly, if the chain operator tightened the franchise contract so that franchisees generated less constructive conflict, then the chain would consequently depend more heavily on the less rich (and sometimes distorted) information produced by the company arrangement and would lose the benefit of postimplementation learning.

Inherent Limits to Creating a Hybrid Form. Chain operators may not need to worry about the tradeoffs and lost plural dynamics that accompany hybrids, since there may be inherent limits on the extent to which company and franchise arrangements can be reconfigured to perform like the other. At a micro level, certain organizational design features may be inherently linked or opposed. For example, in exchange for the capital of franchisees, which enhances local responsiveness, the chain operator must provide franchisees with at least some control over decision making, which slows the adaptation process: capital and control are linked together (Fama and Jensen 1983).[4] In other cases, some characteristics may be inherently opposed. For instance, the MIS linking restaurants to the central office may be inherently inconsistent with the communication of rich information, and more subtly may be incompatible with a manager's sense of autonomy.[5] These examples suggest that certain combinations of characteristics on which a hybrid might depend may be fundamentally incompatible and therefore impossible to implement.

The inherent limits to change in each arrangement also may result from the legal and normative frameworks within which each arrangement operates. Williamson (1991, 274) points out that hierarchical (company) and market (franchise) relationships are embedded in different legal regimes:

> The implicit contract law of internal organization is that of forbearance. Thus, whereas courts routinely grant standing to firms should there be disputes over prices, the damages to be ascribed to delays, failures of quality, and the like, courts will refuse to hear disputes between one internal division and another over identical technical issues. Access to the courts being denied, the parties must resolve their differences internally. Accordingly, hierarchy is its own court of ultimate appeal.

Based on this distinction, Williamson infers that replicating the characteristics of one arrangement in the other is inherently impossible:

> Accordingly, the reason why the market is unable to replicate the firm with respect to fiat is that market transactions are defined by contract law of an altogether different kind. There is a logic to classical market contracting and there is a logic for forbearance law, and the choice of one regime precludes the other. (p. 275)

Although Williamson then goes on—somewhat paradoxically—to "dimensionalize" governance structures across a continuum spanning from market to hierarchy, there is a considerable disparity between the modes of governance that may be supported by these different legal regimes.

Regardless of how the company arrangement is managed and organized, the fact remains that the chain operator (that is, the president, CEO, or any superior) has the right to the last word: the hierarchical superior is the "court of ultimate appeal." Simon (1976, 129) makes this point explicitly when he talks about the nature of authority in a hierarchy: "It is this 'right to the last word' which is usually meant in speaking of 'lines of authority' in administrative organization." But this is exactly what does *not* exist in the franchise arrangement, as Williamson (1991) points out. Conflicts are not ultimately settled by a decision of the chain operator, but instead the parties either work out a solution or appeal to third parties like the courts or arbitrators.[6] And in these cases the outcomes are not assured. While a zone of acceptance characterizes the relationship between the chain and local operators in the company arrangement, in the franchise arrangement that relationship may be better described as a zone of contest, where conflicts lead to negotiation. These different types of zones, predicated on distinct legal regimes, are fundamentally incompatible: a relationship cannot be governed by one party *and* governed by both parties.

A recent initiative by one chain operator in my study to transform its company arrangement to make it more "franchise-like" illustrates how the superior's right to the last word permeates the company arrangement. After buying back a large franchisee, this chain decided to operate the units as a separate company-owned operating entity. In just four months, though, the CEO told me that he had to intervene because local managers were making poor decisions: "They wouldn't use our personnel department for payroll, yet we were the cheapest. I told them I was going to send someone down there to find out what the problem was. They decided to switch after that." This course of events was repeated in another chain that attempted a similar initiative. Williamson (1985) notes that one of the most enduring characteristics of hierarchy is the managers' "propensity to manage." In the company arrangement, this propensity is amplified by the architecture of information, which provides detailed operating information to managers up and down the hierarchy, and a structure built around "roll-ups" of performance measures. Despite the expressed intention of executives to permit the autonomy of a local company entity, the superiors cannot resist intervening in its operation. The legal regime of forbearance coupled with the propensity of managers to manage make it extremely difficult, if not impossible, to make "company people like franchisees."

In contrast, the franchise contract restrains the chain operator from intruding into the franchisee's business. While the franchise contract is typically conceived of as specifying the rights and obligations of each party (Rubin 1978; Hadfield 1991), it serves another crucial function: it *inhibits* the chain operator's propensity to manage. Not only is the franchisee granted the sole right to make many decisions, but the areas of activity not specified by the contract are also outside the realm of the chain operator's dictate. Hence, the contract in essence protects the chain operator from itself by limiting its propensity to manage. Along with the specific provisions of the contract, its long-term nature (typically ten to twenty years) also protects franchisees from reprisals if they refuse to comply with the chain operator's recommendations.[7]

This analysis suggests that governance structures are not easily arrayed on a continuum spanning from high control to low control, from company-owned to franchise. The nature of hierarchy and contract may make each institution quite distinct, and efforts to move from one form to another may be an all-or-nothing proposition. This makes efforts to hybridize these arrangements extremely difficult and likely to meet with limited success.

Conclusion: Hybrid Arrangements. The tradeoffs among performance attributes, the lost plural processes, and the inherent limitations to altering each arrangement combine to affirm a simple but important point about the search for a hybrid form: managerial strategies that attempt to "have it all" in a single structure at best will be ineffective and at worse may harm performance. Organizations may be able to alter each arrangement to improve its performance, but the new arrangement (for instance, a hybrid company form) will not reach the same level of performance as the other (for instance, a franchise form) on the management challenges identified in this book. The primary argument in this book is clear: The benefits of the plural form are derived from the simultaneous operation and interaction of two distinct structures. Chain operators that pursue a strategy of hybridizing one arrangement (usually the company) while shifting the mix away from the other (usually the franchise) may be especially vulnerable to hampering the effectiveness of their organizations.

CONCLUDING THOUGHTS

This book has illuminated a new organizational structure: the plural form. While chain organizations are particularly hospitable to the processes of the plural form—since by definition chains have lots of units engaged in similar activities—there are a variety of other settings with similar features, as noted earlier. The underlying idea of redundancy and variety might also apply more broadly to any managerial activity that is discrete and can be separated to some extent from other tasks. Indeed, the ideas developed in this book have implications for the management of the variety of new forms populating the organizational landscape today like alliances, joint ventures, and outsourcing. Many observers of organizations have noted that these new forms have met with mixed success, and in fact, many organizations are reversing decisions that led them to build these new relationships. Many organizations oscillate between forms, shifting activities from inside the firm to outside and then back in again, searching for a perfect formula. Part of the problem is that people are not noticing the crucial role played by the architecture of relationships in the behavior and performance of these arrangements.

Practitioners and academics alike need to move beyond simple models that search for one best way to organize or that seek to identify the unique fit between certain conditions and certain organizational designs. We must entertain the notion that combinations of structures like the plural form offer attributes not available to any single arrangement. And we need to embrace the counterintuitive idea that redundancy and variety can be intertwined in ways that set in motion a powerful set of dynamics that promote self-correction and self-renewal.

The Literature on Owning or Franchising

Chain organizations are ubiquitous, yet three of the standard books that review the organizational-theory literature mention either chains or franchising only once (Pfeffer 1982; Perrow 1986; Scott 1987). However, there is an ample body of work that discusses why chains utilize different mixes of company and franchise units. The main limitation with this literature is that it focuses on the question of whether to own or franchise a unit, not on how they are managed once they are in place. Furthermore, the two main theoretical approaches that dominate this scholarship disagree about how company and franchise arrangements work and what key challenges they face.

First, *ownership redirection theory* predicts that chain operators will franchise early in their life cycle, a pattern that will be reversed in the direction of company ownership as the chain matures (Oxenfeldt and Kelly 1969; Hunt 1973; Caves and Murphy 1976).[1] Oxenfeldt and Kelly lay out the details of the argument: "[F]ranchising is advantageous to a successful franchisor mainly during the infancy and adolescence of the enterprise and even thereafter for the exploitation of marginal locations" (p. 69). They contend that early in a chain's life cycle, capital is in short supply, rapid growth to achieve economies of scale is critical, and knowledge about local conditions is scarce. Over time, the franchisor's capabilities and resources change, and it is able to overcome these deficiencies: "His capital position and ability to raise additional funds improve with success; some knowledge of local conditions is provided by his intimate contact with the franchisee; his ability to recognize key characteristics required of personnel . . . also grows" (p. 74). At this point, the key management problem facing the franchisor changes:

> Failure to get franchisees to adapt their actions to the franchisor's overall program can be very damaging to the success of those programs . . . (p. 72). [The franchisor] recognizes the need for a flexible and responsive organization through which he can implement policy changes rapidly to meet changing circumstances. One solution for him is to control all his franchise outlets directly (p. 75).

The logic predicts that as chains grow they will move in the direction of becoming mostly company-owned. In ownership redirection theory, franchising is a necessary evil on the way to the optimal form: a company-owned chain. Put another way, the desire for rapid growth leads initially to franchising, while the need for adaptability shifts the chain later toward company ownership.[2]

The *agency cost theory*, on the other hand, argues that monitoring costs are a central determinant of whether a unit will be under a company or franchise regime (Rubin 1978; Brickley and Dark 1987) and presents a more complex picture of each arrangement. The use of company and franchise units is explained by the different incentives, monitoring costs, and decision rights associated with each arrangement.[3] For example, Brickley and Dark (1987) argue that company managers need more monitoring than franchisees because managers receive salaries and therefore pose a risk of shirking. In contrast, franchisees internalize the consequences of their behavior because they receive the profit stream of their units and are also able to benefit from the value of the unit through its sale (subject to the approval of the franchisor). At the same time, franchisees also present an agency problem: free-riding. Because the franchisee benefits from the profits of a unit, he or she has an incentive to reduce quality. This behavior is prevented, the authors and others contend, by the franchisor's right to terminate the contract if it catches the franchisee cheating.[4] These different incentive and monitoring schemes lead, for example, to the prediction that company units will be located near corporate monitoring offices and that franchising will occur in more distant locations. In this theory, a chain's mix results mainly from the balancing of agency costs and benefits of company and franchise units as the chain seeks to maintain uniformity.[5]

Both theories find some support in the literature. Each argument, though, is based on different and even contradictory assumptions about how company and franchise arrangements work. The critical management problem facing chains in the ownership redirection argument is generating growth initially, followed later by the problem of adaptation. The critical management challenge posited by the agency cost argument is preventing behavior that damages uniformity: shirking (company) and free-riding (franchise). Neither theory addresses the problems posed by the other. Yet chains need to be able to manage all of these activities at once.

Furthermore, the basic assumptions about how each arrangement is managed also differ in the two theories. Implicit in the ownership redirection argument is the assumption that adaptation with franchisees is an almost intractable problem. In contrast, agency cost theory views adaptation as unproblematic. In their effort to explain *why* a chain operator uses company or franchise arrangements, these theories make conflicting assumptions regarding *what* chains are trying to achieve and *how* company and franchise arrangements serve those ends. One of the major contributions of this study is that it clarifies how these different ways of organizing are structured in practice.

Appendix B

The Research Design

The objective of this research was to develop a descriptive model of how chains are organized and managed to achieve their aims. My first step was to identify a set of plural-form restaurant chains that would be the subject of the study. I sought chains that were large (over 500 units), well-established (in business over ten years), and in sound financial condition (steady growth in revenue over the prior three years). My objective was to develop an understanding of the plural form, not at this early stage to discriminate between high and low performers, or between large and small firms. I also sought chains in the same basic business. Similarity was desirable because different businesses were likely to face different challenges, adding an unnecessary level of complexity to this investigation. Five firms that fit the criteria agreed to participate in the research: KFC (formerly known as Kentucky Fried Chicken), Pizza Hut, Hardee's, Jack in the Box, and Fishermen's Landing (a disguised name). Table 1-2 presents descriptive information on these five chains.

I conducted field work on the five chains from late 1989 to early 1991. I interviewed a vertical slice of the organization, starting with the chief executive officer and moving down the organization to restaurant managers and franchisees. In each chain, I began with a visit to the corporate headquarters and interviewed the CEO and key corporate staff involved in the management of the chain. I then visited a division office for each chain (except for Fishermen's Landing, which had a centralized structure) and interviewed key divisional staff, personnel who worked in the field and were responsible for company and franchise units, and individual restaurant managers and franchisees. Table B-1 lists the number of people I interviewed from each chain. The company category encompasses all people on the payroll of the corporation, regardless of whether they were involved with managing corporate, company-owned, or franchise activities. The franchise category includes only individual franchisees.

The interviews were unstructured and lasted from one to five hours. I

Table B-1   Distribution of People Interviewed, by Chain

Chain	Company Personnel	Franchisees
KFC	19	5
Pizza Hut	22	5
Hardee's	29	3
Jack in the Box	13	2
Fishermen's Landing	7	6
TOTAL	90	21

typically began by asking each person to describe the key ways the chain managed company and franchise units. The interview generally covered three broad topics: (1) the formal structures, systems, and processes used to manage units, (2) the key challenges of managing company and franchise units, and (3) the rationale for the particular mix of company and franchise units used by the chain. The responses were later augmented with data from several other sources. I was sometimes able to directly observe meetings involving both company people and franchisees: in one case, I attended an all-day regional marketing meeting where franchisees discussed and voted on corporate advertising proposals. I also spent five days on "field visits," joining company managers as they called on company and franchise units. Insights gleaned from these behavioral observations often stimulated new lines of inquiry for future interviews. Also, I interviewed elected representatives of the franchise group, in the four chains where such groups existed, to avoid hearing only the corporate point of view. In addition, data and documents from public sources and from the chains helped to clarify issues raised in the interviews. These multiple approaches helped to ensure the reliability and validity of the findings (Jick 1979).

The first phase of analyzing the data was to build case studies of each chain: identifying the key managerial structures, systems, and processes as well as highlighting gaps in the data that needed to be addressed in subsequent field visits. As I was fleshing out these cases, I sought to understand how the organization actually worked, not simply to describe the formal design. This was facilitated by interviewing a variety of people and by spending time with them on the job. For example, company executives and franchisees described the strategy-making process in ways that oftentimes only partially overlapped; both sides were needed to develop a complete picture of the process. At the conclusion of most interviews and in final visits to the field sites, I shared my preliminary findings. This added to my understanding of the management of chains and led to further refinements of the model.

The first drafts of these cases treated company and franchise arrangements separately. It became clear, however, that another analytic category was needed to explain the management of each arrangement: the role played by the other one. For example, when talking about managing the performance of units, practitioners commonly referred to the relative performance of company and franchise units; one arrangement was used to set the performance targets of the other. It was from this analysis that the underlying processes of the plural form began to emerge. As I began to compare how the five chains pursued uniformity and systemwide adaptation, the viability of the plural form became clear. I saw remarkably similar patterns across the chains. Throughout the research, practitioners frequently remarked that a mixture of company and franchise units made the chain stronger than an exclusive reliance on either one—indeed, that was one of the most intriguing leads that provoked this research. Yet people had difficulty specifying the actual processes that produced the advantage. The model that emerged from the data confirmed their point of view.

Appendix C

The Role of the Field Visit

The field visit was an integral element of the management of units that complemented the formal systems described in Chapter 5. Edwards (1979) argues that "personal control" is the oldest and simplest form of management, one especially suited to managing small and routinized production processes. For the chain restaurants I studied, field visits played the obvious role of helping ensure uniformity in company and franchise arrangements, but in addition such visits had a very different secondary function in each arrangement. In the company arrangement, the field visit focused local managers' attention on the details and generated a sense of excitement in an organizational environment that otherwise sparked little enthusiasm. In the franchise arrangement, the field visit was also a means of monitoring for uniformity, but it was conducted in a way to confirm the autonomy of the franchisee. The choreography of the field visit in the franchise arrangement led to what looked like an interaction between independent entities rather than people in different hierarchical positions. Nohria and Eccles (1992) argue that face-to-face interactions are where and when meanings are created and shared understandings are forged; that was certainly the case in the organizations I studied. In each arrangement, the face-to-face interactions provided an opportunity to create meanings that were crucial to the vitality and sustainability of each organization.

Field Visits in the Company Arrangement

In the case of chain organizations, area managers visited their restaurants at least once a week, and most of them said that they were in phone contact with each unit manager several times a week. The senior levels of the operations organization also had extensive contact with the personnel in the restaurants. Two division vice presidents I interviewed estimated that they spent at least three days a week in restaurants. The difficulty I had arranging interviews in all the chains due to managers being in the field reflected the allocation of their time. The typical field visit to a restaurant ranged from a few minutes (a brief chat with the manager) to a few hours (a formal evaluation), although short visits were more common than long ones. The morning I interviewed Todd Christianson, a district manager for Pizza Hut in Wichita, Kansas, I learned that he was scheduled to visit eleven restaurants in the afternoon with his boss, who had flown in from Chicago.

The activities that occurred on the typical field visit ranged from exhorting crew personnel to work harder and more effectively to conducting formal audits of the operation. As a division manager noted, "The AM and DM need to be in restaurants as much as possible and instill pride in their people." When I visited a restaurant with Ken Tyler of KFC the day after a field visit by an executive, Tyler reminded the unit manager that the vice-president had suggested moving a plant from the center aisle to the corner. The president of another chain and I visited a nearby restaurant for lunch and upon entering he noticed a deviation from the standard: the napkin holders were stacked on each other rather than positioned side by side. He slammed the holder into the correct position and called the manager over to tell him in harsh terms to "get it right." While perhaps not models of managerial etiquette, these vignettes illustrate that the field visit served the function of monitoring and managing the details of the operation.

The pervasive use of field visits as a management technique presented a puzzle: Why do chains rely heavily on senior executives to monitor and manage local restaurants in this way? In many respects their contribution to the management of a chain was ambiguous. Not only were formal monitoring systems already in place to serve this function but less costly personnel than senior people could easily have identified the problems with the details in a restaurant. Additionally, while field visits provided executives with a better understanding of local markets and operational issues, these operation people had little input into the decision-making processes that might have tapped that knowledge, as in the case of the marketing decisions described in chapters 6 and 7. In any case, the executives did not describe their visits as emphasizing those objectives. What, then, was the role played by the field visit in chains?

From what I observed, the field visit created a sense of excitement and purpose in local restaurants. A visit by an executive generated great anticipation at the local level: managers scoured restaurants, needed but neglected improvements were made, and managers coached their personnel on the standards. For example, Ken Tyler visited all of his units the day before the field visit to ensure that the restaurants were prepared. As the executives toured his territory, Tyler called ahead to the next restaurant to warn them of their impending arrival. While the field visit emphasized the importance of standards and uniformity, it was also an opportunity for local managers to transcend the everydayness of their jobs and meet a fresh challenge. These dynamics were magnified in proportion to the seniority of the visiting executive. Of course, field visits were sometimes viewed in less sanguine terms: "[They] are by far the most agonizing and awful part of my job," said one manager. But even this negative reaction is a variation from the monotony of the everyday management of the unit.[*]

Regardless of whether the local reaction to a field visit was positive or negative, it remained a significant event that fostered an attention to operational detail and pushed people to see things they may not have previously noticed. Tyler commented, "You don't want to screw up with some executive in your restaurant. We really make sure everything is right that possibly can be." While the difference between having an executive or a district manager monitor a restaurant may be minimal in terms of detecting actual deviations, the "observer effect" of a visit by an executive may motivate local managers to attend to the maintenance of uniformity more assiduously. More subtly, the field visit may heighten awareness of the multitude of rules that are usually taken for granted and shift people from a "mindless" to a "mindful" mode of thinking and acting (Langer 1989).

Field Visits in the Franchise Arrangement

The field visits by chain-operator personnel, usually the franchise consultant, followed a pattern of less intensive management compared to the company arrangement. The wide spans of control of the franchise consultant ensured that no unit was visited very frequently. In fact, I was once lost for half an hour with a franchise consultant who could not find the location of one of his franchisee's restaurants. Not only were visits less frequent, but their content varied considerably from the field visit in the company arrangement.

To begin with, a field visit in franchise arrangements was often conducted in the franchisee's office across a desk or a conference table. The meetings were initiated at the request of the consultant and scheduled at the convenience of the franchisee. If the meeting was in the restaurant, it occurred at a table in the restaurant. The meetings usually covered an array of topics

---

[*] Richard Sennett's excellent book on authority (1980) made the intriguing argument that strong negative feelings about a boss or an organization can sometimes create bonds of attachment to the authority figure that are as powerful and binding as those produced by affirmative acceptance of authority.

with the focus usually being on upcoming marketing events or particular issues facing a franchisee, which almost invariably revolved around adding units. The franchisee typically asked as many questions of the franchise consultant as the consultant did of the franchisee. While uniformity was one of the issues discussed, particularly if a deviation existed, it was addressed in the context of a broader discussion of the business. If an audit was part of the field visit, then these meetings occurred after the audit was completed.

The boundary separating the chain operator and the franchisee's business was subtly reinforced by the conduct of the field visit. Typically, after sitting down in the franchisee's restaurant, ordering something, and eating, the franchise consultant asked to "take a look around," which meant looking behind the counter of the franchisee's restaurant. During the course of several tours of restaurants, I never heard a consultant tell a franchisee or their employees to do anything even if a deviation was observed. The consultant might ask about an item—which of course drew attention to it—but there was no analogue to the manager in the company unit saying, "Do this; fix that." The franchise consultant sometimes explained a new marketing program or the operation of a piece of equipment, but it was always done in a nondirective way. The entire conduct of the field visit reinforced the understanding that this was the franchisee's business.

The follow-up to the field visit was almost always a written business letter that summarized the meeting and reviewed the issues addressed. The letter focused on the strengths and weaknesses of the franchisee's units and enumerated the action plans that were agreed upon; it documented agreements, obligations, concerns, and more generally, the tenor of the relationship. The formal letter provided a paper trail, which was important in the infrequent cases where a situation entered litigation. A subtle effect of the business letter was to reaffirm the nature of the chain operator–franchisee relationship as one between business partners.

The field visit in the franchise arrangement showed franchisees that the chain operator treated them as independent businesspeople. In a context where every unit was virtually identical, affirming the status of the franchisees through this kind of interaction was important. More generally, the multiple meetings that were held in the franchise arrangement may have had as much to do with providing an avenue for franchisees to feel independent as with the substantive contributions they made to the management of the chain. One franchisee who was a former company employee told me that "after becoming a franchisee, I talked to the top people. The president sometimes called me and once even visited to see how things were going." The field visit did not provide excitement in the same sense as in the company arrangement because the threat connected to the field visit was not as great. Still, it was a significant event that affirmed the independent identity of franchisees.

Notes

CHAPTER 1

1. For an excellent history of franchising in the United States, see Dicke (1992).

2. These data were obtained from Technomic, Inc., a leading consulting firm in the restaurant industry. The list was then cross-checked with rankings published annually in *Nation's Restaurant News* and *Restaurant Business*. The list includes chains that provide customers with a range of products that would constitute a meal. Chains based solely on specialty foods like cookies and ice cream are not included.

3. While the chains in my sample had encountered considerable success in the late 1980s, the mid-1990s have been a challenging time for them and the chain-restaurant industry in general. As the competitive environment has intensified, the fast-food business has had to confront a multitude of obstacles, including market saturation, higher food prices, and health-conscious eating trends that steered customers away from quick-serve restaurants. Throughout the 1990s, the growth in restaurants has outpaced the growth in sales, and the highly concentrated stores have begun to cut into one another's sales. During this era of heightened competition, the management challenges remain compelling objectives for the chains in this sample, as well as for the chain industry as a whole.

CHAPTER 2

1. Steers (1977) enumerates a list of general requirements facing all organizations that echo the four challenges noted here.

2. I discuss this difference in Chapter 1. The U.S. Department of Commerce (1987) makes a similar distinction in its annual survey of chain organizations that utilize franchises.

3. ADVO, the largest direct-mail market-research agency in the United States, obtained this data as an outside consultant for a private company ("When They Eat Out, Most Consumers Request" 1996).

4. Specialization is viewed by scholars as a product of several factors: achieving economies of scale (Chandler 1962; Williamson 1975), managing internal and environmental uncertainties (Thompson 1967; Pfeffer and Salancik 1978), controlling workers (Marglin 1974), and obtaining efficiency (Taylor 1911).

5. The addition of delivery services and drive-through windows are two ways chains try to overcome this constraint. Much of the growth in the chain-restaurant

industry and the chains I studied can be attributed to the addition of these features (Emerson 1990).

6. An important reason why Au Bon Pain, a Boston-based bakery chain, saturated urban markets with its stores was that closely clustered stores advertised themselves and each other. "We've never spent a penny on advertising," said the chain's president (Alexander 1989).

7. See Emerson (1990) for a description of the dynamics of each of these market segments.

8. For a general picture of the fast-food industry in the 1980s, see Emerson (1982), McCarthy (1990), Romeo (1990), and Deutsch (1988).

9. An important qualification needs to be made here. For some major chains, international unit additions remain a crucial engine of growth (U.S. Department of Commerce 1987; McIntyre 1992). The argument made in this chapter relates to the dynamics of the U.S. marketplace.

CHAPTER 3

1. For a discussion of the franchise contract and how it differs from practice, see Macauley (1963), Macneil (1978, 1980), and Hadfield (1991).

2. For scholars that argue that the two arrangements vary mainly in terms of incentives and are otherwise similar, see Rubin (1978), Brickley and Dark (1987), and Norton (1988a, 1988b).

3. Resorting to termination, or even threatening it, fundamentally changed the relationship, said Cranor. "It would be like a husband coming home and saying I want a divorce. No matter what happens afterward, the relationship will never be the same." Some people went so far as to say that even a reference to the contract could contaminate the relationship. Dave Hoban, an area director of franchising at Hardee's, said, "You know you're in trouble if you have to refer to the contract." Macauley (1963) observed a similar dynamic when he found that references to the formal contract were sometimes interpreted by one's partner as a lack of trust.

4. This point has been made before, but it continues to be relegated to a footnote in the existing literature on franchising. A small but growing literature, however, explores the relational aspect of long-term contracts. Macauley's finding (1963) that contractual disagreements were rarely litigated remains true today. Macneil (1978, 898) builds on Macauley and argues that two norms govern "relational contracts" like the franchise contract: "(1) harmonizing conflict within the internal matrix of the relation . . . and (2) preservation of the relation." Over time, says Macneil, the relationship takes on "more and more of the characteristics of minisocieties and ministates" (p. 898). This perspective is applied to franchise contracts by Hadfield (1991, 957), who emphasizes the inevitable incompleteness of franchise contracts:

> The contract supplies the starting points: The frequency of payments, expected training levels, and advertising responsibilities. It also supplies boundaries: some supplies must be forthcoming, some sales must be made and royalties paid, and some distances must be preserved between outlets. However, the incompleteness of franchise contracts consists in either the absence or the intense ambiguity of these starting points and boundaries: How

expensive can promotions be? How often can outlet refurbishing be required? What measures to boost sales can be required? The franchise contract sketches out the bare outline, one which is then filled in by the ongoing balance of the beliefs, powers, and incentives that comprise the relationship.

This description captures the nature of the chain operator–franchisee relationship.

5. Stinchcombe (1990) argues that contracts can serve the same functions as a hierarchy. The point I am making here is a bit different. I contend that some aspects of the chain operator–franchisee relationship are not circumscribed by the contract at all, but rather are governed by norms that sometimes even contradict the contract. See Macauley (1963), Macneil (1980), and Hadfield (1991) for discussions of this alternative view of contract dynamics.

6. One of the other impediments to relying more heavily on bonuses was the hierarchy of authority used in the company arrangement. A pay-for-performance system at the local level could easily lead to subordinates making more money than their superiors. No company arrangement I studied had a system that enabled subordinates to make more than superiors. The powerful impetus to correlate earnings to hierarchical position is described by Frank (1985).

One benefit of the franchise relationship is that it escapes this dynamic by creating a relationship that legitimized this inversion—franchisees usually made more than the franchise consultants—because the franchisee was defined as an independent businessperson. Pfeffer and Baron (1988) report that one of the reasons firms use outside contractors is to avoid the constraints on pay imposed by a hierarchy.

7. Stern and El-Ansary (1988) describe the franchise arrangement in similar terms when they say that franchisees ratify the decisions of the channel leader.

8. See Zuboff (1988) for a detailed discussion of how information technology can create an "information panopticon."

9. The most obvious place that information might be distorted was the reporting of revenue that was the basis of the royalty payment from the franchisee to the chain operator. None of the chains I studied reported that this was a problem, though, and they cited two reasons for this. First, the economic benefit of underreporting revenue was viewed as not enough to risk cheating. For example, underreporting revenue by $100,000, a significant amount, would produce a savings of only $4,000 to the franchisee (4 percent of the revenue would be saved in the royalty payment). A $100,000 underreporting, though, was risky because chain operators were knowledgeable about the relationship between trade areas and revenue, so such gaps were likely to attract someone's notice.

The second factor that inhibited the underreporting of revenue was that there were several other places where the "real" revenue number might appear. To begin with, if the franchisee bought supplies from the chain operator—which most did (see Chapter 5)—then the simple relationship between inputs and outputs could be examined. In at least one chain I studied, it routinely matched these numbers to catch discrepancies. On top of that, the contribution to the advertising funds by each franchisee was based on their revenue. These numbers were often available to the other local participants in the marketing cooperative. Accordingly, a franchisee's local peers, who often could see for themselves how the business was doing, would also notice if reported revenue deviated from what they observed. All of these factors made the underreporting of revenue a relatively small problem in the chains I studied.

10. Nohria and Eccles (1992) note the complementarity that exists between face-to-face interactions and electronically mediated exchanges in network organizations. The same complementarity existed in chains, although only the franchise arrangement could be described as analogous to a network. Their argument bears quoting at length:

> [I]ssues of uncertainty, ambiguity, and risk—the daily fare of a network organization—are difficult to address through electronically mediated-exchange. Effective network organizations also require the kind of rich, multidimensional, robust relationships that can be developed only through face-to-face interactions. Thus electronically mediated exchange cannot and should not replace all face-to-face interaction. However, we do not wish to suggest that there is no role for the former in the network organization. Electronically mediated exchange can increase the range, amount, and velocity of information flow in a network organization. But the viability and effectiveness of this electronic network will depend critically on an underlying network of social relationships based on face-to-face interaction. (pp. 289–290)

The plural-form chain organizations I studied displayed both types of information exchange. However, unlike network organizations, the chains specialized the two flows into different structures: the company arrangement engaged in electronically mediated exchanges and the franchise arrangement in face-to-face exchanges.

In Chapter 8, I offer an argument for why these flows are and should be specialized, at least in chain organizations. To summarize, I concluded from my study that electronically mediated exchanges were incompatible with the face-to-face exchanges that produced rich, specific, and accurate information. The use of MIS *itself* shaped people's feelings of autonomy (highlighted by the quote in the text about what it meant to own one's own business). More subtly, the use of MIS may shape the management of chains by affecting the decision-making process because the "hard" numbers often drive out the "soft" face-to-face exchanges. The consequent loss of meaningful personal interaction may weaken the decision-making process.

11. The language used by executives to refer to the franchise arrangement was revealing: they called it the "franchise community." This reflected the relational nature of the structure.

12. A more useful distinction might be between franchisees who could manage the units themselves, and those who were of a size where an area manager was necessary. My data do not allow for such a fine-grained analysis, but let us assume that, like the company arrangement, the need for hierarchy emerged at about 6 units per area manager. In my sample, the numbers of units under such a regime ranged from 1,249 units at KFC (representing 35 percent of the franchise units) to only 8 units at Fishermen's Landing (representing 2 percent of the franchise units). Even under this assumption, the vast majority of franchise units operate within minichains.

13. See, for example, Brickley and Dark (1987) and Norton (1988a). One industry

publication estimates that the restaurant industry's thirty-six largest franchisees own 5,639 restaurants ("Leading Franchisees" 1989).

14. Like company managers who were promoted, franchisees moved away from local markets as they added units and built organizational infrastructure beneath them. Even with this phenomenon, though, the franchise arrangement had people with more experience and longer tenure much closer to local markets than was the case in the company arrangement. It is also worth noting the different ways company managers and franchisees "grew up and away" from their local markets. The company arrangement forced managers to leap from one unit to six units (from restaurant manager to area manager), a jump that many people remarked was a big one and sometimes led to performance problems. A franchisee's growth was not so "lumpy"—the franchisee added one unit at a time. An interesting empirical study would be to assess the effects of these two patterns of growth and professional development on performance.

15. An inescapable limit to size may result from the connection between the maintenance of personal relationships and the number of relationships. While a chain operator can add franchise consultants to work with franchisees, this solved only part of the management problem. Franchisees often wanted to deal with a peer and only rarely did they view the franchise consultant as such. Instead, a peer was the person at or near the top of the chain-operator hierarchy. This definition of a peer meant that *by definition* it was confined to just a few people in the hierarchy. Given that this peer individual or peer group can manage effectively only a limited number of relationships, it follows that whereas hierarchy can keep adding units and proliferating itself, the franchise arrangement cannot. Multi-unit franchising does, however, enable the franchise arrangement to increase the number of units per relationship, which permits the arrangement to grow larger than would otherwise be possible.

16. The use of company people was also driven by a practical consideration: the paucity of qualified prospective franchisees that had both capital and experience operating a restaurant. The CEO of one chain highlighted a conundrum his chain faced: "People with enough money to become a franchisee usually don't want to run a restaurant." While company people rarely had the required capital, the chain operator or a passive investing partner often assisted them in buying the franchise.

CHAPTER 4

1. Franchisees are typically required by contract to spend a fixed percentage of revenue on advertising, so the addition of a franchise unit automatically added to the pool of funds available for advertising. The chain operator usually used the same percentage to establish its advertising budget for company units.

2. Marketing researchers have studied site-location decisions (see Ghosh and McLafferty 1987; Zeller, Achabal, and Brown 1980). Kaufmann and Rangan (1990) present an interesting model that highlights the advantages and disadvantages of adding new units by noting that a new unit may draw consumers away from existing units, but the addition heightens the visibility of the brand which, under some conditions, counteracts the first effect.

3. For evidence of the dismissal of the significance of multi-unit franchisees, see Brickley and Dark (1987), Norton (1988b), and Hadfield (1991). For an exception to this pattern, see Zeller, Achabal, and Brown (1980), Kaufmann and Dant (1996), and Bradach (1995), who analyze the efficiency properties of growth strategies using all three sources of growth.

4. The limits on growth imposed by the size of the existing organization has been remarked on in the organizational literature. Penrose's argument (1980, 49) about the constraints on organizational growth captures exactly the dynamic at work here: the "services available from the existing managerial group limit the amount of expansion that can be planned at any time because all plans for expansion absorb some of the services available from this group, and the larger and more complex the plans the more services will be required to digest and approve them on behalf of the firm."

5. In all five chains, the franchisees typically used their own capital to build the unit. In some chains, the chain operator owned the land and buildings and leased them to the franchisees. While not common, this latter arrangement is used by some major companies such as McDonald's and Dunkin' Donuts. In these cases, the capital-constraint argument for using franchisees is clearly disconfirmed since franchisees are not the source of the capital.

6. Norton (1988a) posits that one of the benefits of franchising is that people self-select themselves to be franchisees. His study builds on Hallegan's interesting argument (1978) that in situations involving uncertain information—like the quality of a franchisee—a contract can serve as a screening mechanism that encourages efficient self-selection and reduces the burden on chain operators to obtain costly information on quality. Hallegan's empirical case is built on sharecropping, where the interdependence among actors is low. In the case of franchising, the need for uniformity creates interdependencies that must be managed. As we will see, it is not necessarily the case that a chain operator would want all the people interested in joining the chain.

7. See Emerson (1990) for evidence of people's increasingly negative perceptions of the fast-food industry.

8. In a survey taken at a "Franchise Exposition," which provided people with information about franchise opportunities, Bradach and Kaufmann (1991) found that on average attendees were considering 2.2 types of businesses—for example, restaurants and cleaning services. Further complicating the issue was the fact that 84 percent of the people were also considering the possibility of operating an independent nonfranchise business.

9. The desire of the franchisees to build their own businesses often meant that they would take over the overhead functions otherwise provided by the chain operator, like training. While the use of separate trainers could conceivably diminish uniformity, this risk appeared minimized in the cases I observed because franchisees usually relied heavily on the company's training material. The franchise simply wanted "control over my own business," as one franchisee put it. The hidden benefit to the chain operator was that franchisees paid for activities that the chain operator would have otherwise provided—essentially, part of the overhead burden was shifted to the franchisees.

10. Despite the importance of the site-location decision to the success of a chain,

agency theorists have ignored this aspect of chain management (Rubin 1978). It would seem, though, that this decision would fit well with the agency-theory arguments that contend that efficient organizational structures join decision rights with relevant information (Jensen and Meckling 1991).

11. Shane (1996) makes the point. He argues chains utilize franchisees as a way to overcome the managerial limits to company-owned growth.

12. Kaufmann and Rangan (1990) argue that chain operators must balance the advantages that accrue to the system from an intensive location strategy with the disadvantages to an existing store's sales that might develop due to the opening of a new outlet. The authors suggest that franchisors must "compare the potential revenue gains with the method of managing system conflict. One method of managing conflict is to calculate the amount of additional advertising necessary to overcome the effects of spatial competition" (pp. 168–169). Chapter 7 discusses in more detail the conflicts of interest that emerge between franchisees and chain operators.

13. The arguments presented to this point reveal the complexity of trying to explain the mix. The company "seeding" strategy leads to the prediction that markets will tilt heavily toward franchise dominance. The "company-controls-the-market" strategy suggests that company units would be a majority in local markets. The incremental nature of growth further complicates these dynamics since at any given time some units are at the frontier of a chain—and are therefore remote and likely to be franchised—while over time the frontier is extended and what were once remote units may fall into the geographic center of the chain and be likely to be company-owned. The point is that the dynamics of growth are multifaceted and change over time.

14. It is worth noting that this pattern contradicts theories that emphasize capital as the motivation for franchising (see, for example, Oxenfeldt and Kelly 1969).

15. Further confirmation of this notion came from one CEO who observed, "Our problems come with the old-timers who really don't have any interest in growing. There isn't much we can do to move them."

16. Klein (1980) makes a similar argument when he claims that an important reason why franchisees do not deviate from the standards and free-ride on the trademark is that they do not want to lose the right to open more units. Klein also notes that a chain's desire to sell franchises motivates chain operators to manage existing units effectively—that is, accomplish the other management challenges—because otherwise the price prospective franchisees would be willing to pay for a franchise would decline. Although ignored in his argument, the plural form provides a compelling reason for why a chain operator would protect and maintain the trademark: like franchisees, the chain operator that owns units wants to ensure the long-term viability of the enterprise.

CHAPTER 5

1. See, for example, Burns and Stalker (1961), Lawrence and Lorsch (1967), and Thompson (1967).

2. The way Jack in the Box implemented its mystery-guest program also reflected the chain's emphasis on anonymity. Kevin Purtell, a senior QCS&F specialist who

trained the mystery guests, said that "We train people to be as discreet as they can be." In the past, mystery guests often were former assistant restaurant managers and managers, which created a problem because sometimes employees recognized them. In January 1990, the chain implemented a program to hire and train inspectors on ninety-day contracts to reduce the problem of detection. Purtell said that the initial solicitations for people to fill these positions resulted in applications from musicians, teachers, housewives, students, and retired people. The desire to obtain an accurate (and anonymous) picture of how the units performed led to such management strategies.

3. Controlling the controllers ran even deeper in the mystery-shopping program. KFC used both corporate mystery shoppers who were directed out of the corporate headquarters, along with third-party vendors of this service. McCain emphasized that "We train and test the third-party people continuously to make sure that their evaluations are correct." The emphasis on control and on obtaining valid data extends to evaluating the evaluators.

4. The similarity of tasks across hierarchical positions was vividly illustrated in a document from one of the chains that showed the "Field Success Profiles" for each position in the company hierarchy. It listed the skills, abilities, attributes, and knowledge required of people filling the positions of area manager, district manager, and regional manager. Notably, each position description was an exact duplicate of the next lower position except for bold type that identified areas of difference. A review of each page showed a field of regular type, with the bold type reserved primarily for the substitution of the words "district" for "area," and "region" for "district." The job descriptions for all the positions were very similar.

5. Eccles and Crane (1988) describe this dynamic in the investment-banking industry. Similarly, Blau (1963, 45) observed the reversal of ends and means in a public bureaucracy: "Indices are not perfectly related to what they purport to measure. Since interviewers were interested in maximizing their 'figures,' they tried to do so by various means." March and Simon's review (1958) of several classic works on bureaucracy highlights the unanticipated consequences of bureaucratic control. The feedback loops they identify—such as problems with performance leading to tighter control, which in turn exacerbates the performance problems—resemble the feedback loops observed here.

6. Mystery-shopping programs may provide a subtle but important benefit to the company arrangement. These programs may be gamed precisely because they can be easily interpreted as games—quite like the game of hide and seek. Mystery-shopping programs, and the machinations devised to game them, may break the monotony of an otherwise routine job by adding, well, mystery. The lengths people will go to to add meaning and excitement to their jobs is perhaps best revealed by Donald Roy's classic study (1960) of how factory workers break the monotony of their jobs by dividing the day into different periods like "banana time." He argues that job satisfaction was largely derived from these games and the social interactions associated with them. Games of this sort also may divert employees' attention away from fundamental issues surrounding the treatment and management of employees, a dynamic observed by Burawoy (1979) in a factory setting. Appendix C argues that the field visit by executives to local units served a similar purpose.

7. The latter score reported for the company was the average of the first wave of audits after the program was reinstituted. The franchisees in this chain continued to purchase the mystery-shopping service, so it was impossible to compare the impact of halting the audits on both arrangements.

8. One hypothesis for the different usage is that mystery shopping may too closely symbolize bureaucracy and control, which is inconsistent with the identity of franchisees as independent businesspeople. Mystery shopping is the most covert means of evaluation available to the chain operator, and it may be difficult to keep this mechanism from being perceived as anything other than a control mechanism. The mystery-shopping mechanism may also be too intrusive a method to use across a nonhierarchical border; it is an activity over which the franchisee has no control, which vitiates the independence of the franchisee. Appendix C notes that franchise consultants rarely entered the "back end" of a franchisee's restaurant without first asking permission. In that context, mystery shoppers would be inconsistent with the norms governing the relationship.

9. Since this research was completed, Pizza Hut has implemented a program wherein franchisees submitted quarterly profit-and-loss statements in a standard format that enabled comparisons between units.

10. Walton and Hackman (1986) describe two management strategies used by groups that map on the company and franchise arrangements. First, *control strategy organizations* are dominated by "top-down controls, narrowly defined jobs, and close supervision." Second, *commitment strategy organizations* "seek to foster high member commitment and the greatest feasible self-management." The use of both strategies by most chain organizations indicates the range of choice available to chain operators in terms of organizational design, and warns scholars against using simple deterministic models to explain these phenomena.

11. The difference between the two arrangements may have also existed at the level of the individual as well as the system. Langer's theory of "mindfulness" (1989) states that highly specific rules—as are found in the company arrangement—often encourage people to quit thinking actively, which may necessitate the use of more rules and standards that in turn exacerbates the problem. On the other hand, franchisees engaged more "mindfully" in their work because their work was not rewarded based on a narrow set of performance measures but rather was a function of a complex set of management tradeoffs—made by them—that led to their ultimate reward—profit. The mindfulness of franchisees may account in part for the similar level of uniformity compared with company units despite fewer and less intense bureaucratic mechanisms.

12. The existing literature asserts that a primary problem with franchisees is that they have incentives to free-ride on the trademark by providing lower quality and services, which redounds to their benefit, while the consequent cost of lost patronage is borne by the chain as a whole (assuming nonrepeat customers). Assuming this hypothesis is true, a multi-unit franchisee internalizes more of the costs of free-riding because the lost patronage is likely to fall on his or her units, which are usually located in geographic clusters. This subtle argument, coupled with those above in the text, make it clear that multi-unit franchisees need to be incorporated in any analysis of uniformity.

CHAPTER 6

1. An excellent example of these different approaches to accomplishing local responses was described in Chapter 4 in the comparison of the ways company and franchise arrangements add units. Franchisees engaged in these activities locally, while the company arrangement relied on specialized staff and senior executives to approve decisions in this area. The focus in this chapter is on ongoing operating decisions, but it is important to recognize that this pattern extends beyond these decisions.

2. Kaufmann (1989) notes the centrality of this problem to chain organizations when he discusses the tradeoffs between using a standardized product in all units versus adapting products to fit local markets. He argues that in the first case the product does not match all markets but the uniform format is maintained, while in the second case the reverse is true. This tradeoff presents chain operators with the problem of deciding how to make the tradeoff. I return throughout this chapter to examining how the chain operator dealt with this tradeoff in each arrangement.

3. The exception to this statement were market tests of proposed systemwide product introductions. This created an appearance of a local variation, but these variations were temporary and were not viewed as local responses. I discuss this in more detail in the next chapter.

4. Thompson (1967) points to the logic of this organizational design and the use of specialized structure when he argues that organizations must buffer their "core technology" from the vicissitudes of external shocks. The company arrangement is organized with the same basic idea in mind, with the operation of the restaurant viewed as the core. The limits to this approach will be discussed later in this chapter.

5. Hayek (1945) made a similar argument in his critique of centralized economies.

6. The legal status of setting prices for advertising purposes was vague to practitioners. One rule of thumb applied, however: no discussion of product price points between franchisees and the chain operator was allowed in the co-op meeting. The company proposed a price point and it was voted on. Of course, prior to the meeting informal discussions with individuals forged a consensus about a proposed price.

7. The training of franchisees was another service provided by the chain operator. The chain operator encouraged franchisees to use the chain's training programs, and by not charging franchisees for it, attendance increased and presumably problems with uniformity declined. Listen to one franchisee extol the benefits of the chain's training program: "It is free. They teach you how to do everything, and there is a way to do everything." This arrangement clearly was a benefit to both the franchisee and the chain operator.

8. Interestingly, Krueger's study (1991) of labor costs in fast-food chains found that on average, a company unit paid lower wages than a franchise unit. More research needs to be done to understand how the wage rate and the amount of labor vary in these two contexts.

9. An important avenue for future research is to assess these criteria and determine how they work, since they provide a window onto the chain operator–franchisee relationship and constitute a key element of a chain's strategy.

10. Chain operators made little distinction between applying for permission to deviate from the standard format and applying for the right to test an idea that deviates from the standard format. This ambiguity may not be accidental. "Testing"

enabled the chain operator to redefine what might otherwise be called deviations and thereby avoid conflict.

11. Local responses not only affected the performance of the franchise arrangement, but they also played a role in forging the identity of franchisees as independent businesspeople. The significance of local decision making in the creation of an independent identity was vividly apparent in the quotes of franchisees in two chains:

> I am an independent owner, but the company is only a phone call away. They provide staff services but operations is the lifeblood of the business and that is what I have control over.

> I am an independent businessperson, and I make my own decisions on pricing, labor, and suppliers, and somewhat on advertising, although that gets into the image [which is the province of the chain operator].

Mike Walters, a Fishermen's Landing franchisee who had previously worked for the company for fifteen years, elaborated on these sentiments: "I'd been running [company] restaurants for fifteen years so this was essentially the same. The difference is that you're an independent businessperson; you're on your own." He offered several examples of what his new role entailed: he negotiated his own group medical plan, did his own financial statements for his business, had been sued twice, and made "lots of operational decisions." Along with enabling effective responses to local conditions, the local decision making in the franchise arrangement was an integral part of a franchisee's identity as an independent businessperson.

12. This is an excellent illustration of "satisficing" (Simon 1976). Rather than search for the optimal solution to the problem of generating a local response, the franchisee settles on a satisfactory solution.

13. This pattern of transactions does not fit neatly in existing treatments of supplier relationships, although it has some of the characteristics of the mandated market-based transfer pricing arrangements described by Eccles (1985). It appears that the plural arrangement has better performance characteristics than mandated market-based transfers. In the plural form, the market is manifest in the actual choices of franchisees and is not the subject of interpretation and negotiation between divisional managers as is the case with mandated market-based transfers.

In another article, Eccles and White (1988) argue that the seeming incongruity between mandatory transfers and market-based pricing serves the important function of alerting the chain's executives to potential problems. When costs and prices drift outside the bounds of the external market, then conflict between the exchange partners ensues, which eventually is brought to the attention of the chain's executives. This self-monitoring system is activated when disjunctions occur between the internal and external markets. The plural form provides a simpler and continuous measure of the internal supplier's performance: the percentage of franchisees using its services.

CHAPTER 7

1. The existing literature on chains has largely ignored this process. It typically assumes that the chain operator decides on adaptations and uses administrative fiat to implement them (Stern 1971; Rubin 1978). But franchisees are not so easily moved. This literature is also limited, as is the broader economics of organization

literature (Williamson 1975, 1985, 1991; Rubin 1978; Brickley and Dark 1987), by its focus on only the later two stages of the process. By incorporating the dynamics of the entire process—including the first two stages—it is possible to develop a much deeper understanding of why different governance structures exist. Only by including all the steps of the process in the analysis will we gain an understanding of the relationship between organizational design and adaptation.

2. Steven Reinemund, the CEO of Pizza Hut, described the role of the chain operator in similar terms: "With franchisees, the rub is that they worked long and hard to get where they are. It is their business and they have a lot invested in it. Therefore, we can only suggest ideas and not dictate them. On the other hand, we are paid to make decisions. We are the experts."

3. As noted in Chapter 4, Klein (1980) also points out that the difference in interests is reduced if the chain operator seeks to sell more franchises, since the attractiveness of a franchise to buyers is based on its earning potential.

4. In the previous chapter I argued that the quality of the staff department may vary depending on whether company units are present in a chain, but here I want to set that nuance aside.

5. The role prescription of the chain operator made it important that the chain operator maintain the perception that it was leading the process. One reason the chain operator may have excluded franchisees from the process was to ensure that the perception was preserved that the chain operator was contributing to the process and that franchisees were getting something in return for the royalty.

6. In his book on the history of the McDonald's chain, Love (1986) describes the development of the Filet-O-Fish sandwich, which exemplifies this process. A McDonald's franchise in Cleveland was losing Catholic consumers on Friday evenings due to the absence of a nonmeat meal on the menu. Borrowing an idea from a competitor, the franchisee added a fish sandwich to the menu. After extensive haggling with the chain operator about whether he was permitted to continue to serve the product (he already was serving it by the time the chain operator found out), the chain eventually tested it, refined it, and added it to the standard menu.

7. Greg Collins, a franchisee at Fishermen's Landing, recounted how in the 1970s he experimented with a chicken-fried steak. Knowing it was a violation, Collins would take the item off the menu when executives visited his restaurants. Much to Collins's surprise, on one visit the president of the chain pulled him aside and asked him what volume the steak was doing. Collins conceded that it was doing only fairly. Shortly after that Collins received a letter asking him to stop selling the item, but again this was an instance of a deviation providing information about a new product idea.

8. Both perspectives may possess a grain of truth. If we assume that franchisees are more risk-averse than the company, then we might reasonably suppose that franchisees would be less likely to generate revolutionary—risky—adaptations. However, because franchisees stand outside the hierarchy of authority they may be more likely to generate frame-breaking ideas. Also, franchisees may simply generate more ideas, which increases the probability that they will generate the innovative ones.

9. One solution to this tension is to allow for some local variation on the menu. This topic was discussed in Chapter 6. The risk associated with menu variation is similar to the risk related to quality deterioration: the trademark may be weakened

when the customer's expectations are not met (Caves and Murphy 1976). The cost of customer confusion was minimized if customers frequented restaurants within the same market area, but nonetheless the issue of local and regional variation is one that vexed chain operators, who generally felt that it diluted the trademark. This complex issue will not be resolved here, but it is important to note that it may not be necessary or desirable for all new products to be adopted systemwide.

10. Ironically, another franchisee in that same chain told me "the company suffers paralysis from analysis—they test things to death." The diversity of perspectives offered by franchisees in itself poses a formidable challenge to the chain operator in the systemwide-adaptation process.

11. Levitt and March (1990) offer an interesting conceptualization of organizational learning that highlights the potential advantage of utilizing knowledge gleaned in these two different ways. At each of their stages of the learning process—learning from direct experience, interpretation of experience, organizational memory—they describe different strategies that can be loosely mapped on the company and franchise arrangements. For example, the authors distinguish between "trial and error experimentation" and "organizational search" as alternative mechanisms for learning from experience. The franchise arrangement offers the former; the company arrangement, the latter. In another instance, the authors note: "The experiential lessons of history are captured by routines in a way that makes the lessons, but not the history, accessible to organizations and organization members who have not themselves experienced this history" (p. 16). While this was true for the company arrangement with its turnover of people (see Chapter 3), the franchisees usually had long tenures with the chain, so they could draw on history as they assessed new situations and considered changes to the routines. Using the language of the authors, company and franchise arrangement offered "alternative routes to intelligence."

12. Until 1990, Pizza Hut had a voting scheme based on one vote per entity in a market. Each franchisee, regardless of the number of units, had one vote, and if the company participated in the market, regardless of the number of units, it too had one vote. Additionally, each market created its own voting schemes so in some markets a simple majority ruled, in others a two-thirds majority was required, and in still others the company could veto the decisions of the advertising cooperative. These features of the Pizza Hut system were an artifact of the negotiations that concentrated on convincing franchisees to join the advertising cooperatives and contribute funds to them.

13. Along with the difference in the mix, another reason for the different institutional design was that KFC and Pizza Hut created local co-ops *after* the initial contract was signed. Executives in those chains explained that the only way to get franchisees to agree to contribute additional funds for advertising was to give them a voice in the advertising process. At Jack in the Box the initial franchise contract included a provision that stated that franchisees had to contribute money to the advertising cooperatives.

14. The commitment strategy is related to Williamson's argument (1985) about the use of credible commitments to preserve a bilateral relationship. He argued that "hostages"—for example, the reciprocal exposure of specialized assets—can serve as a means to stabilize an exchange. When the chain operator owns units, it is effectively providing a hostage to franchisees. Both the chain operator and the franchisees

have invested in specialized assets whose value, at least to some extent, is contingent on working together to preserve and develop a shared identity.

15. These data raise an important theoretical point. Williamson (1985) argues strongly that one of the benefits of hierarchy is the full and accurate information it provides decision makers. Yet the executives in all the chains I studied emphasized that franchisees were a vital source of information, and one that was not duplicable in the company arrangement. "An owner will always pay closer attention to the business than an employee," said one executive. The tendency of company people to "tell me what they think I want to hear" was remarked on by four of the five executives, and one of the antidotes for that tendency was the presence of franchisees. Transaction-cost theory needs to incorporate into its assumptions that a market boundary protects actors and organizations from this pathology of hierarchy and may therefore produce in some cases more useful information for decision making.

16. The role of the franchisee in the decision process may be likened to the devil's advocate role identified by Janis (1983) in his analysis of the "groupthink" phenomenon. The franchisees serve as an institutionalized source of challenge to decisions in a plural chain. The risks of mindless subscription to the reigning argument and of only providing supporting data for the argument are reduced with the presence of franchisees.

17. John's interesting work on opportunism (1984) reinforces this line of argument. John argues that the use of coercive power leads to negative attitudes between exchange partners, which leads to more opportunism. Rather than view opportunism as an inherent feature of organizational life, as Williamson (1975, 1985) does, John's work suggests that opportunism is a variable affected by the nature of the relationship. Put another way, institutional structures both respond to and create behavior.

18. The background of the chain operator's franchise consultants raises a subtle aspect of the plural form. Virtually all franchise managers were formerly restaurant managers and area managers on the company side of the chain (see Chapter 3). The credibility of the franchise consultant hinged largely on whether they understood the business and could add value to the franchisee. Although it is difficult to see empirically because almost all franchise consultants had company experience, it seems reasonable to assume that their background with the company made it considerably easier for them to earn the confidence of franchisees.

19. Sah and Stiglitz (1986) indirectly make a similar argument for the benefits of the plural form. They compare the strengths and weaknesses of hierarchies (where only a few people can undertake a project) and polyarchies (where several decision makers can undertake projects independently). Although company and franchise arrangements do not conform perfectly to these definitions—a systemwide adaptation cannot occur independently—the breadth of participation in the process does match. Borrowing concepts from statistics, the authors make the following argument:

> [I]n a market economy, if one firm rejects a profitable idea (say, for a new product), there is a possibility that another firm might accept it. In contrast, if a single bureau makes such decisions and this bureau rejects the idea, then

the idea must remain unused. The same, however, is also true for those ideas that are unprofitable. As a result, one would expect a greater incidence of Type-II errors in polyarchy [adopting unprofitable ideas], and a greater incidence of Type-I errors in hierarchy [rejecting profitable ideas]. (p. 716)

The authors specify some circumstances under which one structure might outperform the other, such as the distribution of available projects, but they do not entertain the possibility that both structures operating at the same time might outperform either structure by itself. While in conventional organizations such a structure may be difficult to create and manage—although the literature on organizations is full of examples of organizations trying to do just that (see, for example, Duncan 1976; Eccles and Crane 1988; Kanter 1989)—chains can easily operate these structures simultaneously.

CHAPTER 8

1. I hasten to add that the marketing literature is full of studies of coordination and conflict in distribution channels. Hunt, Rau, and Wood's review of the literature (1985), though, indicates that most of these studies rely on measures of the perceptions of participants. For example, Guiltinan, Rejab, and Rodgers (1980) consider a variety of variables through the eyes of the participants—their perceptions of the helpfulness of the chain operator, for example. What is missing, though, is a simple description and conceptualization of how these channels work.

2. It is worth noting that the next largest pure company chains were Red Lobster (659 units), Chick-fil-A (655 units), and The Olive Garden (463 units). The size of pure company chains dropped quickly.

3. When faced with data that do not neatly fit into this paradigm or fall into a middle range that does not point easily to an either-or answer, researchers typically develop more refined conceptualizations of the governance structures or the conditions assumed to evoke the structures (Moriarty and Moran 1990; Rangan, Corey, and Cespedes 1991; Williamson 1991; Walker and Poppo 1991). This thrust, however, remains blind to the possibility that the plural form may yield benefits that are not attainable by any single institutional design.

4. Fama and Jensen (1983) document how organizations with different ownership structures deal with the classic problem of the separation of ownership and control. There are various ways owners ensure that managers are making good use of capital, but a common thread unites all of the strategies: with ownership comes at least some control over the management of the enterprise. In the case of franchising, an inherent organizational consequence of using the franchisee's capital is that the franchisee will exercise some control over decision making. Essentially, then, the franchise arrangement places owners (franchisees) inside the chain organization to ratify the decisions of the managers (the chain operator).

Although not an inherent feature of each arrangement, the kinds of people attracted to each one differed due in part to the capital requirements. The franchise arrangement, for example, attracted people who almost certainly would not join a conventional company arrangement, especially at the local levels. Along with the data in Chapter 3 about who became a franchisee, several recent articles comment on the career path from corporate senior management positions to local franchisees (see "Corporate Refugees" 1989; "Look Who Likes Franchising Now" 1991; "The Flight to Franchising" 1991; "Franchising: A Recipe for Your Second Career?" 1996). The background of these people enabled them to make sound local responses and contribute to the systemwide-adaptation process. It is unlikely that a chain would be able to attract such people without offering them ownership and the accompanying right to exercise choice over decisions affecting their business.

What emerges from this line of reasoning is a perspective on each arrangement that highlights the reinforcing and mutually dependent nature of each one's characteristics: a capital investment is accompanied by local autonomy, which attracts certain kinds of people that stay with the chain for a long time—and each one of these characteristics affects the performance of a chain organization. I do not mean to suggest that a simple causal model exists, with each characteristic leading inexorably to the other, because one can reverse the order of the variables and tell a similar story. The point is that the characteristics reinforce and depend on each other. This perspective leads to one of two conclusions, both of which suggest the inherent limitations of hybrids: (1) changing a single variable will have little effect on performance because of the reinforcing nature of the characteristics, or (2) changing a single variable will cascade through an arrangement and fundamentally change its performance and in the process diminish the strengths as well as reduce the weaknesses.

5. Handy's comparison of decentralization and federation (1990, 119), which loosely map on a hybrid company arrangement and a typical franchise arrangement, makes the point that the two are quite different:

> Decentralization implies that the center delegates certain tasks or duties to the outlying bits, while retaining overall control. The center does the delegating, and initiates and directs. Thus it is that we have the most consistent of organizational findings: The more an organization decentralizes its operations, the greater the flow of information to and from the center.

Rather than replicate the characteristics of the franchise arrangement, then, the hybrid company arrangement does something different. The empirical question is what impact this difference makes.

6. Given that a long-term franchise contract cannot specify all the contingencies that a chain may face (Goldberg 1980; Hadfield 1991; Williamson 1991), the parties to the contract often confront issues on which they must work together to develop a solution. Even with the provisions specified in the contract, there often are varying interpretations that lead to ambiguities about what is expected of the parties and what the outcome would be if the parties went to court, which also encourage the parties to work together.

7. Of course, the growth of a franchisee can be curtailed. But the cost to the franchisee of less growth is the difference in the return to his or her capital between investing in the chain and investing elsewhere. There may be a lost opportunity, but not a loss in the sense of having your job taken away.

APPENDIX A

1. The label "ownership redirection" comes from Dant, Kaufmann, and Paswan's review (1992) of the literature on franchising.

2. For a useful summary of the empirical work on the ownership redirection theory, see Dant, Kaufmann, and Paswan (1992). The authors report that the theory has received mixed support in the literature. Several studies provide support for the theory (Hunt 1973; Vaughn 1974; Lillis, Narayana, and Gilman 1976; and Caves and Murphy 1976).

Recent research has cast doubt on the ownership redirection theory. Andersen (1984), Martin (1988), and Carney and Gedajlovic (1991) find no such shift from franchise to company ownership. The flaw these scholars find in ownership redirection theory is that it implies an imperfection in the capital market. In this vein, Rubin (1978) argues that franchisees will demand a premium for their investment since they possess relatively undiversified portfolios which makes them a high cost source of capital. Therefore, the idea that chains will seek out franchisees as a source of capital must be wrong.

Despite the recent research, the verdict is still out on this theory, particularly since practitioners so uniformly espouse it. Let me briefly suggest a few reasons why the existing research on this theory has presented a muddled picture. I elaborate on these issues in the book.

First, the "critical" point at which the disadvantages of franchisees outweigh their advantages is never specified in any of these tests of the theory. Depending on the sample being used, researchers compare "old" and "new" firms, or compare the mix of units displayed by an industry at two different points in time. The absence of an observed shift may be a result of the continuing advantage of using franchisees over the life cycle of a chain. If chain growth is a central objective (which later I argue it is), a chain may decide to use its internally generated funds to add new units rather than convert existing franchise units to company ownership. Rather than substitute these two sources of growth, a chain may view them as complements that enable faster growth than would otherwise be possible. This would help explain the absence of a shift over time.

Second, while capital has been conceptualized as the major variable affecting growth, the distinctive process of growth in franchise and company arrangements may affect the use of the forms. While the agency cost theory explanation emphasizes the importance of a franchisee's status as a residual claimant for making efficient local operating decisions, the same logic may hold for the development of new units. The franchisee bears the risk of his or her decision to build a unit and the chain operator therefore need not so closely monitor those decisions. The administrative costs of franchise growth may be less than for company growth, which may tilt the mix in the direction of franchise units. Dant, Kaufmann, and Paswan (1992) essentially make this argument in their review of the literature: "The effect of the precise factors purported to bring about ownership redirection as per Oxenfeldt and Kelly— principally the availability of funds, information, and managerial talent—has yet to be directly tested" (p. 15). Chapter 3 of this book shows the value of examining the process of growth.

Finally, the simultaneous use of the two arrangements—the plural form—may provide a chain with management benefits that stabilize the mix and prevent the shift, regardless of why company or franchise arrangements were added in the first place. This argument is at the heart of this book.

3. For detailed examples of this approach, see Mathewson and Winter (1985); Rubin (1987); Brickley and Dark (1987); Norton (1988a, 1988b); Brickley, Dark, and Weisbach (1991).

4. See Klein (1980), Brickley and Dark (1987), and Norton (1988a, 1988b). In their analyses of chains, they assume the unilateral right of franchisors to terminate franchisees, though they acknowledge that in practice this rarely occurs. Just as Dant, Kaufmann, and Paswan (1992) argued that the underlying mechanisms of the ownership redirection theory have gone unexamined, the same statement can be made about this theory. My data show that the two control mechanisms cited by these authors rarely existed in practice: termination and laboratory inspections of suppliers' inputs. Therefore, it is unclear how chain operators manage franchisees.

Brickley, Dark, and Weisbach (1991) provide a more nuanced view of the termination assumption. They compare states with laws restricting franchise termination to states without such restrictions, and they report that the "findings are consistent with the model that predicts that the laws increase the cost of franchising relative to company ownership by making quality control among franchisees more expensive" (p. 39). Specifically, they report that termination laws are associated with a decrease of 2 to 5 percent in the mix of franchise units in a chain. While termination laws have a significant effect, it is a small one, and in any case it is unclear how the chains operating under laws that restrict termination manage their franchisees.

5. Support for this theory can be found in Brickley and Dark (1987); Norton (1988a, 1988b); Brickley, Dark, and Weisbach (1991); Brickley (1995); and Shane (1996).

References

Alderfer, Clayton. 1983. "Intergroup Relations and Organizations." In *Perspectives on Behavior in Organizations,* edited by J. Hackman, E. Lawler, and L. Porter, pp. 397–407. New York: McGraw-Hill.

Alexander, Suzanne. 1989. "Saturating Cities with Stores Can Pay." *Wall Street Journal,* 11 September, B1.

Andersen, Evan. 1984. "The Growth and Performance of Franchise Systems: Company versus Franchise Ownership." *Journal of Economics and Business* 36: 421–31.

Anderson, Erin, and David Schmittlein. 1984. "Integration of the Sales Force: An Empirical Examination." *Rand Journal of Economics* 15: 385–95.

Argyris, Chris, and Donald Schon. 1978. *Organization Learning: A Theory of Action Perspective.* Reading, Mass.: Addison-Wesley.

Arrow, Kenneth. 1974. *The Limits of Organization.* New York: W. W. Norton.

Assael, Henry. 1969. "Constructive Role of Interorganizational Conflict." *Administrative Science Quarterly* 14: 573–82.

Barabba, Vincent, and Gerald Zaltman. 1991. *Hearing the Voice of the Market.* Boston: Harvard Business School Press.

Blau, Peter. 1963. *The Dynamics of Bureaucracy.* 2d ed. Chicago: University of Chicago Press.

Bradach, Jeffrey. 1995. "Chains within Chains: The Role of Multi-Unit Franchisees." *Journal of Marketing Channels* 4: 65–81.

Bradach, Jeffrey, and Robert Eccles. 1989. "Price, Authority, and Trust." *Annual Review of Sociology* 15: 97–118.

———. "Using the Plural Form in the Management of Restaurant Chains." *Administrative Science Quarterly* 42: 276–303.

Bradach, Jeffrey, and Patrick Kaufmann. 1991. "Franchisee or Independent Businessperson: Some Observations on the Decision Process." In *Research at the Marketing/Entrepreneurship Interface 1991,* edited by J. Hills and R. LaForge. Chicago: University of Illinois Press.

Brickley, James. 1995. "Incentive Conflicts and Contracts: Evidence from Franchising." Working paper FR 95–26, Financial Research and Policy Working Paper Series, Bradley Policy Research Center, University of Rochester.

Brickley, James, and Fredrick Dark. 1987. "The Choice of Organizational Form: The Case of Franchising." *Journal of Financial Economics* 18: 401–20.

Brickley, James, Fredrick Dark, and Michael Weisbach. 1991. "An Agency Perspective on Franchising." *Financial Management* 20: 27–35.

Burawoy, Michael. 1979. *Manufacturing Consent.* Chicago: University of Chicago Press.

Burgelman, Robert A. 1991. "Intraorganizational Ecology of Strategy Making and Organizational Adaptation: Theory and Field Research." *Organizational Science* 2: 239–62.

Burns, Tom, and George Stalker. 1961. *The Management of Innovation.* London: Tavistock.

Cameron, Kim S. 1986. "Effectiveness as Paradox: Consensus and Conflict in Conceptions of Organizational Effectiveness." *Management Science* 32: 539–53.

Carney, Mick, and Eric Gedajlovic. 1991. "Vertical Integration in Franchise Systems: Agency Theory and Resource Explanations." *Strategic Management Journal* 12: 607–25.

Caves, Richard, and William Murphy. 1976. "Franchising: Firms, Markets, and Intangible Assets." *Southern Economics Journal* 42: 572–86.

Chandler, Alfred. 1962. *Strategy and Structure.* Cambridge, Mass.: M.I.T. Press.

"CMR Top 50." 1997. *Mediaweek,* January–March.

"Corporate Refugees." 1989. *Success,* October, 50.

Daft, Richard. 1982. "Bureaucratic Versus Nonbureaucratic Structure and the Process of Innovation and Change." *Research in the Sociology of Organizations* 1: 129–66.

Daft, Richard, and Robert Lengel. 1984. "Information Richness: A New Approach to Managerial Behavior and Organization Design." *Research in Organizational Behavior* 6: 191–233.

Dant, Rajiv, Patrick Kaufmann, and Audhesh Paswan. 1992. "Ownership Redirection in Franchised Channels." *Journal of Public Policy and Marketing* 11: 1–12.

Deutsch, Claudia. 1988. "Why Fast Food Has Slowed Down." *New York Times,* 13 March, C1.

Dicke, Thomas. 1992. *Franchising in America.* Chapel Hill, N.C.: University of North Carolina Press.

DiMaggio, Paul, and Walter Powell. 1983. "The Iron Cage Revisited: Institutional Isomorphism and Collective Rationality in Organizational Fields." *American Sociological Review* 48: 47–60.

Donahue, John. 1989. *The Privatization Decision.* New York: Basic Books.

Duncan, Robert. 1976. "The Ambidextrous Organization: Designing Dual Structures for Innovation." In *The Management of Organizational Design,* edited by Ralph Kilman, Louis Pondy, and Dennis Slevin, pp. 167–88. New York: New Holland.

Eccles, Robert. 1985. *The Transfer Pricing Problem: A Theory for Practice.* Lexington, Mass.: Lexington Books.

Eccles, Robert, and Dwight Crane. 1988. *Doing Deals.* Boston: Harvard Business School Press.

Eccles, Robert G., and Harrison C. White. 1986. "Firm and Market Interfaces of Profit Center Control." In *Approaches to Social Theory,* edited by S. Lindenberg, S. Nowak, and J. S. Coleman. New York: The Russell Sage Foundation.

———. 1988. "Price and Authority in Inter-Profit Center Transactions." *American Journal of Sociology* (Supplement) 94: S17–51.

Edwards, Richard. 1979. *Contested Terrain.* New York: Basic Books.

Emerson, Robert. 1982. *Fast Food: The Endless Shakeout.* New York: Lebhar-Friedman.

———. 1990. *The New Economics of Fast Food.* New York: Van Nostrand Reinhold.

Etgar, Michael. 1978. "Differences in the Use of Manufacturer Power in Conventional and Contractual Channels." *Journal of Retailing* 54: 49–62.

Fama, Eugene, and Michael Jensen. 1983. "Separation of Ownership and Control." *Journal of Law and Economics* 26: 301–25.

"The Flight to Franchising." 1991. *U.S. News & World Report,* 10 June, 68.

Foucault, Michael. 1979. *Discipline & Punish.* New York: Vintage.

"Franchise Offering Circular." 1989. Hardee's Corporation publication.

"Franchising: A Recipe for Your Second Career?" 1996. *Business Week,* 4 March, 128–29.

"Franchising Guide to Small Business Dream Launched on Internet at http://www.entremkt.com/IFA." 1996. *PR Newswire,* http://www.bizserv.com/prnewswire, 12 February.

Frank, Robert. 1985. *Choosing the Right Pond.* New York: Oxford University Press.

Frazier, Gary, and John Summers. 1984. "Interfirm Influence Strategies and Their Application within Distribution Channels." *Journal of Marketing* 48: 43–55.

French, James, and Bertram Raven. 1959. "The Basis of Social Power." In *Studies in Power,* edited by D. Cartwright. Ann Arbor, Mich.: University of Michigan Press.

Ghosh, Avijit, and Sara L. McLafferty. 1987. *Location Strategies for Retail Service Firms.* Lexington, Mass.: Lexington Books.

Goldberg, Victor. 1980. "Relational Exchange: Economics and Complex Contracts." *American Behavioral Scientist* 23: 337–52.

Guiltinan, Joseph, Ismail Rejab, and William Rodgers. 1980. "Factors Influencing Coordination in a Franchise Channel." *Journal of Retailing* 56: 41–58.

Hadfield, Gillian. 1991. "Problematic Relations: Franchising and the Law of Incomplete Contracts." *Stanford Law Review* 42: 927–92.

Hallegan, William. 1978. "Self Selection by Contractual Choice and the Theory of Share-cropping." *Bell Journal of Economics* 9: 344–54.

Handy, Charles. 1990. *The Age of Unreason.* Boston: Harvard Business School Press.

Harrigan, Kathryn. 1983. "A Framework for Looking at Vertical Integration." *Journal of Business Strategy* 12: 30–37.

Hayek, Fredrick. 1945. "The Use of Knowledge in Society." *American Economic Review* 35: 519–30.

Hennart, Jean-François. 1991. "The Transaction Cost Theory of the Multinational Enterprise." In *The Nature of the Transnational Firm,* edited by C. Pitelis and R. Sugden. London: Routledge.

Hirschman, Albert. 1986. *Rival Views of Market Society.* New York: Viking.

Hoffman, Richard C., and John F. Preble. 1993. "Franchising into the Twenty-first Century." *Business Horizons* (November–December): 35–43.

Hunt, Shelby. 1973. "The Trend Toward Company-Operated Units in Franchise Chains." *Journal of Retailing* 49: 3–12.

Hunt, Shelby, and John Nevin. 1974. "Power in a Channel of Distribution: Sources and Consequences." *Journal of Marketing Research* 11: 186–93.

Hunt, Shelby, N. Ray, and V. Wood. 1985. "Behavior Dimensions of Channels of Distribution: Review and Synthesis." *Journal of Academy of Marketing Science* 13: 1–24.

Jacques, Elliot. 1990. "In Praise of Hierarchy." *Harvard Business Review* 68: 127–33.

Janis, Irving. 1983. "Groupthink." In *Perspectives on Behavior in Organizations,* edited by J. R. Hackman, E. Lawler, and L. Porter. New York: McGraw-Hill.

Jensen, Michael, and William Meckling. 1991. "Specific and General Knowledge, and Organizational Structure." In *Main Currents in Contract Economics,* edited by L. Werin and H. Wijkander. Oxford: Blackwell.

Jick, Todd. 1979. "Mixing Qualitative and Quantitative Methods: Triangulation in Action." *Administrative Science Quarterly* 24: 602–11.

John, George. 1984. "An Empirical Investigation of Some Antecedents of Opportunism in a Marketing Channel." *Journal of Marketing Research* 21: 278–89.

Kanter, Rosabeth. 1983. *The Change Masters.* New York: Simon & Schuster.

———. 1989. *When Giants Learn to Dance.* New York: Simon & Schuster.

Kaufmann, Patrick. 1989. "Costs and Benefits of Standardized Franchise Formats." In *1989 Proceedings, Society of Franchising,* edited by J. Brown. Washington, D.C.: International Franchise Association.

———. 1991. "The Impact of Managerial Performance Decay on Franchisor's Store Allocation Strategies." Unpublished manuscript.

Kaufmann, Patrick, and Rajiv Dant. 1991. "Dimensionalizing Contractual Integration Through a Theory of Relational Exchange." Unpublished manuscript.

———. 1996. "Multi-unit Franchising: Growth of Management Issues." *Journal of Business Venturing* 11 (5): 343–58.

Kaufmann, Patrick, and V. Kasturi Rangan. 1990. "A Model for Managing System Conflict During Franchise Expansion." *Journal of Retailing* 66 (2): 155–73.

Kaufmann, Patrick, and Louis Stern. 1988. "Relational Exchange Norms, Perceptions of Unfairness, and Retained Hostility in Commercial Litigation." *Journal of Conflict Resolution* 32: 534–52.

Klein, Benjamin. 1980. "Transaction Cost Determinants of 'Unfair' Contractual Arrangements." *American Economic Review* 70: 356–62.

Klein, Benjamin, and L. Saft. 1985. "The Law and Economics of Franchising Tying Contracts." *Journal of Law and Economics* 28: 345–61.

Krueger, Alan. 1991. "Ownership, Agency, and Wages: An Examination of Franchising in the Fast-Food Industry." *The Quarterly Journal of Economics* (February): 75–101.

Langer, Ellen. 1989. *Mindfulness*. Reading, Mass.: Addison-Wesley.

Larson, Andrea. 1992. "Network Dyads in Entrepreneurial Settings: A Study of the Governance of Exchange Relationships." *Administrative Science Quarterly* 37: 76–104.

Lawrence, Paul, and Jay Lorsch. 1967. *Organization and Environment*. Homewood, Ill.: Irwin.

"Leading Franchisees." 1989. *Restaurants & Institutions* (10 July): 178.

Leonard-Barton, Dorothy. 1992. "Core Capabilities and Core Rigidities: A Paradox in Managing New Product Development." *Strategic Management Journal* 13: 111–25.

Levitt, Barbara, and James March. 1990. "Chester I. Barnard and the Intelligence of Learning." In *Organization Theory: From Chester Barnard to the Present and Beyond,* edited by O. Williamson. New York: Oxford University Press.

Lillis, Charles, Chem Narayana, and J. Gilman. 1976. "Competitive Advantage Variation over the Life Cycle of a Franchise." *Journal of Marketing* 40: 77–80.

Lombardi, Dennis. 1996. "Trends and Directions in the Chain-Restaurant Industry." *Cornell Hotel & Restaurant Administration Quarterly* 37 (3): 67–83.

"Look Who Likes Franchising Now." 1991. *Fortune,* 23 September, 128.

Love, John. 1986. *McDonald's: Behind the Arches*. New York: Bantam.

Lovelock, C. 1984. *Service Marketing*. Englewood Cliffs, N.J.: Prentice-Hall.

Lusch, Robert. 1976. "Sources of Power: Their Impact on Intrachannel Conflict." *Journal of Marketing Research* 13: 382–90.

Luxenberg, Stan. 1985. *Roadside Empires*. New York: Penguin.

Macauley, Stewart. 1963. "Noncontractual Relations in Business: A Preliminary Study." *American Sociological Review* 28: 55–67.

Macneil, Ian. 1978. "Contracts: Adjustment of Long-term Economic Relations under Classical, Neoclassical, and Relational Contract Law." *Northwestern Law Review* 72: 854–906.

———. 1980. *The New Social Contract*. New Haven: Yale University Press.

March, James. 1985. "The Technology of Foolishness." In *Organization Theory,* edited by D. Pugh. New York: Penguin.

March, James, and Herbert Simon. 1958. *Organizations*. New York: John Wiley & Sons.

Marglin, Stephan. 1974. "What Do Bosses Do? The Origins and Functions of Hierarchy in Capitalist Production." *Review of Radical Political Economics* 6: 60–112.

Martin, Robert. 1988. "Franchising and Risk Management." *American Economic Review* 78: 954–68.

Mathewson, G. Frank, and Ralph Winter. 1985. "The Economics of Franchise Contracts." *Journal of Law and Economics* 28: 503–26.

McCarthy, Michael. 1990. "Restaurants Search for Winning Recipes." *Wall Street Journal*, 29 January, B1.

McIntyre, Faye. 1992. "International Franchising of U.S. Firms: A Quasi-Longitudinal Analysis." In *Proceedings of the Sixth Conference of the Society of Franchising*, edited by P. Kaufmann. Washington, D.C.: International Franchise Association.

Merchant, Kenneth. 1982. "The Control Function of Management." *Sloan Management Review* 23: 43–55.

Miles, Raymond, and Charles Snow. 1986. "Organizations: New Concepts for New Forms." *California Management Review* 28: 62–73.

Monteverde, Kevin, and David Teece. 1982. "Supplier Switching Costs and Vertical Integration." *Journal of Law and Economics* 13: 206–13.

Morgan, Gareth. 1986. *Images of Organization*. Beverly Hills, Calif.: Sage.

Moriarty, Rowland, and Ursala Moran. 1990. "Managing Hybrid Marketing Systems." *Harvard Business Review* 68: 146–55.

Nohria, Nitin, and Robert Eccles. 1992. "Face-to-Face: Making Network Organizations Work." In *Networks and Organizations: Structure, Form and Action*, edited by N. Nohria and R. Eccles. Boston: Harvard Business School Press.

Norton, Seth. 1988a. "An Empirical Look at Franchising as an Organizational Form." *Journal of Business* 61: 197–218.

———. 1988b. "Franchising, Brand Name Capital, and the Entrepreneurial Capacity Problem." *Strategic Management Journal* 9: 105–14.

"The NRN Top 100: Big Chains Battle for Market Share." 1989. *Nation's Restaurant News* (7 August): 1.

Ouchi, William. 1979. "A Conceptual Framework for the Design of Organizational Control Mechanisms." *Management Science* 25: 833–48.

———. 1980. "Markets, Bureaucracies, and Clans." *Administrative Science Quarterly* 25: 129–41.

Oxenfeldt, Alfred, and Anthony Kelly. 1969. "Will Successful Franchise Systems Ultimately Become Wholly-Owned Chains?" *Journal of Retailing* 44: 69–83.

Padgett, John. 1981. "Hierarchy and Ecological Control in Federal Budgetary Decision-Making." *American Journal of Sociology* 87: 75–129.

Parsons, Talcott. 1951. *The Social System*. Glencoe, Ill.: Free Press.

Penrose, Edith. 1980 [1959]. *The Theory of the Growth of the Firm*. White Plains, N.Y.: M. E. Sharpe.

Perrow, Charles. 1986. *Complex Organizations*. 3d ed. New York: Random House.

Pfeffer, Jeffrey. 1982. *Organizations and Organization Theory.* Cambridge, Mass.: Ballinger.

Pfeffer, Jeffrey, and James Baron. 1988. "Taking the Workers Back Out: Recent Trends in the Structuring of Employment." *Research in Organizational Behavior* 10: 257–303.

Pfeffer, Jeffrey, and Gerald Salancik. 1978. *The External Control of Organizations.* New York: Harper & Row.

Porter, Michael. 1980. *Competitive Strategy.* New York: Free Press.

Porter, Michael, and Mark Fuller. 1986. "Coalitions and Global Strategy." In *Competition in Global Industries,* edited by M. Porter. Boston: Harvard Business School Press.

Powell, Walter, Kenneth W. Koput, and Laurel Smith-Doerr. 1996. "Interorganizational Collaboration and the Locus of Innovation: Networks of Learning in Biotechnology." *Administrative Science Quarterly* 41: 116–45.

Quinn, Robert E., and Kim S. Cameron. 1988. *Paradox and Transformation.* Cambridge, Mass.: Ballinger.

Rangan, Kasturi, Raymond Corey, and Frank Cespedes. 1993. "Transaction Cost Theory: Inferences from Clinical Field Research on Downstream Vertical Integration." *Organization Science* 4: 454–77.

Raven, Bertram, and A. Kruglanski. 1970. "Conflict and Power." In *The Structure of Conflict,* edited by P. Swingle. New York: Academic Press.

Romeo, Peter. 1990. "Challenge 1990: Thawing Out the Customer." *Nation's Restaurant News* (1 January): 33, 36.

Roy, Donald. 1960. "Banana Time: Job Satisfaction and Informal Interaction." *Human Organization* 18: 158–68.

Rubin, Paul. 1978. "The Theory of the Firm and the Structure of the Franchise Contract." *Journal of Law and Economics* 21: 223–33.

Sabir, Nadirah Z. 1996. "All Aboard the Franchise Express." *Black Enterprise* (July).

Sah, Raaj, and Joseph Stiglitz. 1986. "The Architecture of Economic Systems: Hierarchies and Polyarchies." *American Economic Review* 76: 716–27.

Scherer, Fredrick. 1970. *Industrial Market Structure and Economic Performance.* Chicago: Rand McNally.

Schlesinger, Leonard, and James Heskett. 1991. "The Service-Driven Service Company." *Harvard Business Review* 69: 71–81.

Scott, W. Richard. 1987. *Organizations: Rational, Natural, and Open Systems.* Englewood Cliffs, N.J.: Prentice-Hall.

Sennett, Richard. 1980. *Authority.* New York: Vintage.

Shane, Scott. 1996. "Hybrid Organizational Arrangements and Their Implications for Firm Growth and Survival: A Study of New Franchisors." *Academy of Management Journal* 39: 216–34.

Sherif, Muzafer, and Caroline Sherif. 1953. *Groups in Harmony and Tension.* New York: Harper & Row.

Sibley, Stanley, and Donald Michie. 1982. "An Exploratory Investigation of Cooperation in a Franchise Channel." *Journal of Retailing* 58: 23–44.

Simon, Herbert. 1976. *Administrative Behavior.* 3d ed. New York: Free Press.

Steers, Richard. 1977. *Organizational Effectiveness: A Behavioral View.* Santa Monica, Calif.: Goodyear.

Stern, Louis. 1971. "The Interorganizational Management of Distribution Channels." In *New Essays in Marketing Theory,* edited by G. Fisk. Boston: Allyn and Bacon.

Stern, Louis, and A. El-Ansary. 1988. *Marketing Channels.* 3d ed. Englewood Cliffs, N.J.: Prentice-Hall.

"Strong Franchising Growth Projected for '96." 1996. *PR Newswire,* http://www.bizserv.com/prnewswire, 31 January.

Stinchcombe, Arthur. 1965. "Social Structure and Organizations." In *Handbook of Organizations,* edited by James G. March, pp. 142–93. Chicago: Rand McNally.

———. 1990. *Information and Organization.* Berkeley, Calif.: University of California Press.

Taylor, Frederick. 1947 [1911]. *Scientific Management.* New York: Harper.

Technomic 100. 1989. Chicago: Technomic, Inc.

Thompson, James. 1967. *Organizations in Action.* New York: McGraw-Hill.

"Top 50 Franchisers." 1995. *Restaurant Business* 94: 16 (1 November): 35–48.

Tushman, Michael L., and Charles A. O'Reilly. 1997. *Winning through Innovation.* Boston: Harvard Business School Press.

U.S. Department of Commerce. 1987. "Franchising in the Economy, 1985–1987." Washington, D.C.: Government Printing Office.

Van Warner, Rick. 1987. "Hardee's Launches Attack on Big 3." *Nation's Restaurant News* (14 December): F3–F4.

Vaughn, C. 1974. *Franchising.* Lexington, Mass.: Lexington Books.

Walker, Gordon, and Laura Poppo. 1991. "Profit Centers, Single-Source Suppliers, and Transaction Costs." *Administrative Science Quarterly* 36: 66–87.

Walker, Gordon, and David Weber. 1984. "A Transaction Cost Approach to Make-or-Buy Decisions." *Administrative Science Quarterly* 29: 373–91.

Walton, Richard, and J. Richard Hackman. 1986. "Groups Under Contrasting Management Strategies." In *Designing Effective Work Groups,* edited by P. S. Goodman. San Francisco: Jossey-Bass.

Weber, Max. 1971. "Legitimate Authority and Bureaucracy." In *Organizational Theory,* edited by D. S. Pugh. Baltimore: Penguin.

"Welcome to McDonald's." 1996. McDonald's Corporation publication.

"When They Eat Out, Most Consumers Request the Same Thing: Convenience." 1996. *Research Alert* 14: 24 (20 December): 3.

White, Harrison. 1985. "Agency as Control." In *Principals and Agents: The Structure of Business,* edited by John Pratt and Richard Zeckhauser. Boston: Harvard Business School Press.

Williamson, Oliver. 1970. *Corporate Control and Business Behavior.* Englewood Cliffs, N.J.: Prentice-Hall.

———. 1975. *Markets and Hierarchies.* New York: Free Press.

———. 1980. "The Organization of Work." *Journal of Economic Behavior and Organization* 1: 5–38.

———. 1985. *The Economic Institutions of Capitalism.* New York: Free Press.

———. 1991. "Comparative Economic Organization: The Analysis of Discrete Structural Alternatives." *Administrative Science Quarterly* 36: 269–96.

Wilson, James Q. 1966. "Innovation in Organization: Notes Toward a Theory." In *Approaches to Organizational Design,* edited by J. D. Thompson, pp. 193–218. Pittsburgh: University of Pittsburgh Press.

Yin, Robert. 1981. "The Case Study Crisis: Some Answers." *Administrative Science Quarterly* 26: 58–65.

Zeller, Richard, Dale Achabal, and Lawrence Brown. 1980. "Market Penetration and Locational Conflict in Franchise Systems." *Decision Sciences* 11: 58–80.

Zuboff, Shoshana. 1988. *In the Age of the Smart Machine.* New York: Basic Books.

Index

Additive process, 7, 75–77, 168, 170, 177
Advertising
  advantages for large chains, 18, 76
  the decision-making process for, 47, 153–154
  franchisee's potential control over, 154
  growth and, 76
  of new products, 145
  and shared identity, 18
  television, dominance of, 47, 76, 109, 116
Agency cost theory, 15, 75, 77, 109, 131–132, 188
Alderfer, C., 107
Ambidextrous organizations, 178–179
Andersen, E., 217n2
Anderson, E., 10, 175
Area managers, 31
  becoming franchise consultants, 57–58
  from ranks of restaurant managers, 205n14
Argyris, C., 178
Arrow, K., 56
Assael, H., 41, 156

Barabba, V., 142
Baron, J., 203n6
Bradach, J., 3, 9, 170, 206nn3,8
Brickley, J., 2, 35, 54, 75, 81, 102, 103, 109, 128, 131–132, 170, 188, 202n2, 204n13, 206n3, 218nn3,4,5
Burawoy, M., 208n6

Burgelman, R. A., 133
Burns, T., 9, 176

Cameron, K. S., 176, 178
Carney, M., 217n2
Caves, R., 2, 16–18, 102, 187
Cespedes, F., 176
Chain organizations, 1, 3–5. See also
  Company arrangement; Franchise arrangement
  architecture of information, 41–45.
    See also Information architecture
  balancing local responsiveness and uniformity, 112, 120, 124, 132
  blending characteristics of franchise and company arrangements, 51–58
  built on cloning, 15, 21
  business format as the product, 21–22
  business-format chains, 5, 17
  characteristics of company and franchise arrangements, 31–51
  cross-cutting career paths, 54–58
  economics of, 36
  franchise sales departments, 69
  growth from adding units, 21–22, 62–75
  heightened competition among, 29, 201n3
  increasing sales of, 3
  multi-unit franchisees in, 51–54. See also Multi-unit franchisees
  plural form, 2. See also Plural form
  power from right to award new units, 62, 63

Chain organizations *(continued)*
  role in systemwide adaptation, 134–
    136
  sources of influence and control, 39–
    41, 79–81, 105, 132
  spans of managerial control, 45–46
  structural mechanisms, 45–50
Chandler, A., 47, 201*n*4
"Clan" form of organization, 56, 102–
  103
Company arrangement
  authority, hierarchy and zone of ac-
    ceptance, 33, 39–40, 45, 157, 170,
    181–183
  centralized decision making, 8, 47,
    113–115, 120, 150–152
  external controls, 103
  generating ideas, 138–139
  implementation of new product,
    157–158
  local responsiveness, 111, 113–120
  maintaining uniformity, 85–97
  manager as employee, 1–2, 33, 145
  nature of rewards, 37–38, 132
  process of adding units, 63–68
  "seeding" markets with company
    units, 77
  testing and evaluating ideas in, 143,
    144–146
  types of information from, 42, 44,
    83, 89–91, 143–144, 183
Contingency theory, 176, 179
Contractual relationships, 33–36,
  202*nn*3,4,5
Control by "minimum critical specification," 105
Corey, R., 176
Crane, D., 178

Daft, R., 44, 149, 179
Dant, R., 53, 170–171, 206*n*3,
  217*nn*1,2, 218*n*4
Dark, F., 2, 35, 54, 75, 81, 102, 103,
  109, 128, 131–132, 170, 188,
  204*n*13, 206*n*3, 218*nn*3,4,5
Designated Marketing Areas (DMA),
  116–117, 153–156

Deutsch, C., 29
Dimaggio, P., 108
Donahue, J., 10
Duncan, R., 9, 178–179

Eccles, R., 3, 9, 93, 95–96, 104, 130,
  149, 177–178, 195, 204*n*10,
  211*n*13
Edwards, R., 195
El-Ansary, A., 17
Emerson, R., 5, 16, 18, 20–22, 26
Etgar, M., 160–161

Fama, E., 182, 215*n*4
Fast-food chains, 1
  as business-format operations, 17
  convenience, importance of, 20
  significance of "fast food" label, 17
  successful service at, 19
  weak brand loyalty, 20
Field testing, of ideas, 143, 145
Field visits (audits), 42
  activities occurring on, 196
  and autonomy of franchisee, 195,
    198–199
  involvement of senior executives,
    196
  to maintain uniformity, at company
    units, 86–87, 195–197
  to maintain uniformity, at franchise
    units, 98, 197–199
  the role of, 195–199
Fishermen's Landing
  hybrid ownership of franchises, 78–
    79
  Product Service Analysis field audit,
    86–87
  rarity of systemwide adaptation, 26,
    28, 136
  senior managers working with fran-
    chisees, 57
Foucault, M., 89
Franchise advisory committee, 48
Franchise arrangement, 1. *See also* Franchisees; Multi-unit franchisees
  adding new units, 68–72
  concentration of units, 51, 53

and constructive conflict, 156, 163, 181
and decision making, 8, 152–153, 215n4
federal structure of, 45, 47–49, 170
the franchise contract, 34–35, 73, 80, 183
generating ideas, 139–142
implementation of new product, 158–160
internalized controls, 103
legal restriction of franchise termination, 218n4
local responsiveness, 8, 111, 120–128, 139
maintaining uniformity, 97–103
testing and evaluating ideas in, 146–149
transaction benefits of, 41
type of information from, 43–45, 138
Franchise associations, 48
"Franchise community," 103, 204n11
Franchise consultants, 31, 36, 40, 170
field visits by, 197
from ranks of area managers, 57–58, 205n14, 214n18
relationship with franchisees, 47, 205n15
Franchise conventions, 48
Franchisees. *See also* Franchise arrangement
age and experience of, 49
agreement with the chain, 3
company people as, 55–57, 77–79, 205n16. *See also* Socialization process
contribution to U.S. economy, 3
finding qualified franchisees, 69–70, 75, 76, 77–78
hybrid ownership with chain operator, 78–79
as independent businesspeople, 1, 203n6, 209n8, 211n11
independent thinking as asset to chain, 146, 214nn15,16
inhibitions to underreporting revenues, 203–204n9

in less accessible markets, 77, 150–151
nature of rewards, 37–39, 103, 128
owning an exclusive territory, 74, 80
as partners with chain, 2, 33, 198
personal contacts with chain executives, 44, 48, 141, 149, 150, 170
persuasion as chain's mode of influence, 40–41, 46–48, 54, 69, 132, 150, 152, 157, 159, 170
right to reject chain's proposals, 152, 156, 159, 180
royalty fee to the chain, 3, 35, 36, 43
training provided by chain, 210n7
Frank, R., 203n6
Frazier, G., 159, 161
French, J., 62, 159–160

Gaming the control system, 84, 93–95
defined, 93
Gedajlovic, E., 217n2
Growth by adding units. *See* Unit growth
Guiltinan, J., 160

Hackman, R., 209n10
Hadfield, G., 34, 81, 170, 183, 202n1, 206n3
Handy, C., 11, 216n5
Hardee's
acquisition of Roy Rogers chain, 26
"American Dream Program," 56
biscuits for breakfast, systemwide adaptation of, 140, 144, 146
Business Planning Council, franchisees elected by peers, 147
loans to employees to buy franchise, 78
local responsiveness of menu, 24, 129
Menu Development Team, 151
New Products Group, 138
promotion and turnover of managers, 49
"seeding" markets with company units, 77
sources of unit growth, 62

Hardee's *(continued)*
  SQC field audits, 86–87
  trial period for potential franchisees,
    70
Harrigan, K., 10, 176
Hennart, J. F., 175
Heskett, J., 103
Hirschman, A., 156
Hoffman, R. C., 3
Hunt, S., 159, 187
Hybrid forms, 179–184
  dilutive effect of, 180–181
  inherent limits to creation of, 181–
    184

"In and out" product promotions, 138–
  139
"Informational influence," 160
Information architecture
  effect of chain size on, 172
  field visits, 42, 86–87
  "information richness" of franchisee
    data, 44–45, 138, 204n10
  MIS in company arrangement, 42,
    45, 83, 89–91, 143–144, 183
  and systemwide adaptation, 149
  transparent vs. opaque, 41, 43, 50,
    170
Institutional choice, theories of, 175
International Franchise Association
  (IFA), 4

Jack in the Box
  decision process at, 152–153
  "modeling" by franchisees at, 108
  Product Development Group, 138
  QSC&F field audits, 86, 94, 98
  Quality Assurance Systems & Train-
    ing department, 87
  restaurant-development group, 65
  "seeding" markets with company
    units, 77
  sources of unit growth, 63
  systemwide adaptations at, 26,
    27
Jacques, E., 50, 93
Janis, I., 157, 214n6

Jensen, M., 45, 111, 118, 149, 182,
  207n10, 215n4
Jick, T., 192
John, G., 214n17

Kanter, R., 9, 11, 215n19
Kaufmann, P., 24, 53, 62, 102, 109,
  170–171, 205n2, 206nn3,8,
  207n12, 210n2, 217nn1,2, 218n4
Kelly, A., 2, 187, 217n2
KFC
  advertising budget, 18
  Chicken Little program, 155
  conflict over lunch business, 151
  dealing with franchisee deviations,
    102
  franchisees and new owner Pepsico,
    130
  granting territories to franchisees, 74
  local responsiveness of, 24
  menu variations in company units,
    114–115
  minority franchising program, 56
  mystery shopping at franchise units,
    99
  New Product Development Commit-
    tee, composed of franchisees, 147
  Operations and Facility Review, field
    audits, 86
  Original Recipe chicken, 16
  product innovation at, 139
  specialization of local response at,
    117
  Thanksgiving promotion of stuffing,
    144
  trial period for potential franchisees,
    71
Klein, B., 35, 122, 207n16, 218n4
Knapp, M., 29
Koput, K. W., 176
Kroc, Ray (McDonald's founder), 4, 79
Krueger, A., 210n8
Kruglanski, A., 160

Labor
  in company arrangement, 115
  in franchise arrangement, 122–123

Langer, E., 197, 209*n*11
Larson, A., 58
Lawrence, P., 176, 179
Lengel, R., 44, 149
Leonard-Barton, D., 9
Levitt, B., 131
Local learning process, 8, 112, 129, 169
Local responsiveness, 111–132, 169
  and bounds of the contract, 124
  in company arrangement: central-
    ized, specialized, 111, 113–120
  in franchise arrangement: decentral-
    ized, 8, 111, 120–128
  influences on, 111–112
  as management challenge, 24–25
  and plural form, 128–131
  as source of innovation, 139
  tactical and strategic, 24–25, 112,
    121–126
Location of units, 19. *See also* Site selec-
  tion
  as key to success, 21
Lombardi, D., 5
Lorsch, J., 176, 179
Love, J., 20, 79
Lovelock, C., 23
Lusch, R., 159
Luxenberg, S., 3, 17

Macauley, S., 34, 202*n*1, 202*n*3
McDonald's
  locating of outlets, 20
  Love's book on history of, 79
  net income, 4
  as plural organization, 4
  rate of expansion, 4
  role of consistency at, 17
  sources of increased profit, 21
Macneil, I., 34, 170, 202*n*1,
  202*n*4
"Make-or-buy" approach, limitations
  of, 175
Management challenges for restaurant
  chains, 7–8, 15–29
  characteristics of the business, 16–
    21
  and competitive dynamics, 28, 29

growth by adding units, 21–23, 61–
  82
  local responsiveness, 24–25, 111–132
  managing existing units, 28–29
  plural form and, 168–170
  and size of chain, 27–28, 172
  systemwide adaptation, 25–27, 133–
    166
  uniformity, 23–24, 83–110
Management information system (MIS)
  in company arrangement, 42, 45,
    83, 89–91
  effect on decision making, 204*n*10
  and "management by red pen," 90
  and people's feelings of autonomy,
    204*n*10
  rarity of data from franchisees, 99
  role in evaluating new ideas, 143–
    144
March, J., 131, 178
Marglin, S., 201*n*4
"Marketing cooperatives," 153–154
"Market pressure process," 113, 129–
  131, 169
Mathewson, G., 218*n*3
Meckling, W., 45, 111, 118, 149
Menu
  considered inviolate, 114–115, 124
  formal approval of optional items,
    124–126
  and identity, 26
  research and development on, 145
Merchant, K., 105
Michie, D., 159, 161
Miles, R., 11
MIS. *See* Management information sys-
  tem (MIS)
Modeling process
  by multi-unit franchisees, 54, 84,
    108–109, 168, 169
  uniformity and, 8, 84, 108–109
Model of management in restaurant
  chains, 5–9
Monteverde, K., 10, 175–176
Morgan, G., 105
Multi-unit franchisees
  adding a unit, 72–75, 171

Multi-unit franchisees *(continued)*
    hierarchical management by, 51, 55,
        205*n*14
    as inexpensive source of growth for
        chain, 54, 61, 73
    and level of uniformity, 170, 209*n*12
    managerial significance of, 53–54,
        170–171, 206*nn*3,9
    modeling effect, 54, 84, 108–109,
        168–169
    prevalence of, 51
    role in systemwide adaptation, 162–
        163
    use of marketing specialists, 117, 123
Murphy, W., 2, 16–18, 102, 187
Mutual learning
    in the plural form, 9, 133–134, 170
    in systemwide-adaptation process,
        136–162, 169
"Mystery shopping"
    at company units, 83, 87–89, 207*n*2
    and gaming the system, 94, 208*n*6
    infrequent use at franchise units, 99
    negative aspects of, 89

Network organizations, 11
Nevin, J., 159
Nohria, N., 93, 95–96, 104, 149, 195,
        204*n*10
Noncoercive power (in dealing with
        franchisees), 170
    control of information from com-
        pany units, 161
    defined, 159
    fragility of, 161
    and franchisee satisfaction, 159
Norton, S., 128, 131, 202*n*2, 204*n*13,
        206*nn*3,6, 218*nn*3,4,5

O'Reilly, C. A., 9, 178–179
Ouchi, W., 56, 102, 103
Ownership redirection theory, 15,
        187–188
    criticisms of, 217*n*2
    explanations of mixed research re-
        sults, 217–218*n*2

Owning or franchising, literature on,
        187–189
Oxenfeldt, A., 2, 187, 217*n*2

Padgett, J., 178
Parsons, T., 178
Peer monitoring, by franchisees, 98,
        99–100
Penrose, E., 206*n*4
Performance evaluation
    to maintain uniformity and stan-
        dards, 37, 91–93
    and management, 91–93
    QSC audit, 17, 85, 86
    unintended effects of, 93–97
Perrow, C., 93, 187
Pfeffer, J., 187, 201*n*4, 203*n*6
Pizza Hut
    granting territories to franchisees, 74
    incentive-award program, for new
        ideas, 139
    Joint Advisory Committeee: franchi-
        see input, 147
    new MIS system at, 91
    operation of advertising coopera-
        tives, 213*n*12
    "Pairs" program created by franchi-
        sees, 123, 140, 151
    QSC field audits, 86
    ratcheting process at, 106
    role of company commitment, 155
    sources of unit growth, 62–63
    Standard Exception Test (SET) proc-
        ess, for local responses, 125–126,
        132, 140, 175. *See also* SET (Pizza
        Hut)
Plural form
    the additive process, 7, 75–77, 170,
        177
    advantages, benefits of, 2, 9–10, 135,
        136, 167–171, 175, 213*n*11,
        214*n*19, 218*n*2
    and alignment of chain-franchisee in-
        terests, 36
    complementary attributes of, 2
    conflicts of interest, 150–151

contrasting perspectives and organizational effectiveness, 178
control and innovation in single structure, 176–177
cross-cutting career paths, 54–58, 77–79
and decision-making process, 154–157
defined, 9
effects of local responsiveness in, 112–113, 128–131
intergroup dynamics, 107
managing the mix, 174–175
multiple sources of new ideas, 142–143
and network organizations, 11
as new organizational category, 3, 167, 184
in other settings, 10–11
plural processes and the mix, 171–174
potential pitfalls of, 171
the power of, 175–178, 193
prevalence in large chains, 6
and self-correction, self-renewal, 3, 168, 176–178
significance of, 5–7
and socialization process, 7, 55–57, 58, 61
stability of, 6
and systemwide adaptation, 8, 135–137, 142–143, 149–150, 163–166
and unit growth process, 7, 75–79, 81
Porter, M., 10, 176
"Postdecision learning," 161
Powell, W., 108, 176
Preble, J. F., 3
Pricing policies
in company arrangement, 113–114
in franchise arrangement, 121
Product innovations, 138–143
dedicated restaurants for testing of, 146
and market fit, 143–144
"Proportional response" (to franchisee issues), 84, 100–103

QSC (quality, service, cleanliness) audit, 17, 85, 86
Quinn, R. E., 178

Rangan, K., 176, 205n2, 207n12
Ratcheting process, 170
effect on performance measures, 107
and legal limitations, 107
and uniformity, 8, 84, 106–108
Raven, B., 62, 159–160
Rejab, I., 161
Research design, 191–193
Research project, 11–12
statistics on chains in sample, 13
Restaurant chains, 1
characteristics of, 16–21
focus on management, 5
local production, 18–19
management challenges, 15–29, 201n3
market power of, 5
menu and identity, 26
shared identity, 16–18, 23
small, geographically dispersed units, 20
Reward power, 62
Rodgers, W., 161
"Rotations of control" (cycle of shifting priorities), 84, 93, 95–96
Roy, D., 208n6
Rubin, P., 2, 35, 54, 81, 108–109, 131, 170, 183, 188, 202n2, 217n2, 218n3

Sabir, N. Z., 3, 5
Saft, L., 122
Scherer, F., 10, 176
Schlesinger, L., 103
Schmittlein, D., 10, 175
Schon, D., 178
Scott, W. R., 133, 187
Self-correcting and self-renewing organizations
control and innovation in single structure, 176–177, 185

Self-correcting and self-renewing organizations *(continued)*
and the plural form, 3, 168, 176–178
SET (Standard Exception Test) (Pizza Hut), 132
for considering local responses, 125–126, 175
involvement of senior people, 125
learning opportunities from, 126
product variations resulting from, 140
SET committee, 125
Shane, S., 207*n*11, 218*n*5
Sherif, C., 107
Sherif, M., 107
Sibley, S., 159, 161
Simon, H., 33, 40, 96, 182
Site selection. *See also* Location of units
approval by CEO, 65–66
by franchisees, 71, 75
and operating issues, 68
as a specialized function, 67, 118
and "traffic generators," 65
Size of a chain
effect on information architecture, 172
and management challenges, 27–28, 172
and mediating effect of plural form, 172–174
Smith-Doerr, L., 176
Snow, C., 11
Socialization process (company people as franchisees), 7, 55–57, 58, 61, 77–79, 168, 169, 215–216*n*4
Specialization of local response, 115–119
benefits of, 119
division departments involved, 116
organizational dilemmas created by, 117, 118
Stalker, G., 9, 176
Steers, R., 178, 201*n*1
Stern, L., 17, 134, 170, 203*n*7
Stinchcombe, A., 108, 203*n*5

Summers, J., 159, 161
Suppliers
in company arrangement, 115
in franchise arrangement, 121–122, 130
Systemwide adaptation, 133–166
decision making, 150–157
of franchisee's local response, 120, 127, 212*nn*6,7
generating ideas, 138–143
implementation, 157–162
as management challenge, 25–27
mutual learning in, 136–162, 169
of new product, 25–26, 136
and plural form, 8, 135–137, 142–143, 149–150, 163–166, 213*n*11, 214*n*19
role of chain operator, 134–136, 211*n*1
role of multi-unit franchisees, 162–163
testing and evaluating ideas, 143–150

Tapered integration, theories of, 10
and the plural form, 176
Taylor, F., 201*n*4
Teece, D., 10, 175–176
Thompson, J., 201*n*4, 210*n*4
Trademark
as automatic reputation for new unit, 22
local response and, 112
power of, 17, 109
Transaction-cost economics, 44
Tushman, M. L., 9, 178–179

Uniformity, 83–110, 168
common measures for, 23–24
contrasting strategies for maintenance of, 103–105
and customers' expectation, 16, 109
and the growth process, 66–67
maintaining, in company arrangement, 85–97
maintaining, in franchise arrangement, 97–103

and modeling process, 8, 84, 108–109
and ratcheting process, 8, 84, 106–
108
and shared identity, 23
Unit growth, 61–82, 168
adding new franchisee, new franchise unit, 68–72
addition of company unit, 63–68
and the additive process, 75–77, 168
benefits from expertise of chain, 22–
23, 68
capital and management resources required, 65–66, 68, 72, 76
direct and indirect implications of,
61, 205n2, 207n12
growth and performance, 80
the growth process, 62–75
and management of chain, 9
managing franchisees: control over
growth, 9, 41, 79–81
"maximum attainable sales" and, 21,
22, 201nn5,6
need to grow fast, 76

processes of the plural form, 7, 75–79
unit added by existing franchisee,
72–75

Van Warner, R., 66, 139
Variation-selection-retention framework, 133

Walker, G., 10, 107
Walton, R., 209n10
Weber, D., 10, 107
Weber, M., 39, 167
Weisbach, M., 218nn3,4,5
White, H., 96, 177, 211n13
Williamson, O., 33, 40, 44, 132, 167,
170, 173, 175, 182–183, 201n4,
213n4, 214n5
Wilson, J. Q., 178
Winter, R., 218n3

Zaltman, G., 142
Zone of acceptance, 33
Zuboff, S., 203n8

About the Author

Jeffrey L. Bradach is on the faculty at Harvard Business School. He is an expert on how organizations address the question of when they should conduct activities internally and when they should rely on external, market-based relationships such as franchising. Currently he is extending his research into organizations' use of independent contractors for doing managerial and professional work. Bradach is also deeply interested in the nonprofit sector and is studying the challenges faced by social enterprises attempting to grow.

Bradach has consulted to numerous organizations in the private and nonprofit sectors and has published several articles and cases on franchising and the temporary services industry.